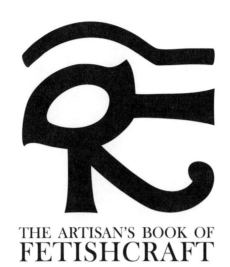

THE ARTISAN'S BOOK OF
FETISHCRAFT

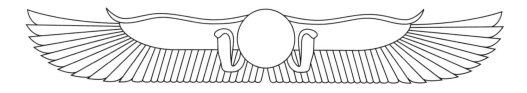

THE ARTISAN'S BOOK OF
FETISHCRAFT

JOHN HUXLEY

greenery press

"Everyone carries a shadow, and the less it is embodied in the individual's conscious life, the blacker and denser it is." - Carl Jung

Readers should be aware that BDSM and fetish play, like all sexual activities, carries an inherent risk of physical and/or emotional injury. While we believe that following the guidelines set forth in this book will minimize that potential, the writer and publisher encourage you to be aware that you are taking some risk when you decide to engage in these activities, and to accept personal responsibility for assuming that risk. In acting on the information in this book, you agree to accept that information as is and with all faults. Neither the author, the publisher, nor anyone else associated with the creation or sale of this book is responsible for any damage sustained.

CONTENTS

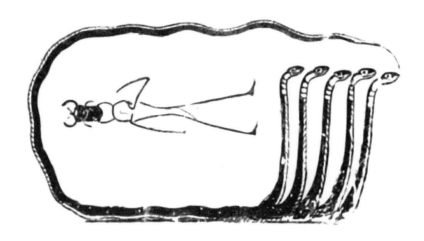

The vignettes found throughout this
book are taken from the Egyptian Amduat, or
"book of what is in the underworld," as painted
on the walls of the tomb of Tuthmosis III.

"Know the way of the Sungod through the beyond!
This is a very true remedy, proven a million times."

For questions, comments and resources:

www.fetishcraft.net

Chapter I

Introduction

Most of us live in a consumer society where we purchase what we need and what we want, leaving the design and construction to someone else, presumably someone with more experience and skill than us. There are, however, certain areas – some might say the most important areas – where we intervene to shape the course of creation. When it comes to our homes, we do not typically ask someone else to choose the decor, nor do we usually leave our tattoo to the artist's discretion.

Our private lives, often the truest possible expression of our inner selves, are where we most desire creative control.

This book was written to assist the reader in designing and constructing fetishwear, restraints, sensory deprivation devices, toys and whips.

When the fit should be precise, as is generally the case with fetishwear, making one's own garments is ideal. Unfortunately, stores that sell fetishwear, where one might try before buying, are not accessible to most at this time. Many products are available on the Internet, but these purchases can often result in sizing problems. Either way the cost can be prohibitive. As more people acquire the kinds of skills taught in this book, though, availability will increase, and cost will decrease.

This book was written to be a creative resource, so think of the projects as simplified designs, or templates. Following the instructions will make a quality product, but I encourage you to customize them, making them look however you want them to look and feel however you want them to feel. The garment projects in Chapters II and III are made to fit the wearer, which means you must first take measurements and then often draft a pattern. The projects in Chapters IV through VII rely less on size and measurement, and allow for more personal customization.

You may notice a vein of Japanese garments running throughout this book. This is partly to do with the elegance, simplicity and practicality of Japanese clothing, but is also a special asset for practitioners of shibari, the centuries-old Japanese art of rope bondage practiced by people all over the world. Projects like the kimono, hakama, samurai gauntlets and tabi can add a certain aesthetic and authenticity to shibari scenes, as well as making unique additions to any wardrobe.

The ideas, techniques and designs presented in this book reflect what I've found to work in my experience. Every effort has been made to universalize the material for a wider audience, but the subjective nature of this topic necessitates a subjective interpretation of this book. Take from it what you will, and make it your own. Please also note that some of clothing, devices and techniques described in this book can be of a psychologically potent and physically intense nature, and should only be used by those of sound mind and body.

How to use this book

This book is broken down into seven chapters. Chapter I introduces the tools and materials used throughout the book, as well as the body dimension legend and pattern expansion technique. The projects are grouped according to their use in the following six chapters, and for the most part they are also grouped according to the techniques used to create them.

The techniques used in making the projects are outlined in the chapter introductions. Chapters II and III present the majority of the techniques, and Chapters IV, V and VI reference and build on them. Chapter VII focuses on plaiting, a skill largely unrelated to the preceding chapters.

Reading the book start to finish is not necessary. You may benefit from reading the following section describing the patterns, but if your skills are well developed, you can then move directly to a particular project. If your skills need to be developed, though, I recommend that you read through the introductions of Chapters II, III and VII, and practice by making the simpler projects.

Patterns

Every effort has been made to present the project patterns in a way that accommodates people of all shapes and sizes. This means that the patterns will look somewhat complicated, and some math will be required. However, the process is really not much more time-consuming than using a commercial pattern.

The English alphabet is used to identify the dimensions in each pattern, and the letters of the Greek alphabet represent the various body dimensions.

The patterns were developed using the metric system, but approximate imperial equivalents have been included for the convenience of U.S. readers. The imperial equivalents will work adequately for most of the larger patterns, but when working in finer detail (such as in the gloves and the plaited projects in Chapter VII), using the metric measurements will ensure accuracy and prevent possible complications.

Most measurements should be made with a measuring tape, though a ruler can be helpful when measuring the jaw, penis and foot. The foot is most easily measured by first tracing it on to a piece of paper, then measuring the tracing. When taking the circumferential measurements, the measuring tape must be held snugly, but not so tightly as to compress the part being measured.

Once measurements have been taken, they can be plugged into the pattern formulas and you can sketch a pattern. Many projects will require that you draft and cut

a full-size paper pattern, whereas for others (such as the robe on page 22), you can just sketch the panels and dimensions out quickly, or skip this step entirely and mark directly on the material.

You'll need a length or roll of meter-wide paper to make patterns for some of the larger projects. Pattern tracing cloth or pattern paper, available at most sewing stores, will also work. Although using a paper pattern will make for greater precision, and will definitely cut the amount of labor if making more than one of a particular project, you can skip this step if the materials are not available. For projects with several identical or mirror-image panels, draw and cut out the first panel, then use it as a guide for the rest. For projects with symmetrical panels, sketching only one half of the panel, then cutting it, folding it over and tracing the cut edge to form the other side of the panel, can help save time and increase symmetry.

If you're using a paper pattern, the best way to ensure an accurate and symmetrical pattern is to first construct a grid. The first step in doing so is determining the height and width of each grid square, or cell. The height of the cells can be determined by dividing the maximum height of the pattern panel by its height in cells. Repeat this process with the maximum width to determine the cell width. Since the pattern will not always meet up with all of the grid lines, you may have to divide the height or width by a fractional number of grid cells. The patterns in this book are presented over a grid whose cells are subdivided in to sixteen small cells. Sketching these smaller cells is not necessary, but can be helpful when constructing patterns with a lot of detail.

Once the cell height and width have been determined, the grid can be drawn by first drawing a box of (cells high x cell height) x (cells wide x cell width), then marking the cell divisions on all of the edges and connecting the dots to make horizontal and vertical lines. Before drafting the pattern, be sure to mark the maximum width and height of the panel on the grid at the appropriate places. The grid expansion method of pattern construction is not perfect, but it does respect the varying dimensions of the human body more than most commercial paper patterns. Projects which include panels for which you should use the grid expansion method are indicated by the expansion symbol (fig 1.1) in the top left corner of the pattern grid.

fig 1.1

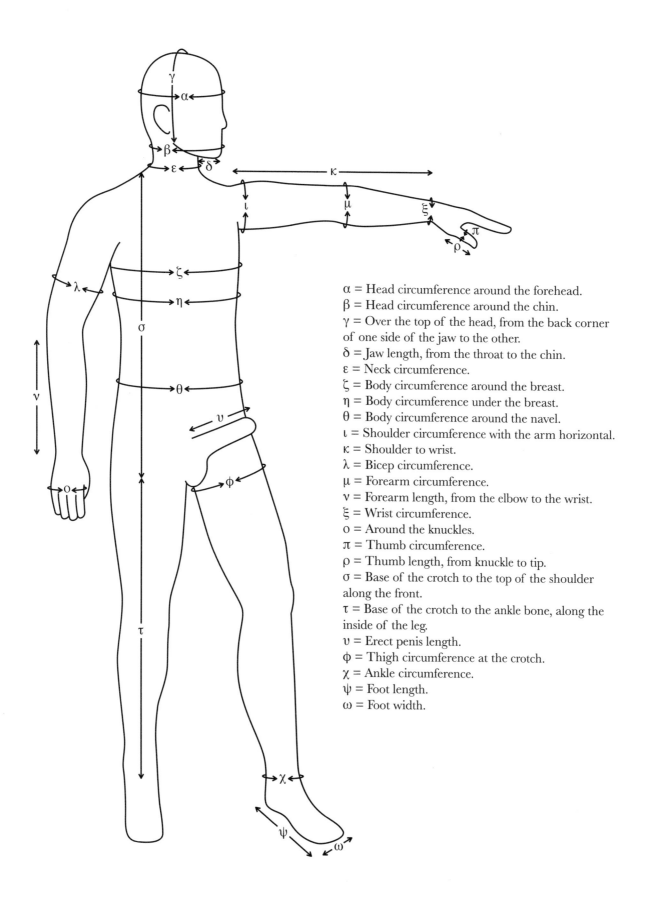

α = Head circumference around the forehead.

β = Head circumference around the chin.

γ = Over the top of the head, from the back corner of one side of the jaw to the other.

δ = Jaw length, from the throat to the chin.

ε = Neck circumference.

ζ = Body circumference around the breast.

η = Body circumference under the breast.

θ = Body circumference around the navel.

ι = Shoulder circumference with the arm horizontal.

κ = Shoulder to wrist.

λ = Bicep circumference.

μ = Forearm circumference.

ν = Forearm length, from the elbow to the wrist.

ξ = Wrist circumference.

ο = Around the knuckles.

π = Thumb circumference.

ρ = Thumb length, from knuckle to tip.

σ = Base of the crotch to the top of the shoulder along the front.

τ = Base of the crotch to the ankle bone, along the inside of the leg.

υ = Erect penis length.

φ = Thigh circumference at the crotch.

χ = Ankle circumference.

ψ = Foot length.

ω = Foot width.

When there is more than one horizontal or vertical dimension given for a panel (such as in the zentai mask neck panel, page 46), use the principal dimensions (C and D) to calculate the cell dimensions, and the supplementary dimensions (E and F) to draft the remainder of the panel without a grid. Supplementary dimensions are indicated by dashes in the dimension arrows (fig 1.2).

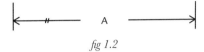

fig 1.2

In panels having only one dimension (such as in the eye mask patterns, page 97), you will have to preserve the aspect ratio. After you calculate one cell dimension you can use it for the other, so they will always be proportional. This is indicated by a small square in the dimension arrow (fig 1.3).

fig 1.3

Alternatively, patterns whose size varies equally in both directions can be re-sized with a photocopier or scanner and printer.

There are also projects where the same cell size, whether the cell is square or not, is used for multiple panels in the pattern (such as in the zentai glove pattern on page 41 and the slipper pattern on page 77). I have done this when there is a precise relationship between the panels that must be preserved when sizing them. This is indicated by a small circle in the dimension arrow (fig 1.4), and is applied to any panels without dimensions.

fig 1.4

Since the zentai mask is the first pattern in the book to use the grid expansion method, and it is also one of the most complex to draft, detailed instructions on this method are given in that section (page 47).

Note that alignment notches are not included in any of the patterns, but can easily be added anywhere desired. (These are small triangular protrusions or cuts in the seam allowances on edges to be sewn together, placed to help you correctly align the layers when sewing. They can be helpful on long seams and when sewing stretch fabrics.)

Anytime a new pattern is drafted, there is always the possibility of a calculation or drafting error, or that the original design was not appropriate for the intended wearer's individual dimensions. With this in mind, you may wish to first make a scrap cloth prototype before using your good material, especially when making the leather projects.

Once the pattern has been drafted, it can be arranged on the wrong side of the material and its edges traced. When your writing instrument makes a wide mark rather than a fine one, take care when cutting to cut inside the marked lines for all outer edges, and outside the marked lines for openings in the panels.

Tools

Sewing machine

A good-quality domestic sewing machine is ideal for many of the projects in this book. A lower-end machine may suffice, as long as it is powerful enough to sew reliably through a half dozen layers of blue jean denim. Be warned, though: using a poorly made machine will inevitably result in wasted time, wasted materials and frustration.

When choosing a machine, look for something simple and powerful. The lower-end Singer sewing machines found in most department stores work well. A serger or overlocker can be helpful for the projects in Chapter I. These can be expensive, though, and are not universally useful, so I will not discuss their use in the instructions. An industrial walking-foot machine is ideal for sewing leather, but is not recommended for sewing delicate or stretch fabrics.

Most sewing machine problems are caused by poor maintenance. If the machine is being used regularly, it should be cleaned and oiled around once a month. Failure to do so can result in poor efficiency and a shorter machine lifespan. Check the instruction booklet for specific cleaning and maintenance procedures, but generally all you need to do is brush away dust and lint from inside the bobbin case, and then oil any of the exposed moving parts. A toothbrush works well for cleaning, and a can of compressed air will also do the job quite efficiently. Be sure to unplug the machine before getting started, and be sure to use only proper sewing machine oil.

Zipper foot

A zipper foot is a smaller presser foot that allows the needle to sew very close to a raised edge, and is particularly helpful when sewing zippers.

Non-stick foot

A presser foot made of non-stick material is indispensable when sewing vinyl, and can be very helpful when sewing leather as well. This kind of foot will not bind to the material when sewing, making for easy, evenly spaced stitches.

Transparent foot

A presser foot made of transparent plastic can be very helpful when sewing seams with very small seam allowances, as in the glove projects.

Straight stitch throat plate

The throat plate is the metal surface on which the presser foot pushes down, with a hole that allows the needle to pass through to the bobbin. Regular throat plates have a wide hole that allows for the three needle positions and zigzag stitches. A straight stitch throat plate, which has only a single small hole (or three small holes), is very helpful when sewing stretch fabrics very close to the edge, as a regular throat plate may allow the fabric to be pushed into the hole.

Machine needles

Although the type of needle used in the sewing machine may not seem terribly important, be assured that it is. Always use the correct needle for the job.

Universal - Pointed tip, used for sewing most woven textiles.

Leather - Wedge-shaped tip, used for machine sewing leather and other heavy unwoven materials.

Stretch - Rounded tip, used for sewing stretch and knit fabrics.

Needles

Small needles - Regular sewing needles. These are used primarily for basting.

Leather needles - Blunt steel needles used mostly for sewing thick leather.

Glover's needles - Three-sided needles used to sew thin leather without pre-punching stitch holes.

Lacing needles - Flat barbed needles that are used for lace work such as turks-heads. (fig 1.5)

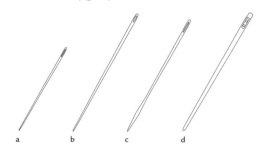

fig 1.5. a: small needle, b: leather needle, c: glover's needle, d: lacing needle

Sailor's palm

This odd-looking device consists of a hard dimpled surface mounted on a leather strap. It is worn around the thumb or finger on the inside of the hand, and used to provide a surface with which to push a needle through leather (fig 1.6).

fig 1.6

Thimble

Thimbles are used in much the same way as the sailor's palm, only generally with smaller needles. They are usually worn on the middle finger, and can be helpful when hand-sewing several layers of material, or even some lighter leathers.

Pins

Although not strictly necessary, pins can be used to hold two or more layers of fabric together prior to cutting or sewing, or even to hold the pattern to the fabric before or instead of tracing. Each pin is stuck through all the layers, then out again, across the direction of the seam. The pins are then removed one by one as the seam is sewn. Some stretch fabrics can be difficult to keep aligned, and pinning the seam can help solve this problem. Using pins is not recommended when working with coated textiles or leather. Leather can be marked up with a pin, however, by pricking the grain side every 5mm (3/16") or so. The obvious disadvantage of this practice is that the marks are permanent, allowing little room for error.

Seam ripper

A seam ripper is a pointed hand tool used to unpick machine-sewn and hand-sewn seams. Having a seam ripper on hand is not necessary, but will save time when undoing errors and removing basting (fig 1.7).

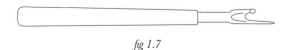

fig 1.7

Shears

Although most fabric can be cut with regular scissors, cutting through almost any kind of garment leather requires something more. Most shears will work well with garment leather, and cut through fabric like a hot knife through butter. The best shears for this kind of work are usually found at sewing stores, or in the sewing section of department stores.

Small scissors

The most readily available and functional scissors for more intricate work are embroidery scissors, which are small, steel, have pointed blades, and can be found at sewing stores. Surgical scissors or appliqué scissors are ideal if you can find them, but any pair of small scissors that keeps an edge after cutting leather will work fine (fig 1.8).

fig 1.8

Snips

This traditional tailor's tool is very useful when machine sewing. Having a pair of snips next to the machine to clip thread is essential, but beyond that they are very helpful in pinning down and maneuvering fabric when machine sewing awkward and hard-to-reach seams (fig 1.9).

fig 1.9

Utility knife

A good-quality utility knife is a must for the plaited projects in Chapter VII, unless you happen to be able to hone the edge of a knife to the point where you could use it to shave. Learning to sharpen knives that well can be time-consuming and not really necessary, unless you're going to do this sort of work professionally. The best utility knives for this type of work have wide snap-off blades (fig 1.10).

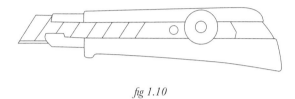

fig 1.10

Hobby knife

A small, scalpel-like blade for delicate work is required for many of the projects in this book, and is a must for every toolbox in any case. These can be purchased from most hobby and hardware stores (fig 1.11).

fig 1.11

Carving knife

A fairly sturdy knife will be required to whittle the handles for the flogger and singletail in Chapter VII. A pocket knife, bowie knife, or even a solid paring knife will do the trick. Should you have access to a wood lathe, however, it is of course preferable.

Rotary cutter

A rotary cutter is a circular blade mounted on a handle, not unlike a pizza cutter. It is not necessary, but will save a lot of time and make for cleaner edges when cutting strapping (fig 1.12).

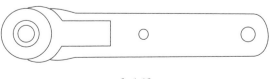

fig 1.12

Australian strander

This little device, used to cut laces, is essentially a blade fixed to an adjustable guide. It can save a lot of time, frustration, and cramped hands when making the plaited projects in Chapter VII (fig 1.13).

fig 1.13

Beveler

This tool is used to round off the edges of latigo and vegetable-tanned leather to give it a cleaner finish (fig 1.14).

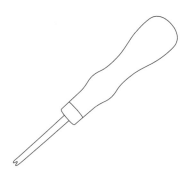

fig 1.14

Awl

An awl is simply a steel spike mounted on a small wooden knob. Although only a few projects in this book actually require the use of an awl, this is a very handy tool to have around when doing any sort of leather work (fig 1.15).

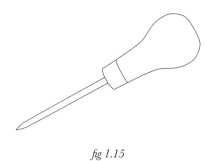

fig 1.15

Stitch chisel

A stitch chisel is used to cut small slots in heavier leather that is to be hand-stitched. They can be found with one blade, or with several evenly spaced chisels in a row. While the latter makes spacing a cinch, the former will be required when making fewer than four stitches in a row, and when going around curved edges (fig 1.16).

fig 1.16

Drive punch

Of the several different styles of hole punches, the most efficient and versatile one is also the simplest. The hand-operated rotary punches tend to be clumsy and only puncture thin leather, and the interchangeable tube variety tend not to be very sturdy. Since all of the projects in this book require making the same size holes, I recommend that you obtain a solidly made ⅛" (3mm) drive punch. If you have a high enough quality punch, you can make holes by simply pushing the punch through the leather, rather than using a hammer (see fig 1.17).

fig 1.17

Stamps

Stamps are used to imprint patterns into vegetable-tanned leather. Some stamps come fixed to a handle, whereas others need to have a handle attached to them before use. Stamps are definitely optional pieces of equipment, but I encourage you to look for a particular stamp that appeals to you so that you can brand your work. To make the sharpest possible stamp imprint, moisten the leather prior to stamping, and stamp it prior to dyeing.

Rivet setter

A rivet setter is simply a small metal rod around 9mm (³⁄₈") in diameter, concave on the end that compresses the rivet. Setters can be purchased from leather stores. Setting is noisy business, and must be done on a solid flat surface such as an anvil (fig 1.18).

fig 1.18

Snap setter

A snap setter is a metal rod with a domed or hexagonal protrusion on the business end (fig 1.19). Small snap setters will often be included in packages of snaps, but I suggest you purchase a setter with a longer handle for increased accuracy and fewer bruised fingers.

fig 1.19

Used in conjunction with the setter, a snap anvil is a small metal disc with a slightly larger diameter than the snap to be set, concave on one side (fig 1.19). The female half of the snap is laid on the concave side of the anvil, which is placed on a hard surface before setting. The male half can be set on the flat side of the anvil, or on a mini-anvil (fig 1.20).

Eyelet/Grommet setter

Like the snap setter, an eyelet setter is a metal rod with a domed tip, used to fix eyelets in place after they have been inserted into the leather. Grommet setters often have wider tips to accommodate larger diameters. Eyelets and grommets should be set on a matching anvil, but a wooden cutting board can sometimes suffice.

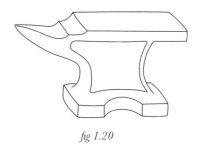

fig 1.20

Anvil

An anvil is a block of hard, flat, solid material on which setting work can be done. It can be anything from a flat piece of stone to a miniature or full-sized blacksmith's anvil (fig 1.20).

Cutting/punching board

A solid cutting board is necessary for most of the projects in this book. Any time you punch a hole in leather, use a cutting board to avoid damaging the punch. Any hardwood cutting board from department or kitchen stores will work. Although only a small board is required, you'll need a larger board if you intend to use a rotary cutter. Rubber punching boards can also work for hole punching, and plastic cutting mats are a viable alternative for rotary cutter work.

Rolling board

You'll need a smaller wooden board, in addition to a cutting board, for making the plaited projects in Chapter VII. It can be of any wood, and should be approximately 300mm x 300mm (12" x 12").

Hammer

Most leather workers use mallets with heads made of rawhide, rubber, or plastic. These will all work fine, and so will a regular claw hammer. Just about any hammer with a flat head will work for the projects in this book.

Pliers/Locking pliers

Every toolbox should contain a decent set of pliers, and needlenose locking pliers are ideal for this kind of work. You'll need pliers for cutting chain, opening D-rings and resetting zipper stops, and also for removing hardware from leather. Having both a pair of pliers and a pair of locking pliers will make some of these jobs easier.

Wire cutter

A wire cutter looks like a pair of pliers with blades where the clamps would be. A wire cutter is only required for the projects that use twist link chain. Some pliers have a wire cutter built in to them, but generally these will not work for cutting chain.

Needle files

Needle files are simply very small metal files, usually a few millimeters in diameter and a hundred or so millimeters long. They typically come in cases of four to a dozen, with flat, curved, triangular, square and round files. They are used to smooth out work in vegetable-tanned leather and to smooth out the welds on metal rings (fig 1.21).

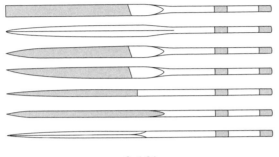

fig 1.21

Rasp

A rasp looks much like a file, but with one side covered with points instead of lines. Rasping surfaces that will be glued together makes for a secure weld.

Drill

A drill is recommended for making the ball gags in Chapter V and some of the whips in Chapter VII. With a bit of patience, you can bore holes through some balls using other methods, but a drill will make the process considerably easier and cleaner. The need for a drill can be circumvented in the whip projects as well if you choose wood that already has an acceptable hole.

Measuring tape

Any flexible measuring tape from a sewing store or sewing section of a department store will work well for both taking measurements and project construction. Steel measuring tapes of the type found in hardware stores will not take accurate body measurements.

Ruler

Aluminum or cork-backed steel rulers are the best for this type of work, as they can also be used as guides when cutting. Having both a small metal ruler and a metal meter stick is ideal; however, any regular plastic or wooden ruler will suffice.

Set square

A set square is a triangular device used to make lines at right angles when drafting. Although not strictly necessary, it can make some jobs easier and more precise.

Small foam brush

Leather dye can be applied with a dye dauber, cotton swab, or even a small sponge, but a small foam paintbrush from the art section of a department store is cheap and just as effective.

Pen

Felt-tip pens can be used to mark up fabric, so having a couple of different colors to contrast with different colored fabrics can be useful. Fine-point black pens can be used to mark up vegetable-tanned leather that will later be dyed black. For other colors, use a pencil.

Pencil

Drafting many of the patterns in this book will require drawing freehand curves. Few people can do this in one line on the first try, so a pencil and eraser will be helpful here.

Water pencil

Although a pencil can be used to mark up vegetable-tanned leather, pencil markings will not be visible on most garment leather. A white watercolor pencil, available at most art supply stores, with a shot glass of water to keep the tip wet, is ideal for marking up most garment leather and some fabrics. Once the cuts are made, the markings can be wiped away with a damp paper towel. A china marker or chinagraph pencil will also work, but their markings do not come off as easily and they can be more difficult to acquire. When marking up stretch fabric, it is often easier to mark a succession of dots rather than lines.

Chalk

Chalk is used to mark up regular textiles and stretch fabrics. Tailor's chalk works well, as does chalkboard chalk, which is cheaper and available in multiple colors. In both cases, the tip of the chalk can be shaved with a knife to make a finer point. When marking up stretch fabrics, it can be helpful to moisten the edge of the chalk to keep it from jumping.

Iron

An iron and ironing board are very helpful when making folds and flattening seams in woven fabric. Unfortunately, stretch fabrics cannot be ironed effectively.

Sandpaper

In this book, sandpaper is only called for when shaping the wooden handle cores of the whips in Chapter VII. Coarse sandpaper can also be used in place of a rasp when roughing up leather prior to gluing.

Rags

Small clean rags are required for some projects made from vegetable-tanned leather. They should be made of cotton or some other absorbent material, as they are used to apply leather conditioner and plaiting soap and for polishing.

Lighter

A small lighter will be required for many of the projects in this book. It is used to melt the ends of fraying synthetic material, such as zipper tape and fabric elastic, after it has been trimmed.

Spoon

A small metal spoon is very helpful when weaving turks-head knots. After you complete the knot, you can rub it with the concave side of the spoon to give it a rounder shape.

Hardware

Rivets

Rivets are small metal fasteners used to keep two or more pieces of leather together (fig 1.22). The post and cap of the rivet are assembled around the leather, and set in place using a rivet setter, a hammer and an anvil. Rivets are made with various metals in a variety of styles, and are generally sized as follows:

	Base diameter	Post height	Cap diameter
Small	6mm (¼")	6mm (¼")	6mm (¼")
Medium	10mm (⅜")	8mm (⁵⁄₁₆")	10mm (⅜")
Large	10mm (⅜")	13mm (½")	10mm (⅜")

Choosing the correct rivet height is just as important as the cap size, as the rivet will not set properly if it is too short or tall for the leather it is fastening. See page 55 for a discussion of rivet techniques.

Most rivets have a steel core and are plated with either brass or nickel. Although brass-plated rivets tend to be more rust-resistant than their nickel-plated counterparts, both have the potential to rust over time. Rivets with a brass core will never rust, and are therefore the ideal choice, and absolutely necessary in any area that may get damp, such as around the buckles of collars.

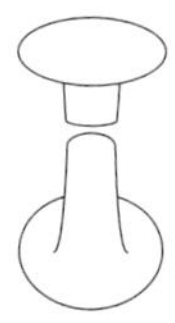

fig 1.22

Once you're comfortable with the relevant techniques, I suggest you use only the highest quality double-cap brass-core rivets. If you're uncertain if a rivet has a steel or brass core, simply hold a magnet up to it: if it sticks, it's made of steel.

Snaps

Snaps come in a few different diameters and post heights, and are usually made of steel plated with nickel, brass or copper. The 14mm (⁹⁄₁₆") wide nickel-plated variety are ideal for the projects in this book. They come in four parts, two for the female half (the button and socket), two for the male (the stud and eyelet), and are set with a snap setter and anvil (fig 1.23).

fig 1.23

Eyelets/Grommets

Eyelets are small metal cylinders used to reinforce holes made in leather. Grommets are simply eyelets with washers placed over the eyelets after they have been pushed through the leather, making for a cleaner, sturdier setting. Eyelets are called for far more frequently, as grommets of the size needed (inside and outside diameters) can be very difficult to acquire. It is, however, easier to find eyelet washers, which you can then combine with a matching eyelet to form a grommet (fig 1.24).

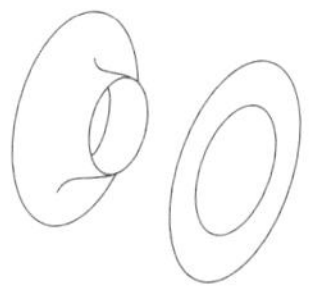

fig 1.24

Eyelets should be used to reinforce any lace holes or buckle pin holes where the strapping is made of more than one layer of leather. Beyond that, you, the designer, can choose when to use an eyelet and when to leave the hole alone - with one exception: the makeshift locking buckle on page 116. Eyelets can be an attractive cosmetic addition to some projects, particularly when using chap leather. But any time you use eyelets to reinforce buckle pin holes, check that the buckle pin will fit through the eyelets before fixing them in place. Also, in small strapping, eyelets in the buckle pin holes can make fastening the buckle a bit awkward.

Eyelets come in a variety of widths, heights and styles. Short, medium and tall eyelets are all called for in this book, but only in a width of ³⁄₁₆" (5mm). One setter can be used with most eyelets of this width, but check with the vendor for the correct setter if you're not sure. Some eyelets will split into tabs when set, which must then be flattened with a hammer.

Embellishments

The most common decorative elements when it comes to leather are spikes and studs, although a wider variety of ornamentation can be found at leather stores or on the Internet. Spikes are typically screwed in place through holes, and studs folded in place through slots.

Rings

Many projects in this book use steel rings. Although some smaller-diameter rings can be purchased at hardware stores, you'll probably need to shop at a leather store for some of the larger ones. And remember: if a body part is going to go in the ring, be sure to file down the weld.

D-rings

A D-ring is quite simply a ring shaped like a capital D. D-rings are used as attachment points on many of the restraints in this book.

Connector rings

These rings are used to connect lengths of chain and to attach spring clips. The simplest and easiest connector ring to acquire is a key ring, and these are often suffi- ciently durable for the projects in this book. Split rings, which are simply metal wires bent into loops, are ideal if their ends are welded together after they are fixed in place. Also worth consideration are small connecting quick links and spring gate O-rings, though these are more costly and difficult to acquire.

Spring clips

These small steel clips are fastened to the ends of lengths of leather or chain so that they can be attached to something else. In this book they are used to make leashes and reins. Having a few different lengths of chain with spring clips on the ends can be useful (fig 1.25).

fig 1.25

Buckles

Buckles are used to connect strapping in many of the leather projects in this book, and are usually fastened to the strapping with rivets. Center-bar buckles have built-in strap keepers, but heel-bar buckles will require that you mount a separate keeper behind the buckle. Handmade leather strap keepers are used in this book. Center-bar buckles are thicker, and thus do not lie as flat as heel-bar buckles. They can cause the wearer discomfort when body pressure is exerted against them – which is why you should use heel-bar buckles when constructing harnesses. Locking buckles are locked in place by slipping a padlock through the ring at the tip of the pin after buckling (fig 1.26).

fig 1.26. Heel-bar buckle, Center-bar buckle – often roller-bar, and Locking buckle.

Slide buckles

Slide buckles are small three-bar devices used to lengthen and shorten strapping. One end of the strap is attached to the center bar of the buckle, and the other end is threaded around it (fig 1.27).

fig 1.27

Zippers

Two types of zippers are used in this book. Nylon chain zippers are used in Chapter I; you should select a

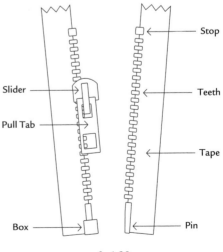

fig 1.28

11

closed-ended zipper that matches the fabric and the length of the opening. The metal type will generally need to be open-ended (separable), and can be resized fairly easily (see page 57). If a new metal zipper is sticky, rub it with beeswax, then open and close it a few times.

Boning

Boning is sewn into fabric in order to stiffen it, as in corsetry. It is purchased in rolls or strips, and can be made from plastic, steel or wood, though at one time boning was actually made from whalebone (baleen). The projects in this book call for the "Rigilene" type of plastic boning, which is made with many small plastic rods woven together to produce boning that is stiff but not rigid. The advantage of using this type of boning is that it can be sewn through with a domestic sewing machine, while other types cannot.

Chain

The only type of chain used in this book is called "twist link," which is the kind that will lay flat. The larger 10mm (³⁄₈") chain is used for leashes, and the 5mm (³⁄₁₆") chain for everything else. Although 10mm (³⁄₈") twist link can be purchased in bulk at most hardware stores, 5mm (³⁄₁₆") can be difficult to acquire (fig 1.29).

fig 1.29

Tacks

Small tacks are used in the flogger and singletail projects in Chapter VII to fix the leather laces and bolsters to the handle cores. They can typically be purchased at hardware stores.

Lag Screws/Washers

Lag screws are large wood screws with hex bolt heads (fig 1.30). They are used in conjunction with matching washers to counterweight the flogger in Chapter VII. When purchasing washers, ensure they fit fairly sungly around the shaft of the lag screw, and also that their outside diameter is not greater than the final diameter of the handle. They can typically be purchased at hardware stores.

fig 1.30

Other Materials

Thread

The best thread to use in a sewing machine is usually mercerized cotton, regardless of what project is being sewn. The color of the thread should be chosen to match the fabric or leather as closely as possible. When working with vegetable-tanned leather, artificial sinew can be a good choice for hand-sewing, as it is pretty much indestructible. Artificial sinew is also ideal for wrapping the bolster on the singletail in Chapter VII, as it lies flat and the wax makes it adhere well to the bolster. Since most leather will be colored, though, using a matching colored thread is generally best. Waxed cotton and the heavy thread used in upholstery are ideal for hand-sewing the leather projects in this book.

Laces

Many of the projects in this book employ lace closures, necessitating shoe or boot laces. Round laces, which can be purchased in standardized lengths at shoe and department stores, are generally best.

Fabric elastic

Fabric elastic can be purchased in a variety of widths at most sewing stores and some department stores. It can typically only be found in either black or white, so keep this in mind when choosing colors for projects that call for it.

Hook-and-loop

Called for only once in this book (see page 167), hook-and-loop fastener consists of two strips of nylon, one with tiny hooks, and the other with tiny loops. I generally avoid it because its lifespan is short compared to that of leather, and its insecure nature makes it inappropriate for the kinds of projects in this book.

Polyurethane foam

A couple of projects in Chapter V call for polyurethane foam, which is the type of foam used in furniture and mattresses. Foam can be purchased at upholstery stores, but since only small pieces are required, off cuts can often be acquired free of charge. Polyurethane foam cannot be glued with contact cement. Polyurethane glue is best for the techniques described in this book (see page 153).

Liquid latex

Latex garments are generally made by either joining panels of latex sheeting, or by dipping molds into liquid latex. I have not discussed the construction techniques used to make latex garments, as they differ greatly from those employed when working with leather and textiles. However, many of the patterns in this book could be used to construct garments out of latex sheeting.

Liquid latex *is* used, however, to seal the ball gag projects on pages 156 and 158. Buy it pre-vulcanized and without color, though it will have a milky appearance. It can often be purchased at art supply stores. It should be colored with a universal colorant (only as much as is necessary), which can usually be purchased at the same place.

Contact cement

Contact cement is a glue that works particularly well with leather. Many products are designed specifically for leather, but regular contact cement from the hardware store works just as well for the projects in this book. Generally, when glue is called for, contact cement is used. It should have consistency of honey, with a solvent smell, and is applied with a glue brush or butter knife in a well-ventilated area. Contact cement can be removed from the grain side of leather by simply rubbing it with your fingers. Contact cement thinner, nail polish remover, or another powerful solvent can help remove it from fabric.

Cyanoacrylate glue

Although completely optional, cyanoacrylate, or CA, glue (also known as "Super Glue") can be used to reinforce the knots made when hand-sewing leather. A small drop of this glue will help prevent the knot from coming untied.

Solvent

When you apply contact cement to leather, be certain that the surface is free of dirt and oily contaminants. Since the leather laces in the plaited projects in Chapter VII are impregnated with a mixture of fat and soap, you must clean these surfaces before the glue can be applied.

This is not difficult: simply wipe the area to be glued with a rag or paper towel, and a solvent such as rubbing alcohol. Contact cement thinner can also suffice, and is also very useful when removing contact cement. Removing contact cement is required in some projects even when no errors are made.

Leather dye

Vegetable-tanned leather is not generally colored at the tannery, and must be dyed by hand if you want any coloring besides its natural tan, which will darken with use to a medium brown. Leather dye can be purchased in a reasonably wide variety of colors from most leather stores. Some water-based fabric dyes will work on leather, though they must be mixed to around eight times their normal concentration.

Leather conditioner

Leather conditioner is useful in treating vegetable-tanned leather, particularly after it has been dyed. You can achieve nice shine by applying it in small amounts and rubbing it in with a cotton cloth. Garment leather does not usually need leather conditioner unless it has been washed.

Plaiting soap

A mixture of fat, soap and water, plaiting soap is used to soften and condition leather, particularly leather laces prior to plaiting. It can not generally be purchased, but a recipe is provided on page 188.

Paper

Since many of the projects in this book require drafting a paper pattern as a first step, paper of a size approximate to the pattern will be required. A large sketchbook will suffice for most of these projects, but it is recommended that a length of meter-wide paper be purchased for the larger ones. (If that is not available, several pieces of paper can be joined together.)

Newspaper

When rolling the plaited whips in Chapter VII, the boards are wrapped in newspaper to provide traction and absorb excess plaiting soap.

CHAPTER II

Clothing

The projects in this chapter are made with fabric, mostly of types found in the average sewing or department store. Although some hand-sewing and other techniques will be used, the majority of the work will be done with a sewing machine. As in each chapter of this book, I'll discuss the techniques you'll use before we get started.

Basic sewing

The first three projects are made of basic woven fabric with very little stretch, the ideal type of fabric to choose when you're learning how to use a sewing machine. When assembling these, use the straight stitch on the sewing machine, leaving a 15mm (⅝") seam allowance unless otherwise specified (fig 2.1).

When starting any stitch, first hold both threads taut and make several stitches forward. Then use a technique called backtacking to prevent the seam from coming undone. To backtack, reverse the sewing machine and go back several stitches over the seam, then forward again. When going forward again, take care not to run in to the seam allowance; it's better to head ever so slightly to the left of the seam, as shown (exaggerated for illustrative purposes). Backtacking is also used to end the seam – though when ending, you should run your backward stitches slightly into the seam allowance, then forward to the end of the seam (fig 2.2).

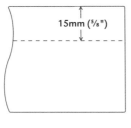

fig 2.1

fig 2.2

Some seams will then be finished with a technique known as topstitching (fig 2.3). To topstitch a seam, first press or glue the seam allowance flat against the material. Pressing the seam allowance to one side and then topstitching it in one seam will strengthen the seam, while spreading the seam allowance apart and topstitching both sides of the allowance will give it a more decorative finish. To use the second method without sacrificing strength, add a strip of material underneath the seam – a technique often used in leather work. It is generally easier to topstitch a seam from the inside of the project unless using a reinforcing strip, in which case sewing from the outside (so you can see the seam you're topstitching) will make for straighter seams. Take care to keep all layers of material flat and taut when topstitching.

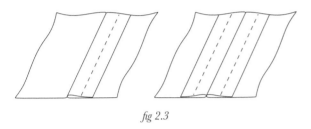

fig 2.3

Another type of seam worthy of note is the French seam, which encloses the raw edges to prevent fraying. To sew a French seam, first sew the fabric, good sides out, 5mm (³⁄₁₆") from the edge. Then, turn the fabric so the good sides are together, press the seam, and sew a second seam 10mm (³⁄₈") inside the first. French seams are only useful on straight runs or gentle curves. They are not called for in this book, but can be used on appropriate runs in the kimono, robe and hakama projects if desired.

Generally, when assembling projects made with stretch fabric (such as the zentai) on a domestic machine, you'll want to use zigzag stitches. To make a strong yet flexible seam, you'll sew two parallel seams in a 15mm (⁵⁄₈") seam allowance, the inside being narrow zigzag stitch and the outside being a wide zigzag stitch (fig 2.4). Although the outside zigzag can be used to overcast the edge of the fabric if desired, in this example the entire stitch is inside the seam allowance. These stitches will collectively be referred to as a stretch stitch. Some sewing machines actually have a special stretch stitch setting, which you can use if desired.

When making the zentai mask and gloves, however, you'll want to use a straight stitch to accommodate more detail; the zentai and gloves do not need to expand as much as the other stretch garments, so you won't need the stretch stitch. Use very short stitches, between one and two millimeters (¹⁄₁₆"). The 10mm (³⁄₈") seam allowance used in the mask is only to allow for easier assembly, and should be trimmed to 5mm (³⁄₁₆") after the seam is completed.

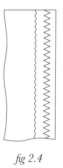

fig 2.4

When making a 90° turn, or any turn where the presser foot must be lifted, make sure the needle is all the way down through the fabric to prevent slippage and missed stitches. Missed stitches can also be caused by an incorrect or bent needle, incorrect threading of the machine, or incorrect tension setting.

Basting and zippers

When installing zippers in the bodysuit and mask, you'll use a hand sewing technique called basting (fig 2.5). First, draw a line with a water pencil on the wrong side of the fabric, 15mm (⁵⁄₈") from and parallel to the opening edge, then hand-sew the opening shut, good sides together, along this line. Take care to sew a straight and even stitch. You can pull the basting thread tight to gather the fabric slightly, thus preventing the zipper from bubbling, if desired.

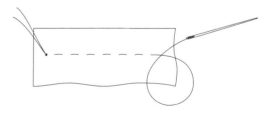

fig 2.5

Once the opening has been basted shut, spread the seam allowance apart and place the zipper inside face down, with the center of the zipper precisely on the center of the seam. Take careful notice of how much of the seam allowance extends beyond the zipper tape. Position the metal base of the zipper just behind where the opening is to start and baste the first side of the zipper tape in place, remembering where on the seam allowance to place it. It is very important that this be done precisely and kept parallel along the length of the zipper (fig 2.6).

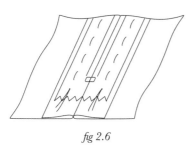

fig 2.6

After the other side of the zipper tape has been basted in the same manner, you can sew the zipper in place from the top side, with a straight stitch and a zipper foot. Although this step is usually fairly straightforward, some fabrics – particularly swimwear fabric, fabric that stretches both ways, and even fabrics with a very high stretch percentage – will tend to stick to the presser foot, stretching the top layer of fabric. This problem can be solved by also basting each side of the top layer to the bottom and zipper tape before sewing it in place.

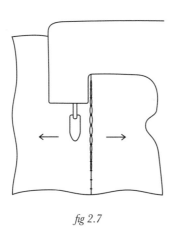

fig 2.7

For the first side of the zipper, start at the base and work up to the top, 3mm (⅛") from the center seam. Be sure to keep the fabric flat, and keep the zipper centered on the center seam by feeling it through the fabric and peeking through the holes in the basting (fig 2.7). For the second side, start at the base about 5mm (³⁄₁₆") inside the first seam, stitch over it until just below the zipper stop, then make a 90° turn and cross over the zipper tape to 3mm (⅛") from the other side of the center seam and up to the top in the same manner as the first side. When installing a closed-top zipper, such as the crotch zipper in the bodysuit, the second seam should meet with the first at the top end in the same manner as the bottom. Once the zipper has been satisfactorily sewn in place, the center and zipper basting can be carefully removed with the help of small scissors or a seam ripper.

Basting can also be used anytime layers of fabric need to be held together precisely before sewing, such as when sewing gloves with fourchettes. Although basting can add a bit of time, it can certainly save on frustration. Try not to sew the basting seam in the same area the machine seam will go though, as doing so can make removing the basting thread difficult.

Easing

Another technique that is useful to know, though never called for in this book, is what is called easing. Easing is done when one layer of fabric is too long at the end of a seam, but both layers must end together. Errors of this nature can happen easily with stretch fabric, as the sewing machine will tend to stretch the top layer of fabric more than the bottom, leaving extra fabric on the top side at the end of the seam. This can often be trimmed off without consequence, but if it is imperative that both layers of fabric end together, you can ease them slightly without consequence. If it is the top layer that is too long, simply pull the bottom layer taut while pushing the top layer towards the presser foot, creating little bubbles. This must be done a little bit at a time, as easing too much too quickly will create pleats or a bubbly seam, which means having to unpick the seam and re-do the ease. If it is the bottom layer that is too long, pull the top layer taut and attempt to feed more of the bottom layer.

KIMONO

This is a good project to start with if your sewing skills need to be developed. It uses straightforward techniques that will be built upon as the book progresses. The seams need not be finished, though French seams (see page 16) could be used for the sides, back and arm openings.

When choosing material, pretty much anything with little or no stretch will work, but some cheaper fabric may be best for a preliminary run if this is your first attempt at using a sewing machine. Ideally, though, this project will look its best when made with some sort of embroidered fabric, such as silk brocade.

The sleeves in this pattern are the more formal furisode sleeves, which fall to the knees and are closed at the front up to the wrist and open at the back. Having the sleeves closed in the back and open in the front, or even replacing them with narrow, cylindrical sleeves, are attractive, untraditional possibilities. Narrow sleeves are more typical of menswear, and this pattern can be further altered to produce a short men's jacket by shortening the front and rear panels to fall just below the crotch.

This project's design is based on that of a traditional kimono, but it deviates from tradition in many respects. This kimono is designed to fall freely to the ankles, where traditional kimonos are as long as the wearer is tall and are folded at the obi, or belt, to the correct length. The pattern can easily be altered to make a traditional kimono by extending the length of the front and rear panels.

Another significant departure from tradition is the way in which the sleeves are attached to the body of the kimono. Typically, the sleeves are not attached all the way around the arm openings, and a small gap remains at the tops of the side seams. This construction style allows for the wide obi that are sometimes worn with the kimonos. However, this style does not produce a very sturdy seam, so in this design the side seams run all the way up to a closed arm opening. To alter this pattern back to the traditional, the sides of the front and rear panels should drop straight from the shoulder to the floor, omitting the indentations and tapers. The sleeves can then be attached in much the same manner as described in this project, though the 100mm (4") seams on the inside of the sleeves are omitted, and 60mm (2½") gaps are left between the top of the side seam and the sleeves.

The four-panel construction style employed here is untraditional as well. Typically, the front and rear of each side of the kimono are cut from one piece of fabric, and small extension panels are sewn along the front meeting edges so that they can overlap under the obi. This construction method is due at least in part to the narrow width of the fabric used to make kimonos in Japan. The four-panel style, with two panels making up the front and two making up the rear, allows for greater flexibility and often less waste when cutting out the panels on western-width fabric. It also makes for a neater appearance, particularly when using fabric with an asymmetrical pattern.

Although the sleeves on the kimono presented here will fall to the same point on the wrist as a traditional kimono, the sleeves are actually larger and the body smaller. The large-body, small-sleeve construction style may be another consequence of the width of fabric used in Japan. I've changed this proportion in the interests of sturdier seams and a more form-fitting garment, but you can change it back by first calculating the traditional rear panel width (approximately half ζ), using that to calculate the front panel size, then finding the difference between the traditional rear panel size and the rear panel size prescribed here, and subtracting that difference from the sleeve width.

Tools

- Sewing machine (universal needle)
- Small needle
- Shears
- Measuring tape
- Chalk
- Iron

Materials

- Embroidered silk brocade (or other woven fabric)
- Matching thread

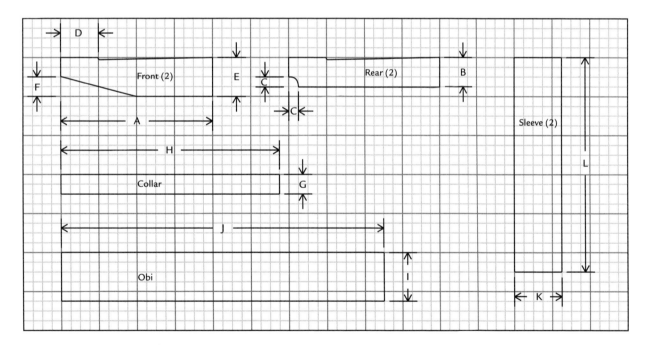

A = σ + τ + 130mm (5")

B = 0.33ζ + 40mm (1½")

C = 0.25ε + 15mm (⅝")

D = ι

E = B + 75mm (3")

F = C + 75mm (3")

G = 170mm (6¾")

H = A + 0.5ε + 300mm (12")

I = 230mm (9")

J = 4θ

K = κ - 70mm (2¾")

L = 2[σ + 0.50τ + 15mm (⅝")]

Instructions

- Mark and cut out all pieces, taking care to make each pair of front and rear panels mirror images of each other. When using fabric with an asymmetrical pattern, ensure that the pattern runs in the same direction along all panels. Because the sleeves are each cut in one piece, the pattern will necessarily run in the opposite direction on one side, so take care to ensure that it runs in the proper direction on the front of each sleeve. Note that the indentations at the base of the arm openings on the front and rear panels are 20mm (¾") deep, and the meeting edge tapers on the front panels begin halfway up their length.

- Sew the rear panels, good sides together, 15mm (⅝") from the edge, from the neck down to the bottom.

- Sew each front panel to the corresponding rear panel along the shoulders, good sides together, 15mm (⅝") from the edge.

- Press open the rear and shoulder seam allowances.

- Lay the kimono body good sides out and front up, fold the sleeves in half widthwise, and arrange them on either side of the kimono body so the fabric pattern runs in the same direction on all panels. Mark the center point on each sleeve, where it will be joined to the shoulder.

- Align the center mark of each sleeve with the corresponding shoulder seam, good sides together, and sew 15mm (⅝") from the edge, from the center down to 15mm (⅝") from the bottom of each indentation.

- Sew each sleeve, good sides together, starting at the wrist opening, 200mm (8") below the fold, 15mm (⅝") from the edge. Sew down the outside of the sleeve and the bottom, forming a gentle curve at the outside bottom corner.

- Sew the top 100mm (4") of the inside of each sleeve, good sides together, 15mm (⅝") from the edge. Do not sew through the front and rear panel seam allowances when meeting the arm opening seam (fig 2.8).

- Sew each front panel to the corresponding rear panel along the sides, good sides together, from the arm opening seam down, 15mm (⅝") from the edge (fig 2.8).

- Turn the sleeves good sides out and press, forming 15mm (⅝") folds at the wrist openings.

- Press 15mm (⅝") folds, good sides out, along the inside edges of the sleeves.

- Press open the side seam allowances.

- Trim the bottom edge straight if necessary and press a 20mm (¾") fold along the edge, good sides out.

- Press 20mm (¾") folds along the vertical portion of the front meeting edges, good sides out.

- Sew the wrist opening folds in place from the inside, folding the raw edge under the fold, 2mm (1⁄16") from the edge of the inside fold (fig 2.9).

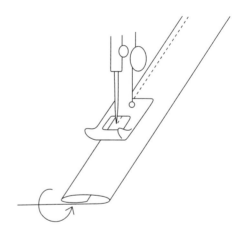

fig 2.9

- Sew the sleeve folds in place from the inside, folding the raw edge under the fold, 2mm (1⁄16") from the edge of the inside fold (fig 2.9).

- Reinforce the points where the wrist openings and inside sleeve openings begin by joining the topstitching on either side with several lines of stitching (fig 2.10, page 21).

- Sew the vertical meeting edge folds in place from the inside, folding the raw edge under the fold, 2mm (1⁄16") from the edge of the inside fold (fig 2.9).

- Sew the bottom fold in place from the inside, folding the raw edge under the fold, 2mm (1⁄16") from the edge of the inside fold (fig 2.9).

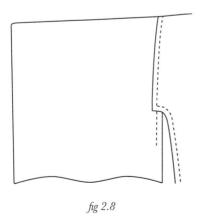

fig 2.8

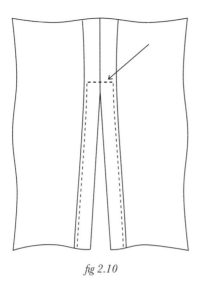

fig 2.10

- Mark the lengthwise center of the collar panel and align it with the top of the rear seam, good sides together. Sew it in place from the center down to where each folded vertical portion begins, 15mm (⅝") from the edge.

- Fold the collar away from the body of the kimono and iron a crease on the collar, 2mm (1/16") from the joining seam, so that the fold covers the seam.

- Press a 45mm (1¾") fold, good sides out, along the outside edge of the collar.

- Fold the remaining width of the collar in half lengthwise, sandwiching the kimono in the center, and press.

- Press 15mm (⅝") folds, good sides out, along all four edges of the obi panel.

- Fold the obi in half lengthwise and press.

- Baste the collar fold in place, taking care to align the folds on the inside and the outside of the kimono. Each end of the collar will need to be trimmed so that it extends 15mm (⅝") beyond the end of the seam. Fold this raw edge inside the collar and baste it together.

- Sew the collar in place from the outside, 3mm (⅛") from the inside fold and the ends.

- Sew the obi on all four sides, 3mm (⅛") from the edge.

- Remove the basting.

- Press the entire kimono, focusing on the folded edges.

ROBE

This simple hooded robe is basically an extension of the previous project. It is constructed with four panels making up the body, one for each of the arms, and four more for the hood. Any natural-fiber fabric will work well for this project; cotton twill is ideal. A painter's dropcloth made of soft natural cotton makes a cheap and comfortable material for this project. The design presented here wraps around the front like the kimono and ties at the sides, but an untied robe can also be made by using the rear panel pattern for both the front and rear panels. This type of robe can be left open, or closed with a belt or a clasp at the neck.

Tools

- Sewing machine (universal needle)
- Small needle
- Shcars
- Measuring tape
- Pencil and ruler
- Chalk
- Iron

Materials

- Natural fiber fabric
- Matching thread
- Paper

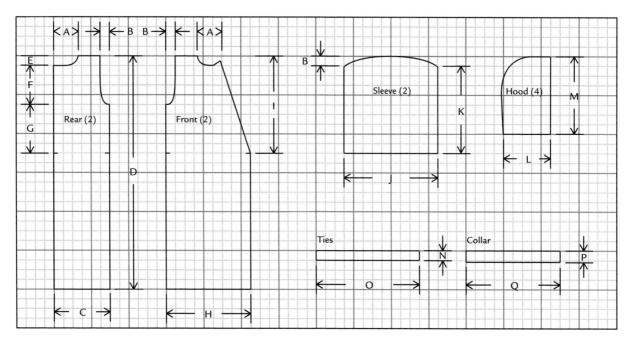

A = 200mm (8")

B = 40mm (1½")

C = 0.25ζ + 200mm (8")

D = σ + τ + 120mm (4¾")

E = 50mm (2")

F = ι - E - 50mm (2")

G = I - E - F

H = 0.50ζ + 130mm (5")

I = 0.85σ

J = 2[ι - 30mm (1¼")]

K = κ + 50mm (2")

L = 330mm (13")

M = 520mm (20½")

N = 45mm (1¾")

O = 720mm (28")

P = 50mm (2")

Q = 700mm (27½")

Instructions

- Mark and cut out all pieces, taking care to make each pair of panels mirror images of each other, and two mirror-image pairs of the hood panels.

- Sew the sleeves, good sides together, 15mm (⅝") from the edge.

- Sew the rear panels, good sides together, from the top down to the bottom, 15mm (⅝") from the edge.

- Sew each pair of hood panels along the curved edge, good sides together, making two identical hoods.

- Press open the sleeve, rear and straight portions of the hood seam allowances.

- Press 20mm (¾") folds, good sides out, along the opening edges of the front panels.

- Press 40mm (1½") folds, good sides out, along the opening edges of the front panels.

- Fold the long edges of the tie piece in to the center, good sides out, and press. Fold it in half along the center line so that all the raw edges are inside, and press again.

- Cut the tie piece into four equal lengths.

- Sew each tie together, 2mm (¹⁄₁₆") from the edge of the first set of folds.

- Sew the opening edge folds in place from the inside, using two seams, 3mm (⅛") from the inside and outside fold edges. Make the folds on the lower half of the panels first, then the top, which will create a downward-facing pocket once the inner seam is sewn.

- Insert a tie in to each of the pockets (an awl can help here if it's a tight fit) and sew in place along the pocket edge. Then sew the tie down in a second seam over the outer opening edge seam (fig 2.11).

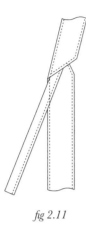

fig 2.11

- Topstitch both sides of the sleeve, rear and hood seams.

- Fold the robe, good sides out, along the back seam, and mark and sew a seam 100mm (4") inside the fold running from the top of the robe down 190mm (7 ½"). This seam helps the back pleat lay flat and straight.

- Turn one of the hoods good sides out and place it inside the other hood, which should be good sides in. Sew the hoods, good sides together, 15mm (⅝") from the front edge (fig 2.12).

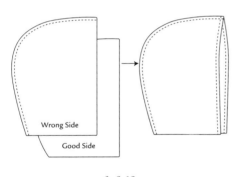

Wrong Side

Good Side

fig 2.12

- Press a 20mm (¾") fold, good sides out, on the cuff of each sleeve.

- Press a 40mm (1 ½") fold, good sides out, on the cuff of each sleeve.

- Form the back pleat in the robe by aligning the back seam over the seam sewn in the rear panels and pressing.

- Topstitch each side of the back pleat from the top down 200mm (8"), 3mm (⅛") from the edge (fig 2.13).

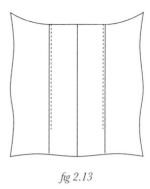

fig 2.13

- Sew the cuff folds in place from the inside in two seams, 3mm (⅛") from the inside and outside fold edges.

- Sew each front panel to the corresponding rear panel along the shoulder, good sides together, 15mm (⅝") from the edge.

- Sew each front panel to the corresponding rear panel along the sides from the top down, good sides together, 15mm (⅝") from the edge. When the tie mark is reached on the left side, sandwich a tie between the front and rear panels so that the edge of the tie is even with the seam allowance.

- Ensure that the bottom edge of the hood, from front seam to front seam, matches the length of the collar. Adjust the front hood seam if necessary.

- Turn the hood right side out, and press the front edge.

- Press open the side and shoulder seam allowances.

- Topstitch both sides of the shoulder and side seams. When topstitching the side seam that does not have a tie sewn in the seam, lay another tie over the seam at the tie mark, on the inside pointing forward so that the edge of the tie lines up with the inside edge of the seam allowance. Sew over it on both sides of the seam. When topstitching the side seam with the tie already sewn in it, lay the tie so that it points to the front on the outside, and sew over it on both sides of the seam.

- Sew the front of the hood 10mm (⅜") from the edge, and along the bottom 5mm (³⁄₁₆") from the edge.

- Align the base of the rear hood seams with top of the back seam good sides together and sew along the collar in two seams running from the center 15mm (⅝") from the edge.

- Press open the collar seam allowance.

- Press 10mm (⅜") folds good sides out along all four sides of the collar panel.

- Press a 20mm (¾") fold, good sides out, along the bottom edge.

- Press a 40mm (1 ½") fold, good sides out, along the bottom edge.

- Sew the bottom edge fold in place from the inside in two seams, 3mm (⅛") from the inside and outside fold edges.

- With the sleeves right sides out and the robe inside out, insert each sleeve into an arm opening, lining up the sleeve seam with the side seam. Sew in place 10mm (⅜") from the edge.

- Sew around the edge of the arm opening seam allowances with a zig-zag stitch.

- Baste collar panel over the collar seam, taking care to keep it centered on the seam (fig 2.14). The raw edge of the collar panel should be folded in at the robe's meeting edges, and will probably need to be trimmed before folding when you reach the far meeting edge.

fig 2.14

- Sew all four edges of the collar panel from the inside, 3mm (⅛") from each edge. The meeting edges of the collar can end up being quite bulky because of the many layers of fabric. Compressing these areas with locking pliers can help get them under the presser foot.

- Remove the basting.

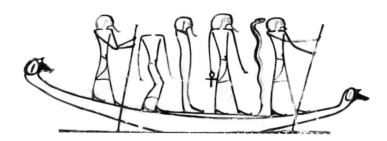

HAKAMA

Hakama are traditional Japanese divided skirts. They are tied at the waist and fall to the center of the ankle. Traditionally worn by the samurai, and worn today by practitioners of the samurai arts (among others), these wide-legged pants allow for freedom of movement and are very comfortable. They work well worn over the zentai in this chapter and can be an authentic addition to shibari scenes.

Although traditional and formal hakama are made of silk, modern hakama for the martial arts are typically made of either cotton, polyester, or a blend of the two. Depending on the material being used, it may be wise to pre-shrink and press the fabric prior to cutting the panels.

Hakama are traditionally made to be open at the sides, so after pleating, the front of the hakama is four-tenths of the waist measurement and the rear is three-tenths. This proportion can be adjusted if desired, though changing these widths will necessitate changing the pleat locations as well.

Hakama typically have a stiff panel, or koshi-ita, sewn in to the rear, which presses against the lower back to straighten the posture. The koshi-ita backing material can be made from just about anything with the required stiffness, though how the hakama will be washed should be kept in mind. Layers of vinyl, canvas or interfacing

are all possibilities. The koshi-ita can actually make the hakama uncomfortable for some, and can be omitted if desired. Early hakama, in fact, did not have koshi-ita panels. To omit the koshi-ita, simply finish the rear of the hakama in the same manner as the front. Without the koshi-ita, hakama allow a full range of movement.

A simpler and more feminine version of this project can be made by omitting the pleats, outer seams and opening edge folds. The edges that would have met in the outer seams are pressed with two 20mm (¾") folds, good sides out, and sewn in place 2mm (1/16") from the inside fold edge, folding the raw edge under the fold. The pants are worn by first wrapping the front straps around the body and tying them in the front, then tying the rear straps just below the front strap tie. The inseams can also be eliminated, if the fabric allows, by making the pants in two panels, taking care to remove the seam allowances for the inseams.

To make economical use of the fabric and to make the strap or himo panels as long as they need to be, you may need to have at least one join in each himo. The joins should be made on a bias, as shown in fig 2.15 on page 27. Avoid joining an even number of panels together, as a join will then be sewn over the center of the hakama; it's better to cut the himo from an odd number of panels.

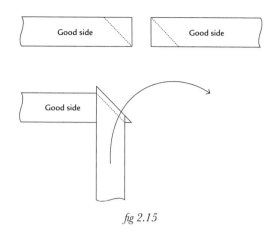

fig 2.15

Tools

- Sewing machine (universal needle)
- Small needle
- Pins
- Shears
- Measuring tape
- Chalk
- Iron

Materials

- Fabric
- Matching thread
- Koshi-ita material (optional)

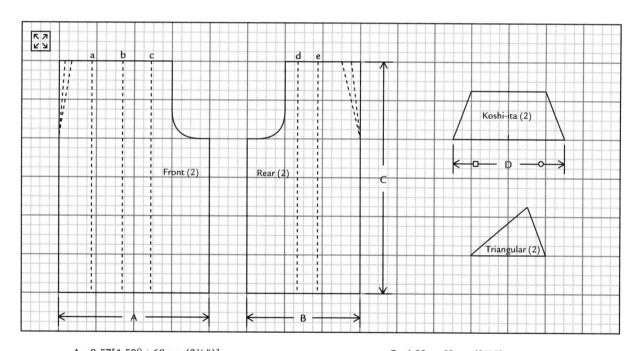

$A = 0.57[1.50\theta + 60mm\ (2\frac{1}{2}")]$

$B = 0.43[1.50\theta + 60mm\ (2\frac{1}{2}")]$

$C = 1.33\tau + 60mm\ (2\frac{1}{2}")$

$D = 0.30\theta + 55mm\ (2\frac{1}{8}")$

Front Himo - 160mm (6") x 4θ

Rear Himo - 160mm (6") x 2θ

Instructions

- Mark and cut out all pieces, taking care to make each pair of panels mirror images of each other. Note that the himo panels are not pictured in the pattern, but the dimensions are provided.

- Press 10mm (⅜") folds, good sides out, at the ends of each himo panel.

- Press 40mm (1½") folds in to the center, good sides out, along the length of the himo panels.

- Mark the lengthwise center of each himo.

- Fold each himo in half along its length and press.

- Finish the opening edges on the rear panels by first pressing triangular folds, good sides out, along the tops of the panels – starting at the tops of the inside dashed lines and ending 15mm (⅝") wide at the opening edges (these fold lines are not marked in the pattern). With those folds in place, fold along each outside dashed line in the pattern, good sides out. Press.

- Fold along each inside dashed line in the pattern, good sides out. Press. Sew the folds in place, 2mm (1⁄16") from the inside, outside and top fold edges.

- Finish the opening edges on the front panels by folding along each outside dashed line in the pattern, good sides out. Press.

- Fold along each inside dashed line in the pattern, good sides out. Press. Then press a third fold on each side – this time good sides together, so that the edge of the first fold is exactly flush with the new fold edge. Sew the outside folds in place first, then the inside folds, both 2mm (1⁄16") from the edge.

- Sew each front panel to the corresponding rear panel, good sides together, along the inseam, 15mm (⅝") from the edge.

- Press the inseam allowances towards the rear of the hakama. Topstitch them from the inside, 10mm (⅜") from the seam.

- Line up the inseams, good sides together. Sew the crotch curve, in two seams each starting from the inseam, 15mm (⅝") from the edge. Go over this seam again with a straight stitch, and then a wide zigzag stitch at the edge of the seam allowance. Alternatively, trim the seam allowances at the top of the inseams and use a French seam (see page 16).

- Press the crotch seam flat at the front and the rear.

- The pleats (vertical dashed lines in the pattern) are described as though looking at the hakama face on, top to bottom (fig 2.16). Bring the top of pleat **c** on the left panel to 20mm (¾") to the right of the center seam, then bring the top of pleat **c** on the right panel to the center seam. Pin in place.

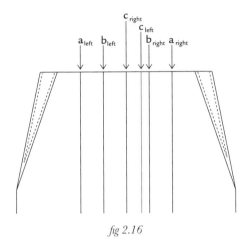

fig 2.16

- Bring the tops of pleats **b** to 30mm (1¼") to either side of the center seam. Pin in place.

- Bring the tops of pleats **a** in toward the center until the length from one opening edge to the other is equal to 0.4θ.

- Adjust the pleats, if necessary, so that they are equidistant. If you have adjusted the pleats, mark them. Unpin them.

- Press each of the pleats good sides out, then rearrange using the previous steps and pin back in place.

- Sew across the top of the pleats, 10mm (⅜") from the top edge.

- A good-sides-together pleat will be created between each set of good-sides-out pleats. Press these pleats.

- Open up the front himo. Place the top front of the hakama on the inside of the fold, lining up the center seam with the center mark on the himo. Carefully baste the himo in place. If the himo is not basted on evenly front to back, the stitches in the next step may not catch.

- Sew the front himo 2mm (1⁄16") from top and bottom edges as well as the ends.

- Sew two additional seams along the length of the himo so that the distance from the top himo seam to the bottom is divided in three by these two seams. These seams are to add strength and keep the fabric inside the himo folded in place.

- Remove the basting.

- Sew the rear himo in four seams along the length as well as the ends in the same manner.

- Make 15mm (⅝") folds, good sides out, along the top and side edges of the koshi-ita panels, and press.

- Make 15mm (⅝") folds, good sides out, along the side edges of the triangular panels. Press. Trim the corners of the seam allowances so that they can be tucked underneath.

- Place the rear himo over one of the koshi-ita panels, good sides together, 25mm (1") from the bottom, lining up the center marks, and sew in place from one koshi-ita fold over to the other on top of the existing himo seams. Take care to go precisely over top of these seams, and not to run them past the fold lines at the ends, as doing so will cause problems when the koshi-ita is assembled.

- Place the triangular panels on the koshi-ita panel with the himo sewn to it aligning the bottom edges and the outside folds of the triangular panels with the fold lines on the koshi-ita, and pin in place.

- Sew the inner sides of the triangular panels 2mm (1/16") from the edge of the folds and the bottoms 5mm (3/16") from the edge (fig 2.17).

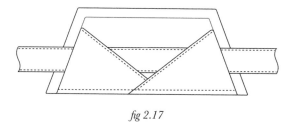

fig 2.17

- Make 25mm (1") folds, good sides out, along the bottom edges of both of the koshi-ita panels. Press.

- Align the koshi-ita panels, good sides together. Sew from the top of the himo on one side, up over the top of the koshi-ita and down to the top of the himo on the other side, 15mm (⅝") from the edge (along the fold lines). Take care not to catch the triangular panels in this seam.

- Trim the top corners, turn the koshi-ita right side out, and turn the side seam allowance folds inside. Baste from the top of the triangular panel down to the bottom of the himo on each side.

- Sew these seams in place 2mm (1/16") from the edge. Do not sew the area below the himo.

- Remove the basting.

- Press the koshi-ita above the himo.

- Trace around the koshi-ita on a sheet of paper, using a ruler to draw a line marking the bottom of the himo, then draw lines 5mm (3/16") inside the outline to create a pattern for the backing material.

- Cut out the pattern, trace it on to the backing material, and sew together if using multiple layers.

- Bring the top of pleat d on the right panel to 10mm (3/8") to the left of the center seam, then bring the top of pleat d on the left panel to the center seam. Pin in place.

- Bring the top of pleat e on the left panel to 10mm (3/8") to the right of the center seam, then bring the top of pleat e on the right panel to the center seam and pin in place. Adjust the pleats to match the koshi-ita width if necessary, keeping the 25mm (1") seam allowances in mind. Mark if necessary, then unpin.

- Press each of the pleats good sides out. Rearrange using the previous steps, and pin back in place.

- Sew across the top of the rear pleats 10mm (3/8") from the edge.

- Press the good-sides-together pleats.

- Align the center mark on the himo side of the koshi-ita with the top of the rear center seam, and pin. Sew the koshi-ita in place 25mm (1") from the edge, taking care not to sew through the himo or the inner koshi-ita panel.

- Insert the koshi-ita backing material and tuck the allowance from the seam joining the koshi-ita to the hakama and the 25mm (1") fold on the inside panel inside the koshi-ita. Trim the seam allowances if necessary. Sew the pocket closed, very close to the fold edge, using a zipper foot.

- Sew each front panel to the corresponding rear panel, good sides together, from the opening down to the bottom, 15mm (⅝") from the edge.

- Press the side seam allowances towards the rear of the hakama and topstitch from the inside, 10mm (³/₈") from the seam.

- Reinforce the bottom of the openings by sewing across from the top of one line of topstitching to the other (fig 2.10, page 21).

- Try on the hakama and check for length, keeping the 20mm (¾") bottom allowance in mind, and trim if necessary.

- Press 20mm (¾") folds, good sides out, along the bottom edges.

- Sew the bottom folds in place from the inside folding the raw edge under the fold, 2mm (¹/₁₆") from the edge of the inside fold.

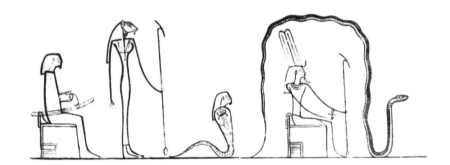

ZENTAI

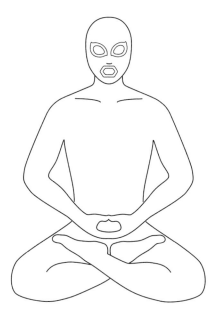

A zentai is a tight-fitting suit that covers the entire body. The term is Japanese and is possibly a contraction of zenshin taitsu or "full-body tights." Zentai are used in the arts to diminish the presence of an actor in a scene, or when chromakeying to digitally remove the actor from the scene.

Wearing a custom-made zentai gives one an experience of total enclosure, which alone can be enough to propel the wearer into an altered state of consciousness. Zentai are used by meditators for a multitude of reasons, and are particularly suitable for zazen and some forms of yoga and tantra. A full zentai can add another dimension to these practices, acting as a symbolic barrier, giving one the sense of being separated from the world. Sitting in front of a mirror, one can experience a loss of individuality and suppression of the ego. And having fabric touch the entirety of one's skin allows for increased body awareness, giving the moment-to-moment sensations that much more flavor.

Traditionally, zentai are made as one-piece suits, complete with gloves, feet, and a hood which covers the entire face and head. There is typically an entry zipper at the rear, which starts at the small of the back and runs up to the back of the head.

The patterns in this section construct the zentai in four parts: the bodysuit, gloves, feet and mask. In a tra-

ditional zentai, the gloves are made from the same panels as the sleeves, the feet are added to the body panels, and the mask is mounted in place of the neck panel. These pattern modifications are detailed further in the gloves and feet sections.

Having a detachable mask gives the zentai greater flexibility, and allows the entry zipper to be placed on the front of the suit instead of the rear. The included crotch zipper can be omitted, which is typical if the zentai is for public rather than private use. This design also calls for openings for the eyes and mouth, but these too can easily be omitted to make a traditional zentai.

It is possible to make a rear-entry bodysuit with no front seam, but this only works with certain body types, as it necessitates a straight-line drop from the neck to the crotch. To do this, draw a fold line parallel to the center line of the pattern, 15mm ($^5/_8$") inside the maximum width. This line will reduce a portion of the front thigh width. The width lost can be added to the rear thigh width if so desired, and any body width lost or gained by the straight line drop can be added or taken away from the rear. Mark the new front thigh point at the same height as the original, and smooth out the front leg curve. The difficulty in doing this lies in that it changes the length of the inseam on the front, which necessitates a change on the rear as well. Measure the front inseam and plot out a new rear inseam to match.

Installing a crotch zipper when the front seam has been eliminated can be difficult, as a cut needs to be made from the crotch of the double panel up 175mm (6¾"), and this half of the crotch opening will have no seam allowances to fold in when installing the zipper. It can be done, though, using the liner technique on page 44. Baste a 30mm (1¼") wide liner along where the opening will be cut, sew seams 5mm (³⁄₁₆") to either side of the center joining the seams at the top, make the cut in between the seams, fold the liner to the underside, and sew in place.

Zentai can be made from pretty much any fabric with a reasonable degree of stretch along the width of the fabric, but ideally should be made from fabric with around 60% stretch, meaning that a piece of fabric 100mm (4") long can be easily stretched to 160mm (6¼"). Stretch percentage can be calculated by stretching a known length of fabric to its reasonable maximum length, then dividing the difference in length by the original length.

$$\text{Stretch Percentage} = 100 \times \frac{\text{Stretched Length - Original Length}}{\text{Original Length}}$$

Stretch microfleece, for example, has a lower stretch percentage, probably closer to 40% – not ideal, but still acceptable. Some swimwear fabrics can also have a lower stretch percentage, but also work fine for this kind of garment. Fabrics with over 100% stretch will work, but can sometimes be difficult to sew: the sewing machine will tend to stretch the seam as it sews. If you're using this kind of fabric, I recommend finishing the cuffs and neck with single 15mm (⅝") folds, held in place by a narrow zigzag stitch 10mm (⅜") from the folded edge. This single-fold finish can be used with any kind of stretch fabric, if desired. With most fabrics, though, folding the edge twice will give a cleaner and more elasticized edge.

The typical zentai material is spandex or elastane, which will make a lightweight suit. Alternatively, they can be made of heavier materials such as cotton stretch or stretch microfleece for a warmer suit. These are well suited to colder climates, as wearing a zentai made of lightweight spandex is almost like wearing nothing at all. (One can remain bound, or go on playing, much longer when one is otherwise comfortable.) Microfleece suits are great for cold weather camping, or even just for lounging around the house. Some may find that cutting the legs and arms full width along their length so there is no taper from shoulder to wrist and crotch to ankle makes for a more comfortable fit. The fit can be relaxed even further by lowering the crotch (extending the distance between the shoulders and crotch points) by 40mm (1½"), and extending the sleeves by 40mm (1½").

When getting started with each part of the zentai, be very careful of the direction of stretch of the fabric. The direction of the greatest degree of stretch should always run horizontally across the body, so keep that in mind when placing the patterns on the fabric. If you want a very tight-fitting garment, you may wish to reduce the size of the pattern pieces by 5%-10% along their horizontal axis. This is called negative ease, and the percentage should be proportional to the degree of stretch of the fabric. If the fabric stretches in both directions, you can also use a vertical negative ease – although to a smaller degree, perhaps 2%-5%.

Having a zipper with two sliders is ideal when making a traditional zentai, which has only one zipper running from the small of the back up to the back of the head. Such zippers can be difficult to acquire. However, if you can find an upholstery or canvas store that sells continuous zip by the meter, you can purchase separate sliders and slide them on to the zipper from each end so as to be in the correct formation. To get the sliders on the zipper, either peel apart the zipper just enough so that the ends can be fed into the slider, then wiggle it on to the zipper, or ask the shopkeeper to take care of it. Alternatively, the mask zipper can be attached to the bodysuit entry zipper with the sliders meeting at the nape of the neck, or you could use a duvet zipper with one slider for the entire length of the opening.

BODYSUIT

Since this portion of the zentai tightly covers the majority of the body, and the sizes, shapes and proportions of the various parts of the body vary greatly from person to person, each person's pattern will be unique. The grid expansion method will therefore not be useful, and the pattern must be drafted from scratch.

While this pattern creation method has been tested on average human body types and sizes, it may not work for everyone as is. This should be kept in mind when choosing fabric for a first attempt. If you encounter a sizing problem, take notes on the problem areas. If the bodysuit can be taken in, do so, then alter the pattern. If it is too small in some way, trace the pattern on to a new piece of paper, correct the problem, then try again.

It should also be noted that the stretch percentage of the fabric can have an influence on how the bodysuit will fit. If fabric with an overly large stretch percentage is used, it may be wise to use a negative ease. Conversely, if the fabric has a very low stretch percentage, it may be wise to extend some of the horizontal measurements.

Tools

- Sewing machine (stretch needle)
- Small needle
- Shears
- Measuring tape
- Pencil and ruler
- Chalk

Materials

- Stretch material
- Matching thread
- 550mm (22") matching nylon zipper
- 350mm (14") matching nylon zipper
- Paper

Drafting the pattern

In this pattern, the gray lines indicate the guidelines that are drafted with a ruler, prior to the actual panel boundaries.

Main panel

- Draw a line in the center of the paper along its length.

- Mark the ankle width A centered at and perpendicular to the bottom of the center line.

- Mark the crotch height B from the bottom of the center line and draw a perpendicular line at that height along the width of the paper.

- Mark the front thigh width D to the right of the center line along the crotch perpendicular.

- Mark the rear thigh width E to the left of the center line along the crotch perpendicular.

- Make a mark C below the rear thigh width, and draw a perpendicular at that height. The value given for C should work for most body types, but can be changed if necessary.

- Mark the top of the panel F above the crotch height on the center line, and draw a perpendicular at that height along the width of the paper.

- Make a mark G below the top of the panel on the center line and draw another perpendicular at that height.

- Mark the arm opening depth H below the G line on the center line.

- Mark halfway between the arm opening depth H and the G line. Draw a perpendicular of width I, centered on the center line.

- Mark a width of I - 20mm (¾") on the G line, centered on the center line.

- Complete the arm opening by first connecting the points on the G line with the maximum width and depth points with a ruler, then sketching a curved line as shown in the pattern. Mark the center bottom of the arm opening.

- Mark the upper maximum width of the panel J at the top of the panel and at the maximum depth of the arm opening centered on the center line.

- Mark the under-breast height K below the arm opening.

- Mark the under-breast width L centered on the center line at the under breast height K.

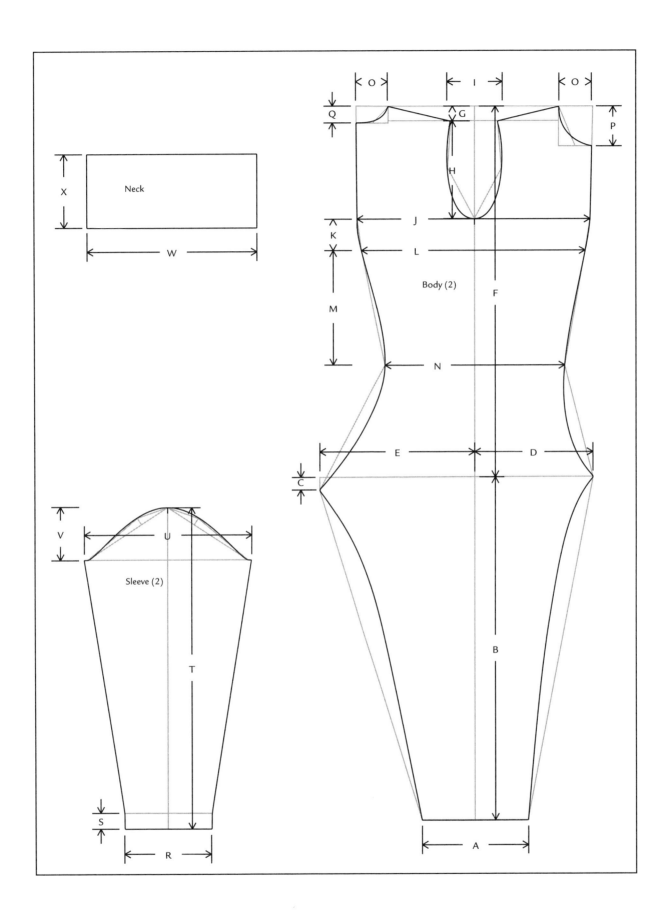

Neck

Body (2)

Sleeve (2)

$A = \chi + 30mm\ (1\,\tfrac14\,")$

$B = \tau + 100mm\ (4")$

$C = 20mm\ (\tfrac34\,")$

$$D = \frac{\phi + 30mm\ (1\,\tfrac14\,") + [\tau - C + 100mm\ (4")]^2 - [\tau + 100mm\ (4")]^2}{2}\ \frac{}{2(\phi - \chi)}$$

$E = \phi - D + 30mm\ (1\,\tfrac14\,")$

$F = \sigma + 90mm\ (3\,\tfrac12\,")$

$G = 30mm\ (1\,\tfrac14\,")$

$H = 0.50\iota + 15mm\ (\tfrac58\,")$

$I = 0.60H$ @ half depth

$J = 0.50\zeta + 30mm\ (1\,\tfrac14\,")$

$K = 0.10\sigma$

$L = 0.50\eta + 30mm\ (1\,\tfrac14\,")$

$M = 0.50(F - G - H - K)$

$N = 0.85\,[0.50\theta + 30mm\ (1\,\tfrac14\,")]$

$O = 70mm\ (2\,\tfrac34\,")$

$$P = \sqrt{[0.30\varepsilon + 17mm\ (\tfrac{11}{16}\,") - 0.50O]^2 - (0.50O)^2}$$

$$Q = \sqrt{(0.22\varepsilon - 0.50O)^2 - (0.50O)^2}$$

$R = \xi + 30mm\ (1\,\tfrac14\,")$

$S = 40mm\ (1\,\tfrac12\,")$

$T = \kappa + 90mm\ (3\,\tfrac12\,")$

$U = 0.90\iota + 30mm\ (1\,\tfrac14\,")$

$V = 0.30U$

$W = \varepsilon + 50mm\ (2")$ *

$X = 150mm\ (6")$ *

* Omit neck panel for traditional zentai.

- Mark the navel height M below the under breast height K.

- Mark the navel width N, centered on the center line at the navel height M. This value has been reduced by 15% to make for a tighter fit around the small of the back. This should work well for fabrics with a stretch percentage of around 60%, but can be altered to suit the fabric or the wearer.

- Mark the neck openings O from each side of top of the the panel. The value given for O should work for most body types, but can be changed if necessary.

- Connect each neck opening point O with the corresponding side of the top of the arm opening.

- Mark the front neck opening depth P below the top of the panel on its right edge, then draw a perpendicular of length O at that height, with a mark at half the length. Connect the end of this perpendicular with the top of the neck opening, and then draw a second line connecting the top of the neck opening to the mark at half the length. Sketch the front neck opening as shown in the pattern.

- Mark the rear neck opening depth Q below the top of the panel on its left edge. Then, draw a perpendicular of length O at that height, with a mark at half the length. Connect the end of this perpendicular with the top of the neck opening, and then draw a second line connecting the top of the neck opening to the mark at half the length. Sketch the rear neck opening as shown in the pattern.

- Connect each of the left panel boundary marks with a ruler, taking care to use the lowered rear thigh width mark, then do the same with the right side of the panel.

- Draw 30mm (1 ¼") x 30mm (1 ¼") right angle triangles at each of the thigh points so that the corresponding perpendicular bisects each triangle.

- Using the right angle triangles and straight boundary lines as guides, sketch the panel boundary as shown in the pattern.

- Make the crotch zipper marks 170mm (6¾") above each thigh point, using a measuring tape.

- Make the entry zipper mark 100mm (4") above the rear zipper mark, or front mark if making a front zip suit.

Arm panel

- Draw a line down the center of the paper along its length.

- Mark the wrist width R, centered at and perpendicular to the bottom of the center line, and again S above it to account for the folds.

- Mark the maximum height T from the bottom of the center line.

- Mark the maximum width depth V below the maximum height T.

- Mark the maximum width U at the maximum width depth V centered on the center line.

- Make marks 15mm (⅝") inside each maximum width mark to account for the seam allowances.

- Connect the panel boundary marks together with a ruler, taking care to use the inner marks made above the wrist and inside the maximum width.

- Make marks on the lines that connect the maximum width to the maximum height one third the length from the top of each line, and draw 20mm (¾") perpendicular lines at each of these points.

- Draw lines connecting the maximum width less the seam allowances to the top of the perpendiculars to the maximum height with a ruler as shown.

Instructions

- Trace all pieces, taking care to make the body panels mirror images of each other. If the fabric is wide enough, it can be easier to fold it lengthwise good sides together, trace the arm and body panels, pin the layers together at regular intervals, then cut.

- Mark the starts and stops of the zippers, the bottoms of the arm openings, and the top center of the arm panels.

- Cut out all pieces.

- Sew each arm panel, good sides together, from the top to the bottom with a stretch stitch.

- Align the body panels, good sides together, and sew the section between the zippers. This seam should be reinforced with several additional lines of stitching.

- Sew the top 100mm (4") of the front, or the back if making a front-zip suit.

- Sew the bottom 100mm (4") of the front (above the zipper mark), or the back if making a front-zip suit.

- Sew the shoulders, good sides together, to create arm openings.

- Align the center mark of each arm panel with the end of each shoulder seam, and sew from the top down to the bottom on either side, good sides together. The arm panel seams should line up with the marks at the bottom of the arm openings.

- Sew each of the inseams, good sides together, from the crotch down to the ankle.

- Sew the neck panel to the neck opening on the body-suit, good sides together. If making a traditional zentai, line up the center of the bottom of the neck panel of the mask (see page 43) with the center front seam, good sides together, and sew in two seams running from the center.

- Using these lines as a guide, sketch the top of the arm panel as shown in the pattern.

- Mark the center top of the arm panel.

Neck panel

- Draw a rectangle of length W and height X.

- Trim the seam allowances down to 5mm (³⁄₁₆") at the final 30mm (1 ¼") of the arm seams, as well as on both ends of the neck seam and leg seams.

- Baste the entry zipper opening shut. Baste the zipper in place, face down.

- Baste the crotch zipper opening shut. Baste the zipper in place, face down (sew the opening shut if making a traditional zentai).

- Sew the entry zipper in place from the top side through the opening left in the front, or back if making a front-zip suit, with a zipper foot, 5mm (³⁄₁₆") from the center seam.

- Sew the crotch zipper in place from the top side through the opening, with a zipper foot, 5mm (³⁄₁₆") from the center seam (not necessary if making a traditional zentai).

- Remove the basting.

- Sew the opening shut.

- Turn the bodysuit right side out.

* *Skip the following four steps if making a traditional zentai.*

- Trim the top of the neck panel to 30mm (1 ¼") from the zipper stops if necessary.

- Make a 15mm (⅝") fold, good sides out, on the top of the neck panel, and sew it in place with a wide zigzag stitch from the inside.

- Make a second 15mm (⅝") fold, but this time sew it in place with a straight stitch 3mm (⅛") from the edge of the first fold from the inside.

- For each of the wrist and ankle cuffs, make a 15mm (⅝") fold, good sides out. Stitch it down with a large zigzag stitch from the inside, then make a second 15mm (⅝") fold and stitch it down in the same manner.

Feet

Fabrics with enough stretch to make zentai tend not to be very robust, and are therefore not entirely suitable for footwear. Although an outer layer of leather can be added to the sole panel, this does not necessarily add much to the project's longevity. If you plan to do much walking in your zentai, I recommend that you cover your feet with some kind of footwear, perhaps the leather slippers in Chapter III.

If the feet will be used as stockings to be worn under footwear, you may wish to lengthen them so that they can be held up by a garter belt. Also, if they will be worn with the tabi in Chapter III, they can be modified to include a split toe, using the gray lines in the pattern.

If making a traditional zentai, the feet top and rear panels are cut from the same panels as the bodysuit. When laying out the bodysuit pattern panels, lay the sole pattern on top of the front half of the bottom of the bodysuit pattern so that the heel curve lies on top of

the bodysuit pattern and the big toe of the sole is on its front edge. Then, lay the rear foot pattern panel on the rear half of the bottom of the bodysuit pattern so that the heel curve extends beyond the bottom of the bodysuit pattern. Use the marks made at the start of the heel curve on the rear and sole pattern panels when lining them up with the bodysuit pattern (see fig 2.18 on page 38).

The width of the bottom of the bodysuit panel may not exactly match twice the foot panel width. If this happens, adjust the width of the bottom of the bodysuit to match the width of the foot panels laying side by side.

When sewing a bodysuit with feet attached, first sew the sole panel on to the bodysuit, good sides together, 10mm (³⁄₈") from the edge along the heel seam. Then sew the sole panel to the top panel, good sides together, 10mm (³⁄₈") from the edge. The inseam can then be sewn from the ankle up to the crotch.

Tools

- Sewing machine (stretch needle)
- Shears
- Measuring tape
- Pencil and ruler
- Chalk

Materials

- Stretch material
- Matching thread
- Paper

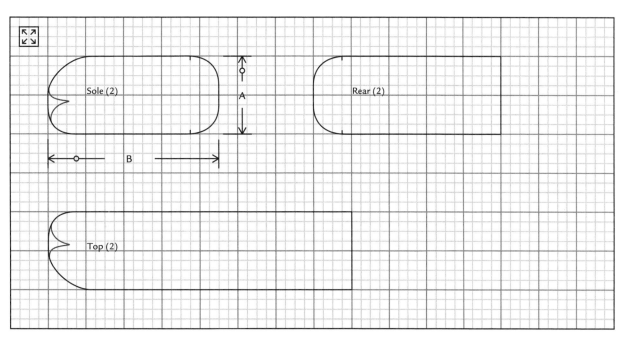

A = ω + 20mm (¾")   B = ψ

Instructions

- Draft the pattern as shown, taking care to mark the start of each heel curve on the back edge of the sole panel and the bottom edge of the rear panel.

- Trace, mark and cut out all panels, taking care to make mirror image pairs of the top and sole panels.

- Sew each sole panel to a rear panel, good sides together, along the heel curve, with a stretch stitch 10mm ($^3/_8$") from the edge.

- Sew each top panel to the corresponding sole panel, good sides together, in two seams, starting from the front and running to each side of the heel curve.

- Sew each top panel to its rear panel, good sides together, in two seams from the heel to the top.

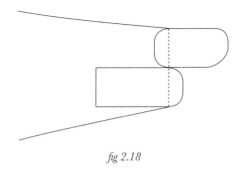

fig 2.18

- Turn the feet right side out. Make a 15mm ($^5/_8$") fold, good sides out, on each cuff, and stitch it down with a large zigzag stitch from the inside.

GLOVES

Making gloves is difficult at the best of times. Making proper gloves with stretch material is difficult and time-consuming, and they do not tend to last due to the fragile nature of the material. For these reasons, two glove designs will be presented here, the first one being a simplified glove, and the second being more complex.

The principle difference in the simplified design is that the gloves do not have fourchettes, the strips of material that run between the fingers to give the glove a third dimension. Installing fourchettes is probably the most difficult part of glovemaking, and since you are using stretch fabric, they are not entirely necessary.

Although these gloves have been simplified, they do use separate thumb panels, which can be difficult to mount on the glove. This step can be made easier by first basting the thumb pieces in place, but the gloves can be further simplified by adding the thumb to the main panel of the glove when tracing the hand, and sewing the glove all in one piece.

If making a traditional zentai, the gloves are made from the same panel as the sleeves. If using the simplified pattern, the glove pattern must have one straight folded edge running from the index finger up the arm to the shoulder. This necessitates a slightly different pattern, with the index finger pointing straight and the rest of the fingers fanning downwards. The pattern can then be traced on a folded sheet of paper with the straight edge flush with the fold, and cut out. Then, when tracing the

arm panels, line the dashed line on the glove pattern up with the wrist edge of the sleeve panel. Center it, then cut the whole panel out in one piece, leaving the area around the fingers uncut, as described in the simplified gloves section. The width of the arm panel wrist edge may not exactly match the width of the glove pattern. If this is the case, the width of the wrist edge should be adjusted to match the width of the glove pattern.

Of course, the ideal way of making gloves a part of the zentai sleeves is to use the complex pattern on page 41, which can be added to the arm panel using the same technique. A similar technique can be used to make attached mitts, using the pattern on page 163.

Another option to consider when opting for a zentai with attached gloves is to make half gloves instead. A half glove covers only the palm and the top of the hand, leaving the fingers and thumb exposed, and can be slid down around the wrist to leave the entire hand exposed if desired. Half gloves are made by extending the sleeve by 80mm (3$^1/_8$") and leaving an opening in the seam for the thumb 40mm (1$^1/_2$") long and 60mm (2$^3/_8$") from the end of the sleeve. Each side of the seam allowance around the thumb opening is folded twice and sewn in place, then the cuff is finished by sewing two 10mm ($^3/_8$") folds.

Finishing attached gloves before attaching the sleeve to the bodysuit is the easier order of operations, as there is less bulk to deal with when assembling the gloves. Using a straight-stitch throat plate can make assembly much easier.

SIMPLIFIED GLOVES

Tools

- Sewing machine (stretch needle)
- Small needle
- Shears
- Snips
- Measuring tape
- Pencil and ruler
- Chalk

Materials

- Stretch material
- Matching thread
- Paper

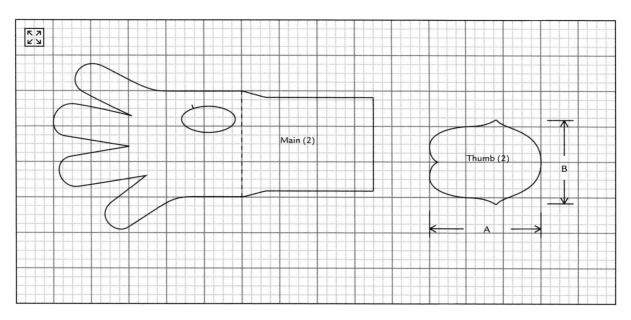

A = ρ + 10mm (³⁄₈")

B = π + 10mm (³⁄₈")

Making the pattern

- Place the intended wearer's left hand on the paper and mark dots to the left of the little finger knuckle and to the right of the index finger knuckle.

- Draw parallel vertical lines intersecting each dot, running the length of the page.

- Place the hand back on the paper, with the fingers a few centimeters (an inch or so) from the top, spread out as widely and evenly as possible. The index and little fingers should be equally over the edges of the vertical lines. Trace over the fingers and make dots at the lowest point between each finger. Omit the thumb.

- Draw a second set of vertical lines 3mm (¹⁄₈") outside of and parallel to the original lines, running from the wrist to just past the knuckles.

- Make a second set of dots, each being 6mm (¼") above the corresponding lowest point dot, centered between each of the fingers.

- To account for the seam allowance, draw a line around the perimeter of the hand, from one wrist edge to the other, 3mm (¹⁄₈") from the outer lines and finger traces, coming to its lowest point between the fingers at the second set of dots.

- Draw the thumb opening 35mm-40mm (1³⁄₈"-1⁵⁄₈") below the lower dot at the base of the index finger and 15mm (⁵⁄₈") from the side. It should be an oval approximately 50mm (2") tall and 30mm (1¼") wide. Although stretch material is fairly forgiving in this situation, these dimensions may need to be adjusted if the thumb panel doesn't fit the opening.

- Mark the thumb panel alignment point as shown in the pattern.

- Draw a horizontal line 120mm (4¾") below the wrist edge.

- Cut out the pattern and the thumb opening.

- Draft and cut out the thumb panel pattern as shown.

Instructions

- Cut two square pieces of fabric large enough, when folded in half, to accommodate the glove pattern.

- With each piece of fabric folded in half across its direction of stretch, good sides together, trace an outline of each glove including the thumb openings and marks, taking care to make them mirror images of each other.

- Use a straight stitch to sew the left border of the first glove from the bottom edge up past the edge of the finger, 3mm (⅛") inside the line, taking care to keep both layers of fabric together and flat.

- Repeat with the right border, again being careful to keep both layers of fabric flat.

- Beginning 20mm (¾") below the tip of the little finger, sew along the edge of the finger, around the tip and down to 6mm (¼") below the lowest part marked on the fabric, always 3mm (⅛") inside the line. Then, with the needle in the fabric, lift the presser foot and turn the fabric around to sew up the next finger. Proceed until 20mm (¾") below the tip of the index finger. This is intricate work, and must be done slowly and with care (fig 2.19).

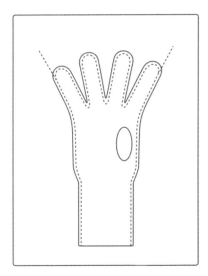

fig 2.19

- Repeat with the other glove.

- Carefully cut out the gloves along the marked lines.

- Make very small 2mm-3mm (⅛") cuts between each finger, taking care not to come within 2mm (¹⁄₁₆") of any seam.

- Cut out the thumb openings, taking care not to damage the other side of the gloves.

- Find two scraps from the remainder of the original square of material large enough to accommodate the thumb panels.

- Fold the thumb panel pattern in half lengthwise, as well as the first piece of fabric good sides together across the direction of stretch. Align the folded edges and trace.

- Sew the top curved portion of the thumb panel from the protrusion to the fold 3mm (⅛") inside the line, taking care to keep the fabric flat and the fold where it should be.

- Cut out the thumb panel along the line.

- Repeat with the second thumb panel.

- Turn the first thumb panel right side out and insert it into a thumb opening, aligning the seam with the marking (fig 2.20).

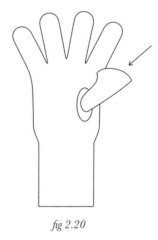

fig 2.20

- Sew the thumb panel in place from the thumb seam around to 15mm (⅝") past the thumb seam from the glove side, 3mm (⅛") from the edge. Again, this is intricate work, and must be done slowly and with care. Basting the panel in place before sewing can help.

- Repeat with the other thumb panel.

- Turn the gloves right side out.

- Make a 15mm (⅝") fold, good sides out, on each cuff, and sew in place with a wide zigzag stitch from the inside.

Gloves

Since these gloves are made with stretch material, a 10% negative ease has been included across the pattern. The negative ease can be removed by using A = o + 6mm (¼") to calculate the vertical cell length, but still using A = .9o + 6mm (¼") to calculate the horizontal cell length.

Though the proportions given in this pattern will work for most hands, adjustments to the finger lengths may be necessary. The thumb measurements are not used, as the

relationship between the thumb panel and the thumb opening is precise. The length and width of the upper portion of the panel (to the left of the protrusions on the pattern) can be adjusted to match, taking the allowances and ease into consideration, if necessary. The pattern can be adjusted before cutting and sewing if desired, but it is best to first make a practice glove, then adjust the glove and pattern if necessary.

Tools

- Sewing machine (stretch needle)
- Small needle
- Shears
- Measuring tape
- Pencil and ruler
- Chalk

Materials

- Stretch material
- Matching thread
- Paper

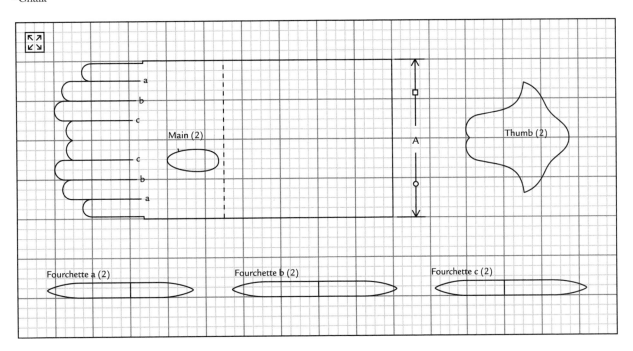

A = 0.90o + 6mm (¼")

Instructions

- Draft the pattern as shown. Note that only one measurement is required and the grid cells are of equal height and width for all of the panels.

- Trace, mark and cut out all of the panels of each glove, leaving the fingers and thumb opening uncut. Leave a 10-20mm (½"-¾") margin at the top of each glove. Take care to make each set of panels mirror images of each other and not to mix them together.

- Sew around the end of each finger division line 2mm (¹⁄₁₆") from the line, up 15mm (⅝") on each side of the line (fig 2.21, page 42).

- Sew around each thumb opening 2mm (¹⁄₁₆") outside the line (fig 2.21, page 42).

- Cut out the fingers by first cutting down the finger division lines, then cutting the tips of the fingers.

- Cut out the thumb openings.

- Fold each thumb panel lengthwise, good sides together, and sew from the folded edge up over the top and down to the protrusion 3mm (⅛") from the edge.

- Turn each thumb panel right side out and insert it into a thumb opening, lining up the seam up with the marking, good sides together, and baste it in place.

- Sew each thumb panel in place, 3mm (⅛") from the edge.

- Fold each glove in half lengthwise, good sides together, and sew the outside of the little finger from the tip down to the bottom, 3mm (⅛") from the edge.

- Sew the outside half of the top of each index finger, 3mm (⅛") from the edge.

- Sew the tops of each middle and ring finger, good sides together, with 10mm (⅜") seams, 3mm (⅛") from the edge.

- Baste each of the fourchettes to the back side of each glove, good sides together, by first lining up the center mark of the fourchette with the end of the appropriate finger slot, and basting from there up to each tip. Take care to orient the fourchettes so that the length of each side matches the finger length. If any of the fourchettes are too long, trim the length and reshape the point.

- Match the center mark on the other side of each fourchette with the end of the matching finger slot on the palm side of the glove and repeat.

- Sew the fourchette seams on the palm side of each glove in three seams, using snips to help maneuver the fabric. One from the top of the index finger to the top of the middle finger, the second from the top of the middle finger to the top of the ring finger, and the third from the top of the ring finger to the top of the little finger.

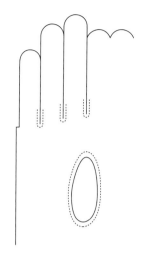

fig 2.21

- Sew the fourchette seams on the back side of each glove in one seam, starting from the top of the little finger to the top of the index finger for the left glove (reverse for the right), using snips to help maneuver the fabric. When going across the tops of the fingers, fold the fourchettes into the middle of the fingers so that they lay flat.

- Sew from the little finger down the length of each glove, 10mm (⅜") from the edge.

- Turn each glove right side out. Make 15mm (⅝") folds, good sides out, on each cuff. Stitch them down with a wide zigzag stitch from the inside. If a straight-stitch throat plate was used, be sure to switch it back before attempting a zigzag stitch.

- Remove the basting.

- Trim the seam allowances at the tips of the fingers if bulky.

MASK

Learning to make the projects in this and the following chapter will help develop a skill set that will enable you to make *your own* clothing. Simply following the instructions will produce a quality garment, but as long as the time is being taken to make something, it might as well be made to fit your ideal. Take some time and sketch out some ideas. The zentai mask is a project that has a lot of room for creativity and personalization.

If opting for a traditional zentai, the mask will be fairly straightforward. If you prefer a more conventional mask, you'll need to choose the shape and size of the leather eye and mouth appliqués. Another option is to make a half mask, exposing the bottom half of the face, either covering or exposing the nose. In that case, you need choose only the shape and size of the eye appliqués. Instead of a mouth appliqué, a 10mm (⅜") strip of black garment leather is used to line the opening. Medium-weight garment leather is the ideal for these appliqués, but lighter garment leather or even 1-2 oz. vegetable-tanned leather will work. Using vegetable-tanned leather gives you the option of customizing the color of the appliqués with dye, though you must condition and wipe them thoroughly before mounting them on the mask. Some sample designs for the eye and mouth appliqués are shown in fig 2.22.

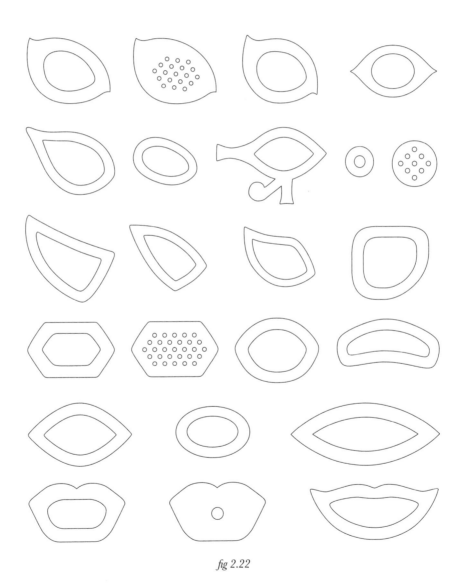

fig 2.22

Generally, for the mask to be comfortable and for the wearer have full vision, you should follow these guidelines:

- The openings in the eye appliqués should be at least 40mm (1⅝") in length and 30mm (1³⁄₁₆") in height.

- The opening in the mouth appliqué should be at least 50mm (2") in length and 25mm (1") in height. Longer openings allow the mouth to be opened wider.

- The width of the eye appliqués should be no less than 10mm (⅜") at any point and no wider than 15mm (⅝") on the inside corner, as the openings in the eye appliqués should be approximately 30-40mm (1³⁄₁₆"-1⅝") apart from one another when sewn onto the mask.

- The width of the mouth appliqué should be approximately 10mm (⅜"), to allow for two seams and an adequate mouth opening.

Another option to consider is having openings for the eyes and mouth that can be closed with a zipper. This can be accomplished by sandwiching a small nylon chain zipper between the mask and the specially shaped garment leather appliqué shown in fig 2.23. The appliqué is longer and thinner than normal. It is designed to stay open when the zip is open, and straight when the zip is closed. A rectangular appliqué with a simple cut through the center will also work, but not as well. Once the appliqué is cut out, the zipper is sewn shut at the appropriate length and the excess zipper tape removed. The corners of the zipper tape are then trimmed so that they will not be exposed behind the appliqué, and all trimmed edges slightly melted with a lighter to prevent fraying. The zipper is then glued to the back of the appliqué before both are then glued to the mask. After drying overnight, the appliqués are sewn in place with one seam around the outside, 2mm (¹⁄₁₆") from the edge, and seams on each side of the zipper, using the zipper foot, 4mm (⅛") from the inside edge.

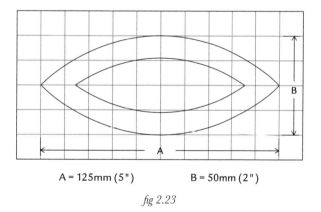

A = 125mm (5")   B = 50mm (2")

fig 2.23

Openings can also be made for the eyes and mouth without using appliqués, using the following procedure. Start by sketching the opening on a piece of paper or tracing the opening from an existing template. Then, sketch lines 5mm (³⁄₁₆") inside and 10mm (⅜") outside the perimeter of the opening, and cut along both of these new lines. Trace the opening template onto some backing material and cut it out. The backing material can be the same material used to make the mask, though using fabric with a bit more stiffness can make this process easier. Place the template over the desired position of the opening and trace around the inner perimeter. Line up the backing liner with the trace, good sides together, and sew along the inner perimeter 5mm (³⁄₁₆") from the edge. Cut a hole through the material to match the hole in the backing liner. Finally, push the backing liner through the hole so that the wrong sides are together. Sew in place from the outside, 2mm (¹⁄₁₆") from the edge, and trim away any excess backing liner from the inside if necessary (fig 2.24).

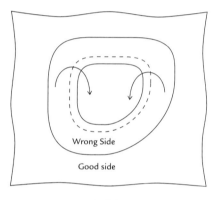

Wrong Side

Good side

fig 2.24

This method can be used quite effectively to make larger openings, such as for a half mask or even an open-faced hood. For larger openings, rather than using an opening template, simply use strips of fabric cut to match the curvature of the opening. These strips can be sewn to the opening, with each piece overlapping the previous by around 2mm (¹⁄₁₆").

The three lines in the front panel of the mask pattern indicate where the panel should be cut in order to make a half mask with the nose covered, a half mask with the nose exposed, and an open-faced hood that leaves the chin exposed. Note that when making a half mask or an open-faced chin-exposed hood, the protrusion on the neck panel is omitted. The opening of an open-face chin-covered hood is best determined experimentally by making a full mask without an opening, trying on the mask, and sketching the desired opening in chalk. The opening of a chin-exposed hood should be lined with two strips of leather, one running along the top and one going under the chin from one side of the top to the other, meeting at 90° angles. If making a chin-covered hood, you may wish to substitute a curved strip, cut to match the curve of the hood opening, for the long straight strip. If the material is thick enough, the opening could also be finished by folding it good sides out.

Leather is an ideal material with which to make an open-faced hood. Use the half mask pattern on page 111, but with the front panel shown in this section. The shape of the top line of the hood may need to be modified to suit the wearer, and can be given a point down in the center for a more stylized feminine look if desired. If making the top line pointed, the opening should be lined with leather, and the top strip should be cut to match the shape of the line.

The mask pattern detailed in this section can be used to make a mask out of any type of material, even if it has little or no stretch. So, when making a mask out of material with a higher stretch percentage, it may be necessary to take the mask in somewhat before installing the zipper. Alternatively, one could use a negative ease of 5%-10% when making the pattern.

Like the bodysuit pattern, this pattern may not work for everyone as is. If you encounter a sizing problem, take notes on the problem areas. If the seams are wrinkled, they should be taken in. Try the mask on inside out, mark where the seam or seams should be sewn, resew, trim, then adjust the pattern panel or panels accordingly. The shape of the nose is fairly regular and will work for most people, but can be adjusted if necessary. If the sizing problem cannot be solved by taking in some of the seams, or if the mask is too small in some way, trace the problem pattern panels on to a new piece of paper, correct the problem, then try again.

Although attaching a mask to a rear-entry bodysuit is fairly straightforward, adding one to a front-entry bodysuit can be a bit problematic. A half mask with the nose exposed or a hood with the chin exposed can be added to a front-entry suit fairly easily though, as the rear mask zipper can be omitted and it can be pulled on over the head like a hood. If opting for this style, extend the liner by 60mm (2½") (one side of the liner if making a hood) and make a 30mm (1¼") fold at one end, so that you can add a snap closure over the top of the zipper after everything is sewn in place. The half mask or hood is made without a neck panel, and the bodysuit is made in the same way as usual – but after the first neck fold is sewn in place, the mask or hood is sewn on to the neck panel, good sides together, 15mm (⅝") from the edge. Each opening edge of the mask or hood should attach to the neck panel 50mm (2") from the panel's meeting edges. This may require that the mask or hood's rear seam be taken in. Then, the second neck fold is sewn in place from the inside, taking care to also sew down the mask or hood's seam allowance.

Latex

It is worth mentioning that crude latex garments can be created by applying layers of liquid latex to prefabricated stretch fabric garments with a foam brush. A zentai mask with eye and mouth openings, perhaps one that is flawed or no longer in use, is ideal for experimenting with this technique.

Having a mannequin head to zip the mask onto can make this process infinitely easier. These can sometimes be purchased from hat, wig and clothing stores, or on the Internet. If the dimensions of the head are much different from the intended wearer's, it can be built up with a layer of modeling clay. Once the clay has been dried or cured according to the package's directions, it can be smoothed with fine sandpaper and sealed with latex paint. This kind of accurate model can be very useful when making masks.

With the mask zipped in place, apply the first coat of latex fairly liberally to the mask with a foam brush, taking care not to cover the zipper or the eye and mouth openings. Depending on the knit and material, the latex may be absorbed quite easily, or the fabric may require more work to impregnate fully. This first coat will take longer to dry, about two hours. The next coat should be applied when the latex is mostly dry but still slightly tacky. Waiting too long could prevent the layers of latex from adhering to one another. Subsequent coats should only take about one hour to dry. The number of coats applied really depends on how heavy a mask you're making, but five coats produces a strong yet pliable mask.

After the final coat has been applied, the mask is left to dry overnight, then cured and dried as described on page 157. The surface of the mask will not likely be smooth because of the brush strokes, but the appearance can be improved by applying some latex polish once the baby powder has been rinsed off and the mask is completely dry. Do not remove the mask from the mannequin head before this process is complete. It is worth noting that when latex dries, it actually shrinks somewhat, which can make for interesting sensations.

Applying this technique to larger garments is also possible, though one would probably need to build or acquire some kind of mannequin. For larger latex garments, you may wish to purchase some latex sheeting and rubber cement.

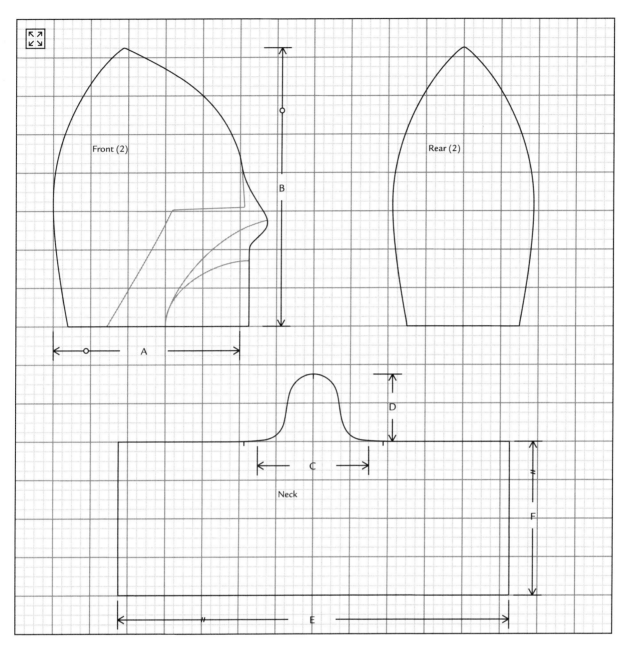

$A = 0.30\alpha + 10\text{mm} \ (\sfrac{3}{8}")$

$B = 0.50\gamma + 10\text{mm} \ (\sfrac{3}{8}")$

$C = 1.50 \ [\delta + 10\text{mm} \ (\sfrac{3}{8}")]$

$D = \delta + 10\text{mm} \ (\sfrac{3}{8}")$

$E = \varepsilon + 30\text{mm} \ (1\sfrac{1}{4}")$

$F = 150\text{mm} \ (6")$

Tools

- Sewing machine (stretch needle)
- Small needle
- Shears
- Small scissors*
- Measuring tape
- Pencil and ruler
- Water pencil*
- Chalk*

Materials

- Stretch material
- Matching thread for stretch material
- Garment leather*
- Matching thread for leather*
- 300mm (12") matching nylon zipper*
- Contact cement*
- Paper
- Cardboard*

Not necessary for a traditional zentai

Making the pattern

Front panel

- Determine the horizontal size of the each cell by dividing A by 5, since A spans five cells.

- Determine the vertical size of the each cell by dividing B by 7.25, since B spans seven and one quarter cells.

- Draw a rectangle that is 6 x (horizontal cell size) wide and 8 x (vertical cell size) high, since the panel occupies that many cells.

- Construct the grid inside this rectangle by first marking out the vertical cell divisions (using the vertical cell size) on both vertical edges of the rectangle, then connecting each pair of marks. Then do the same for the horizontal cell divisions.

- Mark the top of the panel $1\frac{7}{8}$ cells in from the left and $\frac{3}{4}$ cell from the top, and the tip of the nose $\frac{1}{4}$ cell from the right and $2\frac{5}{8}$ cells from the bottom.

- Mark where the panel should intersect each grid line.

- Sketch the panel, using the boundary and intersection marks as guides, so that it resembles the pattern. It is more important that the curves of the panel be smooth than that they go through each marking exactly.

- Measure the height and forehead width of the panel and ensure that they match the desired dimensions. Small inaccuracies in the sizes of the cells can skew the overall size and must be corrected if more than a few millimeters ($\frac{1}{8}$").

- Cut out the pattern panel.

Rear panel

- Because there are no dimensions given for this panel, and the front panel dimension arrows are marked with circles, the cell width and height from the front panel is used for the rear panel.

- Draw a rectangle that is 4 x (horizontal cell size) wide and 8 x (vertical cell size) high.

- Construct the grid inside this rectangle by first marking out the vertical cell divisions (using the vertical cell size) on each vertical edge of the rectangle, then connecting each pair of marks. Then do the same for the horizontal cell divisions.

- Mark the top of the panel on the center grid line $\frac{3}{4}$ of a cell from the top, and the side boundaries $\frac{1}{8}$ of a cell from each side and $3\frac{1}{4}$ cells from the bottom.

- Mark where the panel should intersect each grid line.

- Sketch the panel using the boundary and intersection marks as guides so that it resembles the pattern. Again, it is more important that the curves of the panel be smooth than that they go through each marking exactly. In this particular example, the rear curve of the front panel matches the side curves on the rear panel, so the front panel can be used as a guide if desired.

- Measure the height of the panel and ensure that it matches the desired dimension. Small inaccuracies in the sizes of the cells can skew the overall size and must be corrected if more than a few millimeters ($\frac{1}{8}$").

- Mark the top of the zipper 80mm ($3\frac{1}{8}$") below the top of the panel, using a measuring tape.

- Cut out the pattern panel.

Neck panel

- Determine the horizontal size of the each cell by dividing C by 3, since C spans three cells.

- Determine the vertical size of the each cell by dividing D by 1.75, since D spans one and three quarter cells.

- Draw a rectangle that is 4 x (horizontal cell size) wide and 2 x (vertical cell size) high, since the grid expandable portion of the panel occupies that many cells. The remaining dimensions of the panel, as indicated by the dashes in dimensions E and F, are supplementary and will be sketched without a grid.

- Construct the grid inside the rectangle by first marking out the vertical cell division (using the vertical cell size) on both vertical edges of the rectangle, then connecting the pair of marks. Then do the same for the horizontal cell divisions. It may be helpful to include the cell subdivisions here.

- Mark the top of the panel on the center line $\frac{1}{4}$ cell from the top.

- Mark where the panel should intersect each grid line.

- Sketch the panel using the boundary and intersection marks as guides so that it resembles the pattern. It is more important that the curves of the panel be smooth than that they go through through each marking exactly. Because this panel is symmetrical on the vertical axis, one side of the protrusion can be sketched, then the paper folded along the center line so that the other side can be traced if desired.

- Extend the center line a distance of F below the bottom line of the grid.

- Draw a line perpendicular to the center line at its base, extending E/2 in both directions.

- Extend the bottom line of the grid so that it is E/2 from the center line in both directions.

- Connect the top and bottom lines and ensure that the connections form right angles.

Instructions

- Trace, mark and cut out all pieces, taking care to make the front panels mirror images of each other. Ensure that all of the panels are placed correctly with respect to the direction of stretch.

- Use a straight stitch to sew the front panels, good sides together, 10mm (⅜") from the front edge. When assembling a mask, it is easiest to align the pieces, then start in the middle and sew down to the bottom. Finish the seam by starting from 20mm (¾") inside the existing seam and working up to the top. The ends of each seam segment will still need to be finished by backtacking a few stitches.

- Align each rear panel with a front panel, good sides together, so that the tip extends 10mm (⅜") above the front seam. Sew the panels together, 10mm (⅜") from the edge.

- Trim the side seam allowances down to 5mm (³⁄₁₆").

- Sew the top of the rear panels, good sides together, 10mm (⅜") from the edge, starting at the opening mark and going over the top of the mask.

- Trim the top and front seam allowance down to 5mm (³⁄₁₆"), starting 20mm (¾") from the opening.

- Align the center of the protrusion on the neck panel with the bottom of the front seam, good sides together. Sew in place, 10mm (⅜") from the edge, in two seams, each starting from 20mm (¾") to the far side of the center. If making a half mask or chin-exposed hood, align the left join mark on the neck panel with the corner of the left front panel, good sides together, and sew in place. Repeat with the right side.

- Check these seams for quality and straightness. Re-sew if necessary.

- Trim the circumferential seam allowance down to 5mm (³⁄₁₆").

- Place the front panel on a piece of cardboard, trace, and cut out.*

- Sketch and cut out the eye and mouth appliqué patterns.*

* Not necessary for a traditional zentai

- Try on the mask, still inside out, and check for fit. Since the pattern can be used with any type of material, and masks made of stretch fabric generally need to be slightly smaller than the circumference of the head to fit properly, the mask may need to be taken in a bit. Pinch the meeting edges around the back of the head to a comfortable tension and mark up. Trim, keeping the 15mm (⅝") seam allowances in mind.

* Skip the remaining steps if making a traditional zentai.

- Baste the opening shut and baste the zipper in place face down.

- Sew the zipper in place from the top side with the zipper foot, 5mm (³⁄₁₆") from the center seam.

- Remove the basting.

- Trim the bottom of the neck panel to 30mm (1¼") from the zipper stops if necessary.

- Make a 15mm (⅝") fold, good sides out, on the bottom of the neck panel, and sew it in place with a large zigzag stitch from the inside.

- Make a second 15mm (⅝") fold, but this time sew it in place with a straight stitch 3mm (⅛") from the edge of the first fold from the inside.

- Turn the mask right side out, try it on again, and mark small dots over the eyes and the corners of the mouth with chalk.

- Trace the eye and mouth appliqués on the garment leather, taking care to make the eye appliqués mirror images of each other. Cut out all pieces, using small scissors for the openings. If making a half mask or hood, cut a 10mm (⅜") strip of garment leather.

- Place the cardboard template inside the mask and zip it shut.

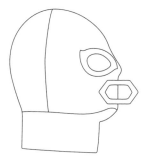

fig 2.25

- Apply contact cement to the flesh side of the right eye appliqué. Place it on the right side of the mask while the contact cement is still wet, taking care to place it around the marking and sufficiently close to the center seam, and press firmly.

- Repeat with the left eye appliqué, taking care to place it in symmetry with the right one. Before pressing, remove the cardboard from the mask and check for symmetry. If it is a bit off, remove it, replace the cardboard, and try again. Contact cement can be easy to remove from some fabrics, but impossible from others; consequently it will be necessary to get this right the first time. Once satisfied, replace the cardboard and press firmly.

- Apply contact cement to the flesh side of the mouth appliqué and place a little less than half of it on the right side of the mask (fig 2.25). Place the appliqué around the markings and close to the eye appliqués, usually no further than 10-30mm (³⁄₈"-1¼"). Remove the cardboard from the mask and check if the center seam runs through the center of the mouth appliqué. If it is a bit off, try again. Doing this correctly takes practice. Once it is centered, press firmly.

- If making a half mask, apply contact cement to the flesh side of the liner and press it down around the perimeter of the opening, starting at the base. If the nose is exposed, the liner should touch the eye appliqués. If not, the liner should run as close to the base of the nose as possible. If aligning it this way leaves a section of the fabric exposed outside the liner, it can be trimmed off. Overlap the liner at the base by 15mm (⁵⁄₈").

- Let the mask dry overnight. Sewing through leather that is still wet with contact cement should be avoided.

- Sew the eye and mouth appliqués (or liner) in place with two seams, one 2mm (¹⁄₁₆") from the outside edge and another 2mm (¹⁄₁₆") from the inside edge. This is intricate work and must be done slowly and with care. It may help to adjust the needle position so that the edge of the leather can be seen through the presser foot, or you can use a transparent presser foot.

- With the stitches firmly in place, pull the fabric inside the openings of the eye and mouth appliqués away from the leather and clip it from under the appliqués with small scissors.

Chapter III

Leather

Leather is a marvelous material, in many ways ideal for fetishwear. It is one of the most common fetishes, probably because leather garments have a transformative quality, giving one the feeling of having a sort of second skin. Although leather garments of any color and style can be the object of fetishes, tight-fitting black leather is the most popular and arguably the most stimulating. One advantage to making your own leather garments is that you can design them to be unlined, allowing contact between the soft flesh side of the leather and the wearer's skin.

Second skin

When leather is pulled tight over the body, it produces a sheen equalled only by latex, adding visual stimulus to the physical sensations. Tight-fitting, black, shiny clothing is a consistent fetish theme: a dominant dressed in leather tends to receive both respect and lust, a potent combination.

Dressing a submissive in leather can also be effective. Being dressed head to toe in tight-fitting leather can actually feel like a form of bondage in itself.

Beyond the visual and sensual factors, there is something psychologically stimulating to donning a second skin. One undergoes a sort of transformation, becoming of

something more primal. Animal skin is common to all human cultures. It was the first material used for clothing, and remained predominant until the Bronze Age, when we began to spin yarn and weave cloth.

If the brain is the most powerful sex organ, the skin is not far behind. Showing a lot of skin can of course provoke a sexual response. Showing form but no skin can also provoke a response, although a somewhat different one. Sexually speaking, we expose our skin in an attempt to remove as many barriers as possible to becoming one with the other. Covering the skin, on the other hand, reinforces the boundaries: a different kind of experience, but often just as intimate and even more exciting.

We are born without boundaries. As infants, we cannot tell the difference between ourselves and the outside world. As we grow, we build boundaries, as they are a prerequisite to learning. The ego can be thought of as the part of our selves created by the boundaries we put up. The ego wants pleasure, feels pride, gets angry and gets hurt. To "lose one's ego" means removing boundaries, typical of most mystical states. Although covering the skin can be seen as reinforcing one's boundaries, having the skin completely covered can create boundary loss. With no skin there are no boundaries, with no boundaries there is no ego, and suppressing the ego is the first step towards higher consciousness.

Although leather garments are not generally a good choice for long periods of meditation, they can make a sensuous addition to certain yogic exercises and breathing techniques. With each breath, the body expands against the leather which constricts it, providing a constant reminder of its presence. This can be a stimulating and rewarding experience. Wearing a zentai along with the body harness described in Chapter IV is also effective in conjunction with these practices.

Varieties of leather

Two types of leather will be used to construct most of the projects in this and the following chapters: vegetable-tanned leather and garment leather. Only cow leather is called for in this book, but deer, pig, lamb and others could also be considered. Vegetable-tanned leather is made by treating the skin with materials derived from tree bark and various plants. It is fairly rigid, usually undyed, and comes in a variety of thicknesses measured in ounces, meaning the leather weighs so many ounces per square foot. For the purposes of this book, "light" weight will mean 1-2oz, "medium" 3-5oz and "heavy" 6oz or heavier. Generally, one ounce per square foot is approximately 0.4mm (approximately ¹⁄₆₄") thick, and this proportion can be used to calculate the weight of any vegetable-tanned leather (see Appendix III on page 213). The heavier skins will be used to make the eye mask projects toward the end of this chapter and some of the restraints in Chapter IV, and the lighter variety is used for plaiting some of the whips in Chapter VII.

A special type of vegetable-tanned leather called "latigo" is worth considering when it comes to projects which incorporate strapping. Latigo is generally made from heavy (6-10oz) skins that have been drum dyed and dipped in hot oils after tanning. Latigo is a very sturdy and durable leather, which makes it rather stiff at first, but once worked it becomes quite comfortable. Although latigo is purchased already dyed, the cut edges will still require coloring.

Garment, or chrome-tanned, leather is treated with chromium sulfate, making it soft and supple. As its name suggests, it is primarily used to make clothing, and it is usually dyed since the chromium process turns the skin blue. There are many different types and weights of garment leather, some more appropriate for these projects than others. Two and a half ounce pebble grain garment leather skins are ideal for any of the projects in this book that call for garment leather. Many of the projects in this and the following chapters call for chap leather, which is basically very heavy (around 5oz) garment leather. Lighter chap skins can be used for clothing, although they can be difficult to sew, whereas the heavier skins make luxurious strapping.

Another type of leather worth considering is suede, which is produced by splitting the skin and then ruffling up the fibers. Because suede no longer has a smooth outer layer, it is not as durable as garment leather, and is therefore not recommended for the majority of the projects in this book. It can, however, be very effectively used to make the falls for the flogger in Chapter VII.

Leather made for the upholstery industry can sometimes be used in place of chap and garment leather, and one can often obtain very high quality leather at upholstery stores.

Finally, sheepskin is also worth consideration, as it is generally tanned with the fleece intact. Fleece is useful for lining cuffs and blindfolds, though with sheepskin the hair may need to be trimmed prior to mounting. To shorten the pile, first cut the panels to size from the flesh side with a utility knife. Then, go over each panel with an electric hair clipper and guide comb, or trim the hair to the desired length by hand with a comb and scissors.

For the most part, leather is purchased by the "side," which is half a cow's skin (fig 3.1). They can be purchased at leather stores, or on the Internet if there are no stores nearby. Different parts of the side have different properties, but generally the best leather is found in the center section. The back tends to be heavier, and the belly tends to be wrinkled and has a lot of stretch. The belly should be used for unimportant or non-visible panels, such as the tongues on the mask, hood and tabi. There are often other wrinkled sections on the front and rear of the side, which should be treated the same way as the belly. Be sure to check the side for scars, brands and nicks before purchasing if possible, and definitely before tracing out a pattern. When tracing patterns onto leather or cutting strapping, one should endeavour to use the leather as economically as possible. This means laying out the pieces in such a way that waste is minimized before beginning to cut the skin.

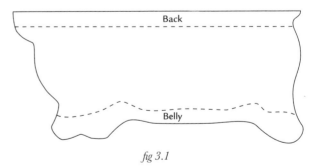

fig 3.1

You might also consider using synthetic materials such as engineered leather, pleather, or upholstery vinyl in place of leather. These can be purchased from upholstery stores in a wide variety of colors, and are generally a lot cheaper and more readily available than leather.

Although they are no substitute for the real thing, they can be useful for practice, as many of these materials have much of the same properties as actual leather.

Marking and cutting

Garment, chap and latigo leather can be marked up very easily with a white water pencil. Suede can be difficult to mark up, as the water pencil marks may not rub off. So, water pencil is fine to mark outlines that will then be hidden, but otherwise mark suede by scratching it with an awl. It is best to mark up vegetable-tanned leather with a pencil, though a free flowing ink pen matching the dye works well if the leather is to be dyed. Vegetable-tanned leather can also be marked up with a stylus or like tool after moistening it with a sponge.

Garment leather, light vegetable-tanned leather and suede can be cut easily with a sharp pair of shears. However, this may not be an option with some heavier vegetable-tanned and latigo skins. Also, most of the panels and straps cut from vegetable-tanned and latigo skins involve long straight edges. The easiest and most accurate way to cut straps and panels of that nature is to use a steel ruler and utility knife or rotary cutter. Simply place the skin over a cutting surface, align the ruler along the edge to be cut, press firmly down on the ruler, and insert the blade in to the leather next to the ruler. Slowly cut down the edge, pressing firmly down on the ruler and pressing the blade against the edge of the ruler.

Cut chap leather with a blade and ruler where possible, but shears will work and will be necessary for curved edges. The same applies to heavy vegetable-tanned and latigo skins; to cut curved edges, make do with a pair of shears if possible, or cut freehand with a knife as a last resort. When cutting freehand, first cut lightly over the marked curve, about halfway through the skin. Then, go over it a second time, this time trying to make it all the way through – but not putting too much pressure on, as the more pressure on the knife the greater chance there is for the knife to slip outside the cut line. After two cuts, the leather should be mostly if not completely separated. If it is still joined in parts, pick the leather up off the cutting surface, push the knife through the cut, and push the knife slowly along the cut line. The cut already achieved will act as a guide for the knife.

Machine-sewing

Garment leather is usually sewn with a straight stitch on a sewing machine. To sew a strong seam, pay close attention to the spacing of the stitches and the pacing. If the stitches are too close, the thread will slice through the leather. When sewing leather with a machine, a slow and consistently smooth pace will make a more even seam than one made with short bursts of speed.

The presser foot can sometimes complicate matters by sticking to the leather. If this happens, the leather is probably just moist and needs to be left to dry for a few hours or overnight. A non-stick presser foot also helps.

Sewing leather with a domestic sewing machine can be difficult. However, with a solidly built machine, two or three layers of garment leather can be sewn together without too much trouble. To make the process easier and more precise, the leather can be glued with contact cement before sewing it in place. This technique is often used along meeting edges and hems; the contact cement holds the fold in place prior to sewing. It can be helpful, particularly when making very wide folds, to draw a line on the flesh side of the leather, twice the fold allowance width from the edge, to use as a guide when making the folds. When a fold is made along a concave curve, such as on the thongs and gothic gauntlets, small incisions half the depth of the fold allowance must be made so that it will lay flat. For a convex curve, the incisions must be wedge-shaped.

Always make sure the contact cement is completely dry before attempting to sew through it. Also, be sure to clean off any contact cement that may have gotten on the surface that will face up when sewing, as it could cause the leather to stick to the presser foot.

Although using contact cement on these folds is recommended, it is not strictly necessary, particularly if using a sewing machine that was made to sew leather. Using contact cement to secure folds in any kind of synthetic leather or vinyl is not recommended, as it does not dry well.

Leather panels that are joined with a machine are typically aligned grain sides together and sewn with a leather needle and a straight stitch. Because leather needles are wedge-shaped, they will make the stitch holes less visible. Although this single-stitch construction method is sufficiently rugged for most purposes, these seams can be topstitched for increased durability or a neater finish if desired (fig 2.3 on page 16). Topstitching for durability in leather work usually involves folding both layers of the seam allowance to one side and sewing them in place from the top side, with one seam close to the first seam and often a second close to the edge of the seam allowance (if the seam is straight and the allowance wide enough). Topstitching a straight seam is reasonably easy, but it becomes more difficult with the degree of curvature of the seam.

A common problem, when sewing leather with a machine not designed for it, is missed stitches. If the stitches stop catching, the first thing to look at is the needle. If it is bent, even slightly, or if it has become dull, the machine will begin to miss stitches. Also remember that trying to sew a fold before the glue is dry can cause a similar problem. Over time and use, however, the sewing machine may actually develop a timing problem. When the machine hits an obstruction with the needle, or when you're sewing materials with a lot of resistance such as leather, the top thread may fail to form a loop around the bottom thread. So unless you're using an industrial leather sewing machine, do not sew through more layers of leather than necessary.

Something else to try when dealing with missed stitches is changing the position of the needle. Most machines have three needle positions: left, center and right. When sewing leather, the needle should usually be in the center position. But if the machine gets out of sync, try the left and right positions as well as positions in between the three, as this could potentially make the stitches catch again.

Binding

A new sewing technique will be used in this chapter: binding an edge. Binding, in terms of sewing, means to sew a strip of material around the length of an edge (fig 3.2). This can be accomplished freehand by pinching the binding around the edge with the right hand and feeding the material into the machine with the left. It is not as difficult as it looks, and you can achieve excellent results by sewing slowly, little by little. Alternatively, the binding can be glued or basted in place prior to sewing. Gluing is usually less time-consuming and works very well with leather, but not with synthetic material. Basting can be done with a glover's needle and a sailor's palm, and will also produce excellent results. Pre-cut fabric bias binding can be purchased in wide variety of colors and widths, but strips of matching garment leather can also be used and are often preferable for the projects in this book. When using strips of leather to bind leather, at least three layers will have to be sewn through in order to secure the binding. While this may not pose a problem with some lighter leathers, sewing through three layers of a heavy garment skin can be difficult with a domestic sewing

machine. With this in mind, when you're working with a heavy garment skin, you may wish to cut the binding from a lighter skin.

If you're using a binding material with an unsuitable raw edge, you may wish to make the binding twice as wide, glue and fold the raw edges into the center, then bind the folded material to the edge. If only one side of the material will show, the binding can be cut extra-wide (and only folded on one side, if folding) to allow for easier sewing. You don't need to baste when using this method, and you can achieve a tight, even finish on the front, and trim the rear after sewing.

When the binding starts at a corner with an angle other than 90°, be sure to cut the edge of the binding to the proper angle before starting to sew. When this happens at the end of the binding, take the work off the machine 40mm (1½") away from the corner, trim the binding appropriately, then finish the seam. Since strips of binding leather are often very long, it can be necessary to join two or more lengths together. Do this by laying the edge of one length over the edge of another so they overlap by 5mm (¼") and sewing in place.

Hand-sewing

Some of the projects in this chapter will also involve hand-sewing. Before you can sew leather by hand, you will have to punch stitch slots. (The exception is the gloves, which require skins light enough to be punctured by a glover's needle.) With the slots punched, the leather can then be sewn with a leather needle and waxed cotton or heavy thread. You'll then use a saddle stitch, which is a simple over and under stitch that is doubled over when the end is reached, filling in the gaps on both sides to complete the seam (fig 3.3). Two needles, one on each end of the thread, can also be used to work the saddle stitch from one end of the seam to the other without having to double back. Using one needle or two is simply a matter of comfort and preference.

When you complete the seam, double-knot the ends of the thread and clip them. Apply a drop of cyanoacrylate glue to the knot, if you like, to ensure it stays knotted.

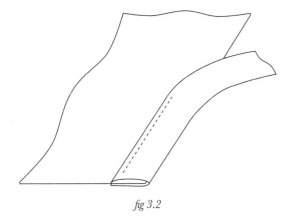

fig 3.2

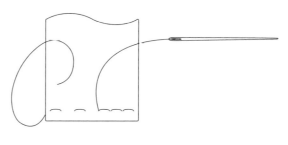

fig 3.3

Rivets

Although rivets will primarily be used to assemble the projects in Chapters IV and V, buckles are fixed in place with rivets, so I'll discuss them here.

Setting a rivet well requires some practice. To achieve a satisfactory result, the height of the rivet post should match the overall thickness of the leather reasonably well. Adding a small square of leather to the underside of what is to be riveted together can help solve some thickness problems, and can also strengthen the join when riveting light- to medium-weight leather.

Before you set the rivet, you must first mark and punch holes in all layers of the leather. The holes must be punched at precisely the right locations or the riveting can look untidy, particularly when there are several rivets in a row. So before you punch the holes, I suggest placing the rivet caps over the markings and nudging them into position, then pushing them into the leather. You can then punch the holes at these indentations.

With the holes punched, push the rivet post through each consecutive layer's flesh side, starting from the bottom, and place the cap on top. Finally, set the rivet with a hammer and rivet setter on an anvil. When setting rivets, grip the setter at its base so that the thumb and index finger are also touching the rivet cap. Strike the setter with medium force, taking care to drive it directly downwards. Once you're satisfied that the rivet is on its way to being properly set, strike it again to set it completely.

It is best to practice this process on some scrap a few times before attempting to set a rivet in a project. Rivets are difficult to remove without damaging the leather once they have been completely set in place.

When setting some brass-core rivets, the post of the rivet can damage the cap somewhat when set, giving it a rather unattractive finish. This happens more often with brass-core rivets as the cap is made of softer metal, and when the degree of curvature of the rivet setter is too great for the rivet. An easy solution to this problem when using double-cap rivets is to insert the rivet backwards, so that the base of the post rests on the grain side, and set it in place from the flesh side. The post will still damage the cap, but it will not be on the visible side of the project, and the base of the rivet, which will be visible, will be set perfectly.

Another approach to solving this problem is modifying a rivet setter so that its curve better suits the brass-core rivets. Rub the concave end of the rivet setter on a piece of medium sandpaper in small circles, taking care to ensure that the rivet setter stays vertical. Check your

work periodically by looking at the underside and by seeing if the setter will stand straight up on its own. Once you've taken off a sufficient amount of the curve (you'll have to determine this amount experimentally, but start when there is a flat ring around the underside around 2mm ($\frac{1}{16}$") wide), the curve must be made smooth again by pressing a small piece of sandpaper into the curve with your finger or thumb, and working it in a rotating motion. Once you've attained a smooth concave curve, smooth the curved surface with a small piece of fine wet and dry paper, and test out the new setter. If the rivet post still protrudes, then more of the curve must be taken off; if the rivet cap has been marked up otherwise, the curve must be smoothed further.

Eyelets

Setting eyelets is comparatively easy. Once the hole has been punched, insert the eyelet from the grain side and place the washer around it on the flesh side. If the hole does not seem quite large enough for the eyelet, use a drive punch to stretch it slightly. Then, place the eyelet on the eyelet anvil, hold the eyelet setter vertically inside the eyelet, and strike it straight down with a hammer until it curls back flush with the leather.

Snaps

Setting snaps is also fairly straightforward. Once you've punched the holes, push the cap through the grain side of the top layer of leather. Then place it on a snap anvil so the leather is flesh side up, top it with the socket that completes the female half, and set it in place with a snap setter. Set the male half by pushing the stud through the flesh side of the bottom layer of leather, placing it on an anvil, topping it with the eyelet and setting it in place with a snap setter.

Errors

Rivets, eyelets and snaps are designed to be set in place permanently, and as long as you've selected the correct height, they will generally hold fast. The downside is that if you've made an error or need to effect a repair, removing them can be rather difficult. With a pair of locking pliers and a good sharp wire cutter, though, it is possible.

To remove rivets or snaps, begin by clamping the cap of the rivet with locking pliers, compressing more and more and pulling until the cap comes off. Then you'll need to compress the underside of the cap with locking pliers until it is small enough to be pushed through the hole. To remove eyelets, make four shallow cuts around the top of the eyelet with a wire cutter (taking care not to damage the leather), then push the four separated edges of the eyelet in towards the middle and pull it through from the other side. Alternatively, use an eyelet removal tool, though these can be difficult to obtain.

Buckles

When fixing a buckle to a leather strap, holes are punched for the rivets and a slot is cut for the pin. The length of the slot will depend of the size of the buckle, but they are usually around 25mm (1") long. When you're using a new type of buckle, cut the slot before punching the rivet holes so you can check the buckle for fit. Special punches can be purchased to cut slots, but these tend to be a bit flimsy and are difficult to keep sharp. The best way to cut a slot is to punch holes at both ends and connect them with two cuts made with a hobby knife (fig 3.4). The sides of the slot can then be finished with a needle file if working with vegetable-tanned leather. If the strap is cut from chap leather and is 13mm (½") wide or thinner, the holes can be omitted, as a single cut with a hobby knife will suffice.

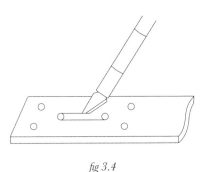

fig 3.4

Because the length of the slot can vary, the placement of the rivet holes can as well. There will always be one hole (or one set of holes for wider straps, see Appendix I on page 213) punched near the end of the strap, but the location of the other one (or set) varies with the size of the buckle and the length of the slot. The same principle applies when mounting rings: the thicker the ring, the greater the distance between the holes (or sets of holes). Although in most cases these rivet holes are marked on the patterns, the inside hole (or set) should be marked and punched to match the hardware that will be mounted on the strap.

Slots are also necessary when using locking buckles, as the loop on the end of the pin will not fit through a regular buckle pin hole. First, punch an even number of holes where the buckle pin holes would be, 10mm (⅜") apart. Then, connect each pair of holes in the same

manner. Regular buckle pin holes are generally spaced 15mm (⅝") apart.

Strap keepers are called for whenever heel-bar buckles are used, and are often used in conjunction with center-bar buckles. A keeper is simply a thin (7mm-12mm, ¼"-½") strip of leather, long enough that it wraps around the buckle strap with the ends meeting on the underside. Punch holes in the buckle strap first, and then punch matching holes in the ends of the keeper strap. To install the keeper, place it under the buckle strap, flesh sides together, lining up the holes. Then push the rivet through the underside and set in place. Wrap the keeper around the buckle strap and repeat the process on the other side. Setting the second rivet is more difficult, as the keeper strap must be pushed out of the way of the rivet so that it can be set. With the second rivet in place, the keeper can be twisted straight. The keeper can be sewn in place instead with artificial sinew or waxed cotton and a leather needle: first punch two small holes at each end of the keeper strap with an awl, then punch matching holes on the buckle strap. Then line up the holes and sew the keeper in place with a square seam (fig 4.6, page 142). Alternatively, the keeper can be sewn end-to-end with a square seam, the distance between the buckle rivet holes and keeper rivet holes extended, the buckle end of the strap extended and matching holes punched so that keeper can be slid onto the strap, sandwiched between the layers of the fold and fixed in between the sets of rivets.

For the projects involving straps and buckles, the ends of the straps should be rounded to make inserting them in to the buckles easier. As special tool with a curved blade can do this easily and well, but if you don't have such a tool, you can also do it manually with a hobby knife. Start by cutting off the corners of the end to be rounded. The cut sections should be isosceles triangles whose equal sides have a length equal to one third of the width of the strap. Then, cut off each of the four corners created by the two previous cuts, creating an arc of eight straight lines which will appear as a curve.

D-rings

D-rings are generally fixed in place with small retainer straps and rivets. The number and size of the rivets used depends on the width of the D-ring and retainer strap (see Appendix I on page 213). The distance between the holes or sets of holes for smaller D-rings is generally 20mm (¾") on the base material, and around 25mm (1") on retainer strap. When using lighter leather for the retainer strap, the ends are folded in to the center, necessitating four holes (or sets of holes) rather than two.

If you're using heavier leather that can not be folded easily, use just a single rectangular panel for the strap, but nip off the corners with a hobby knife as they will tend to protrude after the rivets are in place.

Zippers

Many of the projects in this chapter require metal zippers. The method used to install metal zippers in leather is somewhat different from what was described in Chapter II. The length of the zipper needs to be precise, particularly when installing open-ended (separable) zippers. Since zippers can only be purchased in certain lengths, they will often need to be shortened.

To shorten a zipper, first lay it on the opening and determine which teeth would make ideal zipper stops (see fig 1.28, page 11). Then, use a pair of pliers to remove these teeth and the next four or five towards the end of the zipper (fig 3.5). Also, pull off the teeth next to the zipper stops to make removing them easier. Remove the zipper stops by grabbing them from their sides so as not to damage them, and gently pull them off the zipper tape (fig 3.6).

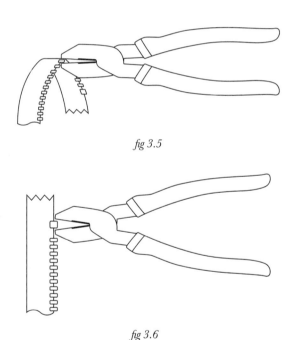

fig 3.5

fig 3.6

Spread the zipper stops apart slightly with your fingers, then squeeze them in place just above the last teeth on each side of the zipper tape. When clamping the zipper stops in place, use a piece of scrap leather between the stops and the pliers to avoid damaging the stops. After the stops are in place, the zipper tape can be trimmed to 2mm (¹⁄₁₆") from the stops and melted with a lighter to prevent fraying.

To allow for an easy and precise installation, always glue the zipper in place with contact cement before sewing. When placing the zipper on the leather, align either the backs or tips of the teeth with the edge of the leather. Once it is dry, it can then be sewn in place 2mm-8mm (¹⁄₁₆"-⁵⁄₁₆") from the edge of the leather.

Studs

Setting a stud in leather is a very simple operation. First, hold the stud over the leather where it will be placed, and press the stud into the leather making two small indentations (fig 3.7). Use a stitch chisel to cut slots at these indentations. Then, insert the stud and fold in the legs to the flesh side and press them into the center of the stud (fig 3.8).

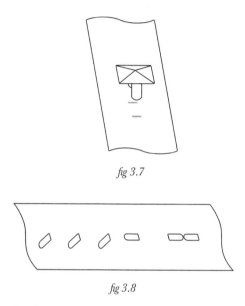

fig 3.7

fig 3.8

Hardening

Leather hardening techniques are used to make the eye masks at the end of this chapter. These techniques have been used for thousands of years in the manufacture of molded leather armor. Various degrees of rigidity can be achieved by changing the temperature, duration and composition of the dip. The process used in this chapter involves simply dipping vegetable-tanned leather in hot water, forming it in to the desired shape, then leaving it to dry at room temperature.

When leather is hardened in this manner, its structure is fundamentally changed. When the piece is dipped in hot water, a portion of the chemicals in the skin will melt, which then realign themselves in to a polymer structure upon drying. The hotter the water, the more the leather turns to a polymer. Boiling the piece actually cooks the skin, shrinking it down to a misshapen brittle mass with which nothing much can be done.

Before the piece is hardened, first cut it to the desired shape and finish its edges. Then, heat a pot of water to around 60°C (140°F), or until you can no longer dip your fingers in it. Remove the pot from the stove and submerge the piece in the water. It will bubble and fizz as the air in the leather comes to the surface, and will need to be held down for the first few seconds. Keep it submerged for around fifteen minutes, after which you can remove it from the water and mold it into the desired shape.

When medieval armorers made breastplates and helmets and the like, they would drop the sogged leather on a mold and work it into all the mold's features. Eye masks are considerably smaller pieces, and can be more effectively molded by hand. Since there is no form for the piece to dry on, though, you must continue molding it to lesser degrees as it dries until it gains some rigidity.

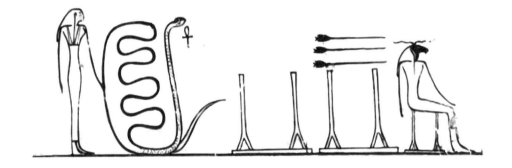

BRACER

This simple unisex bracer is a unique yet subtle piece of leather to wear anywhere. It can easily be made longer or shorter, although with each additional 15mm (⅝"), another eyelet should be added (note that you may need a longer shoelace). The pattern can also be easily resized and modified with parallel edges to make an attractive hair tie.

This project can also be made with medium to heavy vegetable-tanned leather. When making the pattern, though, omit the fold allowances, as no folds will be made. Simply cut out the bracer, bevel the edges, punch the holes, dye and condition it if desired, and fix the eyelets in place.

Tools

- Sewing machine (leather needle)
- Shears
- Drive punch
- Eyelet setter and anvil
- Cutting board
- Hammer
- Measuring tape
- Pencil and ruler
- Water pencil

Materials

- Garment leather
- Matching thread
- 760mm (30") shoelace
- 10 x short eyelets
- Contact cement
- Paper

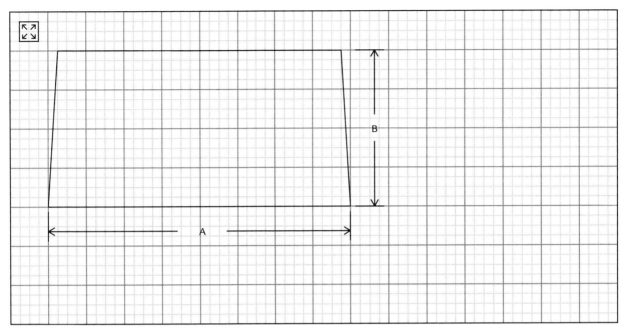

A = ξ + 30mm (1¼")   B = 110mm (4⅜")

Instructions

- Draft the pattern as shown.

- Trace and cut out the bracer.

- The corners of the panel must be cut so that when you make the folds, only two layers need to be sewn through. With 90° corners, the cut portions are isosceles triangles with sides equal to twice the fold allowance, but the slanted sides on this panel mean irregular triangles. Make marks 30mm (1¼") from the top and bottom corners on the slanted sides, 35mm (1⁷⁄₁₆") from the corners on the long side and 25mm (1¹⁄₁₆") from the corners on the short side. These modified distances are estimates, so test them out by folding in the corners and folds on the pattern before cutting the leather. When you're satisfied, draw lines connecting each pair of marks and cut off the corners.

- Apply contact cement to the outside 30mm (1¼") of the flesh side.

- Make 15mm (⅝") folds flesh sides together (fig 3.9), press firmly, and allow to dry overnight.

- Sew around the circumference of the bracer from the grain side, 10mm (⅜") from the edge.

- Mark five evenly spaced holes for the eyelets on both slanted sides starting 10mm (⅜") from the top and ending 10mm (⅜") from the bottom, taking care to keep them symmetrical.

- Punch all holes where marked.

- Insert the eyelets and set.

fig 3.9

GOTHIC GAUNTLETS

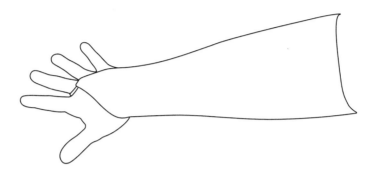

These simple feminine lace-up gauntlets make an elegant addition to any leather ensemble, and can also make an eye-catching accent when worn with other types of clothing. Boning is sewn into each meeting edge to prevent the gauntlets from bunching up when worn, and a triangular protrusion extends over the top of the hand with a loop of leather lace at the tip for the middle finger.

Tools

- Sewing machine (leather needle)
- Shears
- Drive punch
- Eyelet setter and anvil
- Cutting board
- Hammer
- Measuring tape
- Pencil and ruler
- Water pencil

Materials

- Garment leather
- Matching thread
- 2 x 1200mm (47") shoelaces
- 28 x short eyelets
- Boning
- Contact cement
- Paper

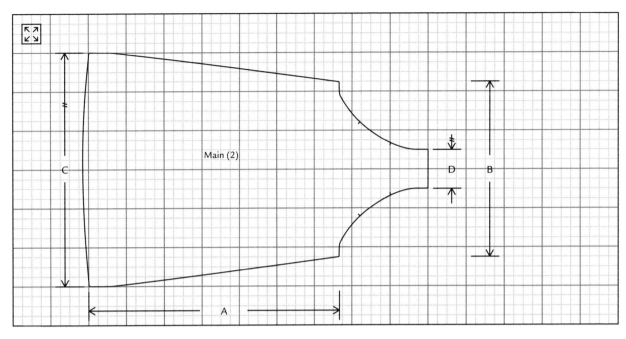

A = ν + 40mm (1½")

B = ξ + 60mm (2½")

C = μ + 60mm (2½")

D = 30mm (1⅛")

2 x 120mm (5") of 3mm (⅛") leather lace

Instructions

- Draft the pattern as shown.

- Trace and cut out both gauntlets making 5mm (³⁄₁₆") incisions along the curved edges where marked.

- Mark an inner perimeter on the flesh side of each gauntlet that lies 60mm (2½") from each meeting edge, 40mm (1½") from the rear edge, and 20mm (¾") from each curved edge.

- Cut four pieces of boning, the length of the meeting edges less 20mm (¾").

- Apply contact cement to the areas between the inner perimeter and the edge.

- Place a piece of boning 5mm (³⁄₁₆") inside each meeting edge perimeter line and 20mm (¾") from the rear edge.

- Fold the meeting edges in to the inner perimeter lines and press firmly.

- Fold the curved edges in to the inner perimeter lines and press firmly.

- Trim off any excess from the meeting edge folds. Then fold the rear edges in to the inner perimeter lines, press firmly, and let dry overnight.

- Use the zipper foot to sew a seam on both sides of each piece of boning from the grain side, from 6mm (¼") from each curved edge to 15mm (⅝") from each rear edge.

- Sew each rear fold between the boning seams from the grain side, 15mm (⅝") from the edge.

- Sew each curved edge from the end of each meeting edge seam to the top of each gauntlet, 6mm (¼") from the edge.

- Mark seven evenly spaced eyelet holes along each meeting edge, starting 10mm (³⁄₈") from the triangular protrusion and ending 10mm (³⁄₈") from the rear edge.

- Punch all holes where marked.

- Insert and set the eyelets.

- Trim the tip of each triangular protrusion straight if necessary.

- Make a fold 15mm (⅝") from the tip of each triangular protrusion and sew in place 10mm (³⁄₈") from the fold. If this is too thick to sew with a machine, hand-sew with waxed cotton.

- Thread the leather laces through each fold and tie the ends together loosely. Check each for fit, adjust the loop size if necessary, then tighten the knots and clip off the ends of the laces.

SAMURAI GAUNTLETS

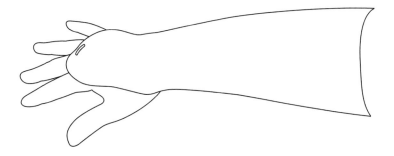

The samurai of feudal Japan typically wore six pieces of armor collectively called the rokugu. These were the helmet, the mask, the body armor, the armored sleeves, the thigh pieces and the shin guards. The design for this project was inspired by the kote, or armored sleeve. Like the hakama in the previous chapter, the samurai gauntlets can make an authentic addition to shibari scenes.

Although this design is for simple leather gauntlets, armor plates can be added to the forearm and hand for a more authentic and functional look. This can be done by sewing leather panels over the arm and hand sections on three sides, creating pockets. Hardened leather, molded polymer or other material can be inserted into the pockets, which can then be sewn shut.

Tools

- Sewing machine (leather needle)
- Shears
- Drive punch
- Snap setter and anvil
- Cutting board
- Hammer
- Pliers
- Measuring tape
- Pencil and ruler
- Water pencil
- Lighter

Materials

- Chap leather
- Matching thread
- 4 x short snaps
- 2 x 300mm (12") open-ended metal zippers
- Contact cement
- Paper

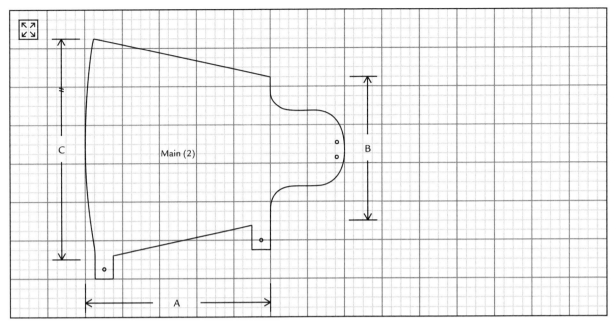

A = v + 10mm (³⁄₈")

B = ξ + 10mm (³⁄₈")

C = μ + 10mm (³⁄₈")

2 x 120mm (5") of 3mm (¹⁄₈") leather lace

Instructions

- Draft the pattern as shown.

- Trace, mark and cut out both gauntlets, taking care to make them mirror images of each other.

- Check the gauntlets for fit keeping a 6mm (¼") gap between the meeting edges to allow for the width of the zipper, and adjust if necessary. If too small, the adjustment can be made by leaving a gap between the edge of the leather and the back of the zipper teeth.

- Shorten each zipper to match the length of the meeting edges. Turn the slider on one of the zippers around, front to back, before reattaching the stop.

- Apply contact cement to the outside 10mm (³⁄₈") of the flesh side of each meeting edge.

- Slowly press each length of zipper tape in place so that the slider sides of the zippers are on the sides without the snap protrusions, the zipper boxes and pins are at the wrist, and the backs of the teeth are flush with the edge of the leather, starting at the wrist and working up to the top. Press firmly and let dry overnight.

- Sew the zippers in place from the grain side 8mm (⁵⁄₁₆") from the edge.

- Sew 30mm (1¼") reinforcement seams 4mm (³⁄₁₆") inside the top and bottom of each seam (fig 3.10).

fig 3.10

- Punch all holes where marked. Zip up gauntlets and use the holes in the protrusions to mark holes in the opposite corners. Punch.

- Set the female halves of the snaps in the protrusions and the male halves in the opposite corners.

- Trim the ends of the protrusions around the snaps.

- Thread a leather lace through each pair of holes and tie the ends together loosely. Check each for fit, adjust the loop size if necessary, then tighten the knot and clip off the ends of the laces.

FEMALE THONG

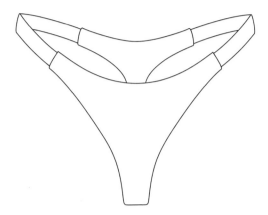

The thong presented here is a fairly classic design with front and rear leather panels connected at the base of the crotch (can be altered to be made in one panel if desired) and fabric elastic waistbands. The pattern is a basic template which can be easily embellished upon. The front panel could connect to the straps with rings and rivets, the thong could be fastened with two buckled straps as in the ring harness on page 174, or it could be altered to include the easy removal snaps described in the male thong project on page 67 (works well in conjunction with a garter belt).

Tools

- Sewing machine (leather needle)
- Leather needle
- Shears
- Stitch chisel
- Cutting board
- Measuring tape
- Pencil and ruler
- Water pencil
- Lighter

Materials

- Garment leather
- Matching thread
- Matching waxed cotton
- 13mm (½") fabric elastic
- Contact cement
- Paper

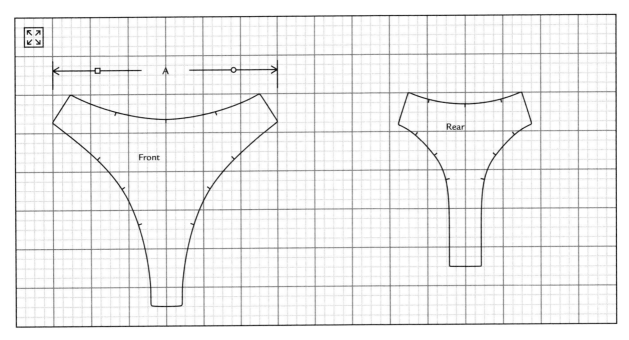

A = 0.40θ

Fabric elastic = 2 x 0.25θ

Instructions

- Draft the pattern as shown.

- Trace and cut out both panels, taking care to make make 5mm (³/₁₆") incisions along the curved edges where marked.

- Cut two lengths of fabric elastic as prescribed above, and melt the ends.

- Apply contact cement to the outer 20mm (¾") of the flesh side of both panels.

- Make 10mm (⅜") folds along all the curved edges. Let both panels dry overnight.

- Sew the folds in place from the grain side, 6mm (¼") from the edge.

- Punch two rows of four slots at the bottom of the front panel. Lay the bottom of the front panel over the bottom of the rear and mark the stitch slots in the rear through the slots in the front. Remove the front panel and punch the slots in the rear panel where marked.

- Punch two rows of three slots at the two remaining raw edges of each panel.

- Hand-sew the bottom of the front panel over the bottom of the rear panel.

- Hand-sew a length of fabric elastic to each set of stitch slots in the rear panel.

- Try on the thong to ensure a good fit. Trim and melt the fabric elastic if necessary.

- Hand-sew the other end of each length of fabric elastic to the corresponding stitch slots in the front panel (fig 3.11).

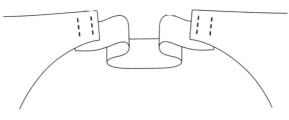

fig 3.11

MALE THONG

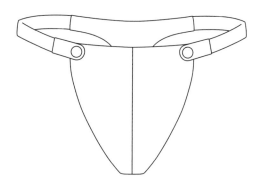

Like the female thong, the male pattern is a template which can be expanded upon. The front panel is based on a designer undergarment for maximum comfort. The waistbands are fixed to the front panels with snaps to allow for easy removal. Although this can work well when wearing chaps, keep in mind that snaps may make the thong uncomfortable to wear as an undergarment. The male thong can of course be altered to the snapless style of the female thong if desired.

Tools

- Sewing machine (leather needle)
- Leather needle
- Shears
- Drive punch
- Snap setter and anvil
- Stitch chisel
- Cutting board
- Hammer
- Measuring tape
- Pencil and ruler
- Water pencil
- Lighter

Materials

- Garment leather
- Matching thread
- Matching waxed cotton
- 2 x short snaps
- 19mm (¾") fabric elastic
- Contact cement
- Paper

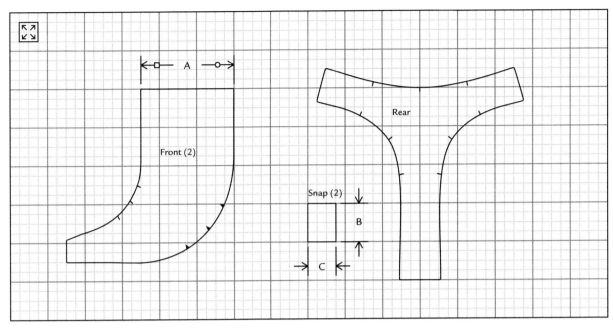

A = 0.12θ

B = 50mm (2")

Fabric elastic = 2 x 0.18θ

C = 40mm (1½")

Instructions

- Draft the pattern as shown.

- Trace and cut out all pieces, taking care to make the front panels mirror images of each other. Make 5mm (³⁄₁₆") incisions along the curved edges where marked. The incisions along the front of the front panel should be cut in small wedges.

- Cut the fabric elastic to the prescribed lengths and melt the ends.

- Sew the front panels grain sides together along the front, 10mm (³⁄₈") from the edge.

- Trim the top 10mm (³⁄₈") of the front seam allowance down to 2mm (¹⁄₁₆").

- Clip off 10mm (³⁄₈") squares from the top corners of both front panels.

- Apply contact cement to both sides of the front 20mm (¾") and fold the seam flat.

- Apply contact cement to the outside 20mm (¾") of the flesh side of the inside curved edges on the front panels and make 10mm (³⁄₈") folds. Start each fold at the bottom so the inside edge meets the edge of the center fold, which may not make a 10mm (³⁄₈") fold at first, but gradually change the size of the fold until it is 10mm (³⁄₈") wide.

- Apply contact cement to the outside 20mm (¾") of the flesh side of the rear panel and make 10mm (³⁄₈") folds. Press firmly and let dry overnight.

- Sew both sides of the flattened seam from the grain side, 6mm (¼") from the center.

- Sew all the other folds in place from the grain side, 6mm (¼") from the edge.

- Straighten the top of the front panels if necessary.

- Apply contact cement to the top 20mm (¾") of the flesh side of the front panels and make a 10mm (³⁄₈") fold.

- Apply contact cement to the flesh side of the snap panels and fold the long edges in to the center. Press firmly and let dry overnight.

- Sew the top fold in place 6mm (¼") from the edge.

- Sew the snap panel folds in place 3mm (¹⁄₈") from the edge.

- Punch two rows of four slots at the bottom of the front panel and all three protrusions of the rear panel.

- Punch two rows of four slots on one side of each of the snap panels.

- Hand-sew the bottom of the front panels over the bottom of the rear panel.

- Hand-sew a length of fabric elastic to each side of the rear panel.

- Try on the thong to ensure a good fit. Trim and melt the fabric elastic if necessary.

- Hand-sew the other ends of the fabric elastic to the snap panels.

- Mark and punch holes for the snaps at the top corners of the front panels and on the ends of the snap panels. Set the male halves in the front panels and the female halves in the snap panels.

- Trim a curved edge on the ends of the snap panels.

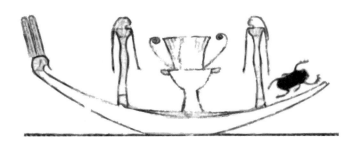

Heavy thong

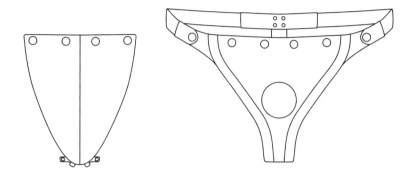

This unique garment was designed to be worn with the male harness in Chapter IV, but can serve a number of functions. Like a thong made with the snap option, it can provide easy access regardless of what one is wearing by removing the front piece. The snap panels on the fabric elastic are included to make it easier to put on and take off.

Like the female chastity belt, this project was not designed to be lockable, but can be made to lock with a few alterations. The row of snaps along the top can be replaced with two more separable zippers and a zipper cover. Those zippers meet in the middle and are locked

together by slipping a padlock through their pull tabs. The side zippers are locked in place by slipping a padlock through their pull tabs and eyelets set in the top zipper cover. Although it is very difficult to remove this garment while it is zipped shut, it still may be possible. This possibility can be removed by changing the style of the frame from fabric elastic to a buckling style, like the female chastity belt or ring harness with locking buckles. Keep in mind, though, that using buckles can make the thong uncomfortable to wear as an undergarment.

Tools

- Sewing machine (leather needle)
- Leather needle
- Shears
- Stitch chisel
- Drive punch
- Rivet setter and anvil
- Snap setter and anvil
- Cutting board
- Hammer
- Pliers
- Measuring tape
- Pencil and ruler
- Water pencil
- Lighter

Materials

- Chap leather
- Matching thread
- Matching waxed cotton
- 4 x medium rivets
- 6 x short snaps
- 2 x 300mm (12") open-ended metal zipper
- 25mm (1") fabric elastic
- Contact cement
- Paper

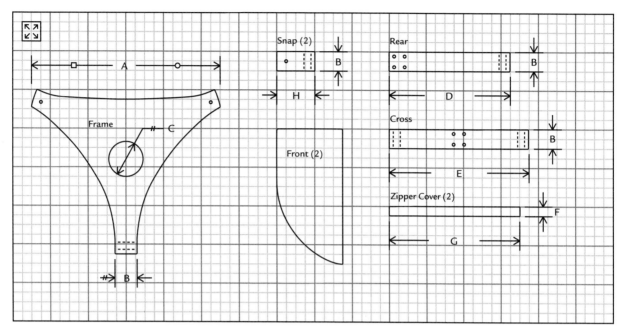

A = 0.33θ + 20mm (¾")

B = 30mm (1¼")

C = 55mm (2¼")

D = 0.25σ + 20mm (¾")

Fabric elastic = 2 x (θ - A - E)/2

E = 0.30θ

F = 18mm (¹¹⁄₁₆")

G = 240mm (9½")

H = 60mm (2½")

Instructions

- Draft the pattern as shown.

- Trace, mark and cut out all pieces, taking care to make the front panels mirror images of each other. Although the hole is meant to be snug, you can widen its diameter if desired.

- Cut the fabric elastic to the prescribed lengths and melt the ends.

- Shorten each zipper to match the length of the front panels. Turn the slider on one of the zippers around, front to back, before reattaching the stop.

- Use contact cement to glue the sliderless sides of the zipper tape to the frame, with the pins at the bottom. Add the zipper covers on top of them (fig 3.12).

- Sew the front panels, grain sides together, along the curved edge, 5mm (³⁄₁₆") from the edge. Depending on the weight of the leather and the power of the sewing machine used, you may wish to glue down and topstitch this seam, but be sure to add 5mm (³⁄₁₆") to the width of the panels and the seam allowance. Also, if you want an odd number of snaps and thus need a center snap, you

can accomplish this by leaving a 5mm (³⁄₁₆") gap in the center seam, 8mm (⁵⁄₁₆") from the top edge. After you have topstitched the seam, you can push the button through the gap, top it with a socket and set it in place.

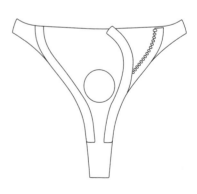

fig 3.12

- Apply contact cement to the outside 8mm (⁵⁄₁₆") of the flesh sides of the flat edges of the front panels. Press the zippers in place, with the pulls facing each other at the bottom and the tips of the teeth flush with the edge of the leather. Let all pieces dry overnight.

- Sew the zippers on the frame in place, 5mm (³⁄₁₆") from the outer edge.

- Sew the zippers on the front panels in place, 5mm (³⁄₁₆") from the edge.

- Mark and punch four equidistant holes in the front panel (see project image).

- Zip the front panels onto the frame and align the top edges. Mark dots on the frame through the holes in the front panels. Punch holes at each of the markings.

- Unzip the front from the frame and set the male halves of the snaps in the frame, and the female halves in the front panel.

- Punch holes in the straps where marked.

- Fix the cross strap to the rear strap with medium rivets.

- Punch two rows of four slots at the bottom of the frame and the rear strap.

- Punch two rows of four slots at the ends of the cross strap and at one end of each snap panel.

- Hand-sew the bottom of the frame over the bottom of the rear strap.

- Hand-sew a length of fabric elastic to each end of the cross strap.

- Try on the thong to ensure a good fit. Trim and melt the fabric elastic if necessary.

- Hand-sew the other ends of the fabric elastic to the snap panels.

- Punch the holes for the snaps at the top ends of the frame and at the ends of the snap panels.

- Set the male halves in the frame and the female halves in the snap panels.

- Trim a curved edge on the ends of the snap panels.

GARTER BELT

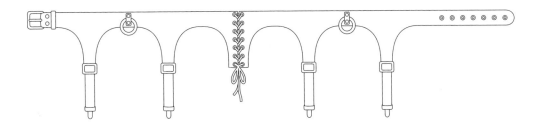

This project is probably closer to a utility belt than lingerie, but does include four stocking garters. The lacing is decorative and allows the project to be cut from a shorter piece of leather, but can easily be omitted. The rings are also optional, but can be used as restraint points or to hang one's implements from. They can also be used as join points to allow the project to be cut from even smaller pieces of leather.

Garter grips can be difficult to acquire, but the clips from sheet grippers can be used in their place. Sheet grippers are lengths of fabric elastic with clips on the ends used to keep bedsheets in place, and can be purchased from linen and department stores. The width of **D** and the width of the ribbon and slide buckles should be chosen to match the width of the garter grips.

Tools

- Sewing machine (leather needle)
- Small needle
- Shears
- Drive punch
- Rivet setter and anvil
- Eyelet setter and anvil
- Cutting board
- Hammer
- Measuring tape
- Pencil and ruler
- Water pencil
- Lighter

Materials

- Garment leather
- Matching thread
- Matching ribbon or fabric elastic (garter grip width)
- 1200mm (47") shoelace
- 8 x medium rivets
- 21 x short eyelets
- 2 x 25mm (1") rings
- 1 x 25mm (1") heel-bar buckle
- 4 x slide buckles (garter grip width)
- 4 x garter grips
- Contact cement
- Paper

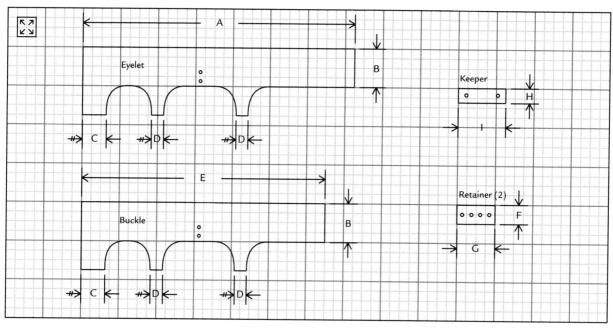

A = 0.50θ + 120mm (4¾")
B = 60mm (2⅜")
C = 40mm (1½")
D = 20mm (¾")
E = 0.50θ + 50mm (2")

F = 30mm (1¼")
G = 70mm (2¾")
H = 20mm (¾")
I = 80mm (3⅛")

Instructions

- Draft the pattern as shown.

- Trace, mark and cut out the panels. Cut rectangular sections 20mm (¾") wide and 27mm (1 1⁄16") deep from the top rear corners of the eyelet and buckle panels.

- Apply contact cement to the flesh sides of the belt portion of both halves, the outside 40mm (1½") of the meeting edges, the ring retainers and the keeper (fig 3.13).

fig 3.13

- Fold the belt portion of the eyelet and buckle panels in half lengthwise, then the meeting edges inward to make 20mm (¾") folds, and fold the long edges of the ring retainers and keeper to the center. Press firmly and let dry overnight.

- Trim the end of the buckle panel flat and cut a rounded edge at the end of the eyelet panel.

- Sew two seams along the belt portion of each panel 5mm (3⁄16") from the folds, raw edges and ends.

- Sew the meeting edge folds 15mm (⅝") from the edge.

- Sew the retainer and keeper folds in place 2mm (1⁄16") from each fold edge.

- Mark seven evenly spaced eyelet holes on the eyelet panel starting 30mm (1¼") from the curved edge, and on the meeting edges of the eyelet and buckle panels.

- Mark the rivet holes and buckle pin slot at the end of the buckle panel (see page 56).

- Punch the holes where marked and cut the buckle pin slot.

- Cut four 250mm (10") lengths of ribbon and melt the ends.

- Wrap the end of each piece of ribbon around the center bar of a slide buckle and hand-sew in place.

- Thread the other end of each ribbon through a garter grip, under the first bar of the slide buckle, over the middle, then under the third. Machine-sew each end to the bottom of a protrusion, 3mm (⅛") from the edge (fig 3.14).

- Insert and set the eyelets in the meeting edges and buckle pin holes.

- Fix the buckle and keeper in place with medium rivets.

- Fix the rings in place with retainers and medium rivets.

- Assemble garter belt with the shoelace.

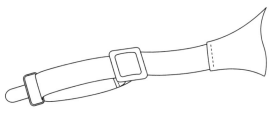

fig 3.14

SLIPPERS

These slippers are more leather socks, but are called slippers because of their functionality. They can be worn with the laces loose so that they can be slipped on and off easily, or they can be laced up to provide a snug fit.

Leather footwear makes a worthwhile addition to a full leather ensemble, and this project provides a more comfortable alternative to boots. Although they provide warmth on their own, they can be worn over socks or the zentai feet in Chapter II.

Although this project calls for the slippers to be made from garment leather, some lighter skins may not be appropriate. For long-lasting slippers, use a heavier garment leather skin, even light chap leather, or any skin which is durable and somewhat supple.

Soles are not included in this design, but they can be added to increase durability or for limited outdoor use. Soles can be purchased from shoe repair or knitting shops, and must be shaped to fit the slipper. Alternatively,

soles could be cut from garment, chap, or medium vegetable-tanned leather or rubber. Once the soles are cut to shape and dyed to match if necessary, both the inside of the soles and the bottoms of the slippers should be roughed up with a rasp or coarse sandpaper, and then glued together with contact cement. Using suede for the sole panel of the slipper can make for an excellent bond with the sole, if it is available.

Since the shape and proportions of the foot and ankle can vary greatly, I recommend that you first make a practice slipper with scrap cloth. If adjustments are necessary, take notes on the problem areas, trace out the pattern on a new piece of paper and make corrections. If the ankle width needs to be increased, move the top rear point backward on the new pattern, but if it needs to be decreased, move the top forward point and the top rear point in towards the center equally.

A zipper can be used in place of the lace closure as shown in the tabi project on page 79 if desired.

Tools

- Sewing machine (leather needle)
- Shears
- Drive punch
- Eyelet setter and anvil
- Cutting board
- Hammer
- Measuring tape
- Pencil and ruler
- Water pencil

Materials

- Garment leather
- Matching thread
- 2 x 1370mm (54") shoelaces
- 24 x short eyelets
- Contact cement
- Paper

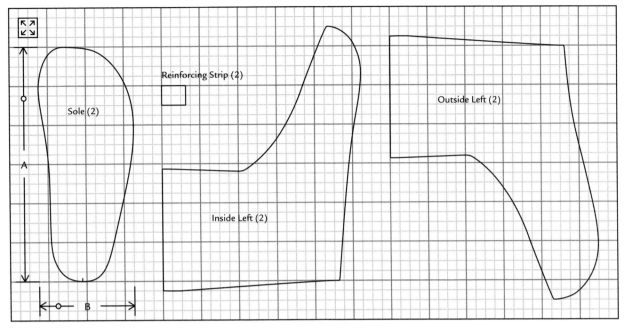

Sole (2)

Reinforcing Strip (2)

Outside Left (2)

Inside Left (2)

A = ψ + 10mm (³⁄₈")

B = ω +10mm (³⁄₈")

Instructions

- Draft the pattern as shown. The top and rear of both the inside and outside panels are identical, so once one panel has been sketched and cut out, it can be used as a guide for top and back of the other. Label the top side of each panel with "left," and the underside with "right." The smaller rectangular panel will reinforce the rear seam and should measure approximately 20mm (¾") x 25mm (1").

- Trace and cut out all pieces, taking care to make one set using the "left" sides of the pattern pieces and one set with the "right" sides. Be sure to transfer the center marks on the sole panels.

- Sew 25mm (1") seams joining each inside panel to its outside panel at the base of the heel, good sides together, 10mm (³⁄₈") from the edge.

- Clip off 15mm (⁵⁄₈") square sections from the top rear corners of both inside and outside panels. This is to minimize the layers you'll have to sew through once the meeting and top edges have been folded.

- Apply contact cement to the outer 20mm (¾") of the flesh sides of each 25mm (1") sewn portion, and to the outer 30mm (1¼") of the flesh sides of the remainder of each rear meeting edge. Make 10mm (³⁄₈") folds along the sewn sections, then move to 15mm (⁵⁄₈") folds for the remainder of the rear meeting edges.

- Apply contact cement to the flesh side of each reinforcing strip, and place them over the sewn portions of the heel bases. Press all edges firmly and let dry overnight.

- Sew each fold in place from the grain side starting from the heel base 7mm (¼") from the center seam, then moving to 10mm (³⁄₈") from the meeting edge for the remainder of the seam.

- Sew reinforcing seams on each heel base 3mm (¹⁄₈") to each side of the center seam.

- Line up each heel seam with the center mark on the corresponding sole panel, grain sides together, and sew from the mark up either side to just below where the toes would begin, 5mm (³⁄₁₆") from the edge. Ensure that the smaller inside panel is on the big toe side of the sole before sewing, otherwise the panels will be mismatched.

- Sew each inside panel to the outside panel, good sides together, from the points to the top, 5mm (³⁄₁₆") from the edge.

- Trim the front 10mm (³⁄₈") of the top seam allowances down to 2mm (¹⁄₁₆").

- Sew around the front of each slipper 5mm (³⁄₁₆") from the edge.

- Trim the top 30mm (1¼") of the top seam allowances down to 2mm (¹⁄₁₆").

- Apply contact cement to the outer 30mm (1 ¼") of the flesh side of each the top edge.

- Make 15mm (⅝") folds along each top edge. Press firmly and let dry overnight.

- Turn the slippers right side out and sew each top fold in place, 10mm (⅜") from the edge.

- Mark and punch six evenly spaced eyelet holes in each meeting edge.

- Insert and set eyelets.

- Thread a shoelace through each set of eyelets and tie knots in the ends.

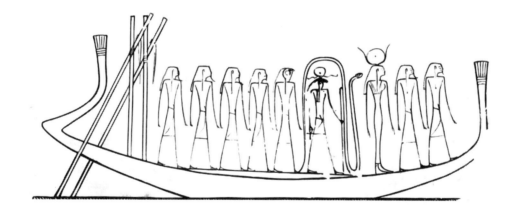

TABI

Tabi are split-toe footwear, part of formal Japanese dress for both men and women. The first tabi were made of leather, but silk and cotton became standard as woven fabrics became more prevalent. The design presented here is for unlined leather tabi. Though tabi typically only cover the foot and the bottom of the ankle, this design rises above the ankle, though it can easily be altered for a more traditional cut or to rise even higher. They fasten at the back with a zipper closure, but this can be changed to a lace closure as described in the slipper project on page 76. The zippers could also be mounted on the sides by sewing the rear seams shut and cutting new openings on the sides.

As in the slipper project, I recommend that you first make a practice tabi with scrap cloth. If adjustments are necessary, take notes on the problem areas, trace out the pattern on a new piece of paper and make corrections. If the ankle width needs to be increased, move the top rear point backward on the new pattern, but if it needs to be decreased, move the top forward point and the top rear point in towards the center equally.

Like the slippers, soles are not included in this design, but can easily be added in the same manner. If attaching soles, the sole panel of the tabi should ideally be made from suede, and a layer of garment or chap leather cut to

the same shape and size as the sole panel less the 5mm (³⁄₁₆") circumferential seam allowance is glued on after assembly, flesh sides together. The suede allows for maximum glue adherence, which is especially crucial around the toes of the tabi. Garment leather can be used for the sole panel if the grain side is roughed up with a rasp or some coarse sandpaper. Lighter garment skins work better for tabi, making soles often a good idea, but the split-toe design allows the tabi to be worn with zori or thong style sandals, which can negate the need for soles.

Although all the seams on the tabi are machine-sewn, the section around the toes must be basted in place prior to sewing. Depending on the weight of the leather, a regular needle and thimble may suffice for this, though most skins will require a glover's needle and a sailor's palm. In both cases, though, use regular sewing thread.

The addition of the reinforcing strip at the bottom of the opening on this and the previous project is necessary because of the stress that will be placed on the seam under the strip. When sewing the strip area in place, three layers of leather in addition to the zipper must be sewn together – so if the leather is fairly heavy, you may wish to cut the reinforcing strip from a lighter skin, allowing the area to be more easily machine-sewn.

Tools

- Sewing machine (leather needle)
- Glover's needle and sailor's palm
- Shears
- Pliers
- Measuring tape
- Pencil and ruler
- Water pencil
- Lighter

Materials

- Garment leather
- Matching thread
- 2 x 300mm (12") open-ended metal zipper
- Contact cement
- Paper

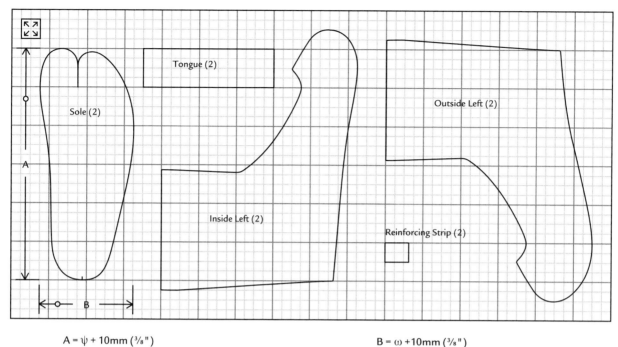

Tongue (2)

Sole (2)

Outside Left (2)

Inside Left (2)

Reinforcing Strip (2)

A = ψ + 10mm (³⁄₈ ")

B = ω +10mm (³⁄₈ ")

Instructions

- Draft the pattern as shown. The top and rear of both the inside and outside panels are identical, so once one panel has been sketched and cut out, it can be used as a guide for top and back of the other. Label the top side of each panel with "left," and the underside with "right." The smaller rectangular panel will reinforce the rear seam and should measure approximately 20mm (³⁄₄ ") x 25mm (1"). The larger rectangular panel is a tongue to go under the zipper, and is optional.

- Trace and cut out all pieces, taking care to make one set using the "left" sides of the pattern pieces and one set with the "right" sides. Be sure to transfer the center mark on the sole panels.

- Sew a 25mm (1") seam joining each inside panel to its outside panel at the base of the heel, good sides together, 10mm (³⁄₈ ") from the edge.

- Adjust the length of the zippers to match the meeting edges less 15mm (⁵⁄₈ "). If using open-ended zippers, sew the bases of the zippers together with heavy thread (fig 3.21, page 112).

- Clip off sections 10mm (³⁄₈ ") long and 15mm (⁵⁄₈ ") deep from the back top corners of both panels (the 15mm (⁵⁄₈ ") side should be along the meeting edge of the panel). This step minimizes the layers to be sewn through once the meeting and top edges have been folded.

- Apply contact cement to the outer 20mm (³⁄₄ ") of the flesh side of each rear meeting edge (including the 25mm (1") sewn portion). Make 10mm (³⁄₈ ") folds.

- Apply contact cement to each meeting edge fold allowance. Press the zippers in place so they are centered over the meeting edges.

- Apply contact cement to the flesh side of each reinforcing strip, and place it over the sewn portion of a heel base.

- Apply contact cement to the outside 5mm (³⁄₁₆ ") of one of the long grain sides of each tongue, and fix it to the inside of each outside panel meeting edge over the zipper, so that the bottom of the tongue meets with the top of the reinforcing strip. Press all edges firmly and let dry overnight.

- Sew each meeting edge from the grain side 5mm (³⁄₁₆ ") from the edge, from the top all the way to the base of the heel. Take care to fold the tongues out of the way when sewing the inside panels.

- Pull each zipper back from the edge and the tongue and rub off the contact cement. Use contact cement thinner very sparingly and only if necessary.

- Line up each heel seam with the center mark on the corresponding sole panel, grain sides together, and sew from the mark up either side to just below where the toes would begin, 5mm (³⁄₁₆ ") from the edge. Ensure that each smaller inside panel is on the big toe side of the sole panel before sewing, otherwise the panels will be mismatched.

- Sew each inside panel to the outside panel, good sides together, from the points that protrude at the ends of the curved sections to the top, 5mm ($\frac{3}{16}$") from the edge.

- Line each center seam up with the end of the split between the toes, pinching the sole and inside panels together around the top and down to the side seam to see if gathering is necessary. Repeat with the outside panels. If gathering is necessary, use a glover's needle and a sailor's palm to baste the unsewn portion of the inside panel approximately 2mm ($\frac{1}{16}$") from the edge. Pull the thread to gather the leather so that it fits the sole panel, and then tie it off. Repeat with the outside panels.

- Baste the unsewn portion of each inside panel to the sole panel, from the center, good sides together, 2mm

($\frac{1}{16}$") from the edge, with a glover's needle and a sailor's palm. Repeat with the outside panels.

- Sew the basted seams with the machine, 3mm ($\frac{1}{8}$") from the edge. Reinforce the points between the toes with another line of stitching if necessary.

- Remove the basting.

- Trim the top 30mm (1 $\frac{1}{4}$") of the top seam allowances down to 2mm ($\frac{1}{16}$").

- Apply contact cement to the outer 30mm (1 $\frac{1}{4}$") of the flesh side of each top edge.

- Make a 15mm ($\frac{5}{8}$") fold along each top edge. Press firmly and let dry overnight.

- Turn the tabi right side out and sew each top fold in place 10mm ($\frac{3}{8}$") from the edge.

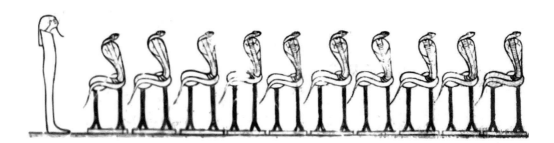

CORSET

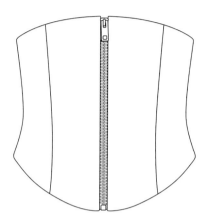

The design presented here is for a simple under-bust corset, or waist cincher. It only covers the waist, not the breasts or hips, but the design can be expanded upon to create larger and more complex pieces.

To construct a corset which covers the breasts and hips, extend the panel lengths and adjust their widths to accommodate the hip and breast measurements. When making an over-bust corset, the shape of the upper part of the front and front side panels should be cut to match the breasts of the intended wearer, using the breast measurement ζ as a guide. The location of the front/front side seam may have to be altered as well so that the seam runs in the middle of the breast. This is usually done by decreasing the width of the front panels and increasing the width of the front side panels. When extending down to the hips, the increase in width can be distributed about the panels uniformly.

Extending the length of the panels will mean adding eyelets to the lace edges, which will then necessitate using a longer lace. If laces longer than 1830mm (72") are not available, buy a pair of shorter laces and fuse them together. This is a relatively easy task, and when you do it correctly the joint will barely be noticeable and will not compromise the overall strength of the lace.

To fuse two laces together, first cut an aglet from each lace. Hold both laces in one hand around 20mm (¾") apart from each other, with the clipped ends extending around 20mm (¾") away from the hand. With a lighter in the other hand, melt the ends over a sink to the point where they start to bubble (be very careful if they start to drip; the melted lace is dangerously hot). After removing them from the flame, immediately transfer one lace to the other hand and press the ends together. After a few seconds, the molten plastic should be cool enough to touch but still warm enough to be malleable. Roll the joint between the thumb and index finger and ensure there are no jagged edges. Once the join has fully cooled, test it for strength and smoothness. Cut and rejoin if necessary.

This design has a separable zipper on the front and lacing on the back. The zipper is not only decorative, but also allows the corset to be laced up and easily removed by the wearer. The zipper can be omitted, if you like, by changing the seam allowances of the front panel meeting edges to match the rest of the panels and joining them together in the same manner. Alternatively, the zipper could be replaced with a busk or more lacing.

With most leathers, the boning on the meeting lace edges should be sufficient reinforcement for the eyelets mounted inside it. When using light leather or other materials, though, you may wish to reinforce the meeting edge with nylon webbing or another layer of leather, between the layers of the boning fold or under it, then mounting the eyelets through all the layers.

Inserting the boning into the pockets can sometimes be difficult, especially if the pockets are too small. The solution to this predicament is to employ the same method used to thread the strap through the ball on page 156. Thread a leather needle with a long length of artificial sinew or waxed cotton, tying the ends together so that the thread is doubled over. Push the needle and thread through the pocket, through one end of the boning, then back through the pocket again. Then, push the boning into the pocket while pulling on both the knotted and needle ends of the thread.

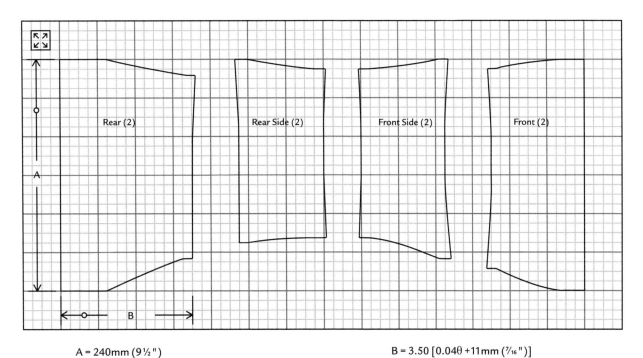

A = 240mm (9½")

B = 3.50 [0.04θ +11mm (⁷⁄₁₆")]

2m (79") x 22mm (⁷⁄₈") matching garment leather binding

Tools

- Sewing machine (leather needle)
- Shears
- Drive punch
- Eyelet setter and anvil
- Cutting board
- Hammer
- Pliers
- Measuring tape
- Pencil and ruler
- Water pencil
- Lighter

Materials

- Garment leather
- Matching thread
- 1830mm (72") shoelace
- 28 x short eyelets
- 300mm (12") separable zipper
- 2.5m (8') boning
- Contact cement
- Paper

Instructions

- Draft the pattern as shown.

- Trace and cut out all panels, taking care to make two mirror images sets of panels.

- Draw lines parallel to the straight edge of each rear panel, on the flesh side, 60mm (2½") from the edge. Use these lines to sew 30mm (1¼") folds 2mm (¹⁄₁₆") from the edge.

- Sew second seams 9mm (³⁄₈") from the fold edge (adjust if boning is wider than 7mm (¼")).

- Draw lines parallel to the straight edge of each front panel on the flesh side, 30mm (1¼") from the edge. Use these lines to sew 15mm (⁵⁄₈") folds 2mm (¹⁄₁₆") from the edge.

- Resize the zipper to match the length of the front panel meeting edges.

- Apply contact cement to the fold allowance on each front panel and press the zipper in place with the back edges of the teeth flush with the fold edge. Allow to dry overnight.

- Sew the zipper in place 2mm (¹⁄₁₆") from the fold edge.

- Sew each set of panels together 3mm (¹⁄₈") from the edges.

- Sew a second seam 9mm (³⁄₈") inside each 3mm (¹⁄₈") joining seam.

- Topstitch each seam from the inside just outside the first seam, with the pockets folded toward the rear.

- Trim the top and bottom edges at the joins to make a smooth curve if necessary.

- Insert boning into each of the ten pockets and trim to size.

- Cut binding strips to match the top and bottom edges, apply contact cement to the flesh side of each, and fold the binding over the top and bottom edges of both sides. Press all edges firmly and let dry overnight.

- Sew the binding in place 2mm (¹⁄₁₆") from the edge of the binding.

- Mark seven evenly spaced eyelet holes on the rear meeting edges between the seams starting 15mm (⁵⁄₈") from the top and ending 15mm (⁵⁄₈") from the bottom, taking care to ensure symmetry.

- Punch all holes where marked.

- Insert and set the eyelets.

VEST

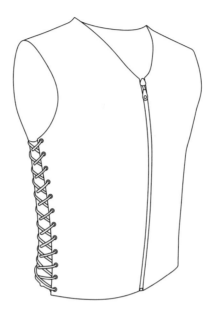

This project is a simple biker style vest with a long zipper closure on the front and lacing on the sides. It is meant to fit fairly snugly with the laces loose, so that it can be cinched down for a tight fit if desired. An even tighter fit can be achieved by adding boning to the eyelet panels.

A belt and belt loops made of chap leather can be added to the vest if desired, and hardened leather or molded polymer plates can be mounted under leather panels in the same manner as the samurai gauntlets for an armored look.

Tools

- Sewing machine (leather needle)
- Shears
- Drive punch
- Eyelet setter and anvil
- Cutting board
- Hammer
- Pliers
- Measuring tape
- Pencil and ruler
- Water pencil
- Lighter

Materials

- Garment leather
- Matching thread
- 2 x 1830mm (72") shoelaces
- 48 x short eyelets
- 550mm (22") open-ended metal zipper
- Contact cement
- Paper

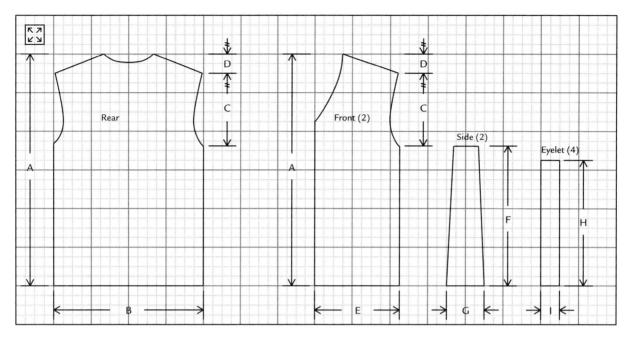

A = 0.85σ + 60mm (2¼")

B = 0.50ζ - 20mm (¾")

C = 0.50ι + 20mm (¾")

D = 50mm (2")

E = 0.25ζ - 10mm (⅜")

F = A - C - 40mm (1⅝")

G = 100mm (4")

H = F - 70mm (2¾")

I = 30mm (1¼")

Instructions

- Draft the pattern as shown.

- Trace and cut out all pieces, taking care to make the front panels mirror images of each other. Mark both sides of each side panel 20mm (¾") from the top and 50mm (2") from the bottom.

- Sew each front panel to the rear panel at the shoulders, grain sides together, 20mm (¾") from the edge.

- Apply contact cement to the outside 40mm (1½") of both flesh sides of the shoulder seams and fold them flat.

- Apply contact cement to the flesh side of the eyelet panels and fold them in half lengthwise. Press firmly and let all pieces dry overnight.

- Mark twelve evenly spaced eyelet holes on each eyelet panel 5mm (³⁄₁₆") from the fold, starting 15mm (⅝") from the top and ending 15mm (⅝") from the bottom, taking care to ensure symmetry between each pair of panels.

- Punch all holes where marked.

- Topstitch both sides of each shoulder seam from the grain side 10mm (⅜") from the center seam.

- Align each side panel with a front panel, grain sides together, with an eyelet strap in between, fold facing inwards between the marks on the side panel. Sew each in place 5mm (³⁄₁₆") from the edge.

- Align the other side of each side panel with the corresponding side of the rear panel, grain sides together, with an eyelet strap in between, fold facing inwards between the marks on the side panel. Sew each in place 5mm (³⁄₁₆") from the edge.

- Apply contact cement to the outside 20mm (¾") of flesh side of the arm openings, including the tops of the side panels.

- Make 10mm (⅜") folds around the arm openings and press firmly.

- Apply contact cement to outside 20mm (¾") of the flesh side of the collar.

- Make a 10mm (⅜") fold along the edge of the collar and press firmly.

- Apply contact cement to the outside 30mm (1¼") of the flesh side of each meeting edge.

- Make 15mm (⁵⁄₈") folds along each edge and press firmly.

- Apply contact cement to the bottom 80mm (3") of the flesh side of the vest.

- Make 40mm (1½") folds along the bottom and press firmly.

- Adjust the zipper length to match meeting edges.

- Apply contact cement to each meeting edge fold allowance.

- Press the zippers in place so the backs of the teeth are flush with the edge of the fold, and let dry overnight.

- Sew the zippers in place from the grain side, 6mm (¼") from the edge.

- Sew the arm openings from the grain side, 6mm (¼") from the edge.

- Sew the collar from the grain side, 6mm (¼") from the edge.

- Sew the bottom of each panel individually from the grain side, 30mm (1¼") from the bottom edge.

- Insert and set the eyelets.

- Thread a shoelace through each pair of eyelet straps from the top down to the bottom. Tie knots in the ends.

CHAPS

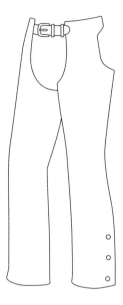

This project is a pair of basic biker-style chaps, made of garment leather in two pieces that lace together in the back. Although most chaps typically have a liner under the leather, this has been omitted here. Without a liner, the leather can either be felt directly on the skin, or through another garment such as a bodysuit – in which case the liner serves no purpose anyway.

As with the vest and samurai gauntlets, molded plates can be mounted on the thighs and shins for an armored look. If this option is taken, open areas should be left behind the knees, which also allows for increased movement and easier kneeling. The leg zips should then each be made in two parts on the back of the chaps rather than the sides, and the snaps omitted. This modification can be worthwhile whether or not plates are used, as they make for a unique, tighter-fitting garment. Also, if the belt and upper leg openings are reinforced with vegetable-tanned leather or nylon webbing and rigged with D-rings, the chaps could be used as a suspension harness (after careful testing a few inches from the floor to ensure safety).

The pattern depicts the chaps in two main panels, but panel division lines are also marked since it is not always possible or economical to cut the each panel in one piece. If using an eight-panel construction as opposed to four, add a 15mm (⅝") seam allowance to the bottoms of the top panels and the tops of the bottom panels, and join them in the same way the front panels are joined to the rear.

When drafting the inner panel pattern, it is much less labor intensive and more accurate to simply trace around the top of the rear panel rather than using the grid expansion method. Use the dashed line one full cell's width from the top of the front panel as the bottom border of this panel.

Note that the protrusion on the zipper side of the front panel should extend 35mm (1⅜"). To change this if required, keep A as the panel width and change the depth of the protrusion. Note also that the protrusion on the zipper side of the rear panel should extend 50mm (2"). To adjust this, change the base width rather than the depth of the protrusion.

There are two ways of mounting the inside panels on the front panels. The method described here involves folding the raw edges of both panels inside first, then glueing the panels flesh sides together, and finally sewing around the perimeter. The other way this can be approached is to sew around the perimeter grain sides together first, then turning grain sides out and sewing around the perimeter again. With the seams in place, glue the front panel to the inside panel, then sew along the bottom of the inside panel after drying overnight.

There are many places in this project where four layers of leather must be sewn through. With heavier skins this will be difficult or impossible, even with an industrial machine. If a heavy skin is used, omit the fold allowances on the inside panel and the corresponding edges on the front panel, make the strap panels at half width with no folds, make the protrusion incision horizontal rather than on a angle, and clip the bottom corners off of the zipper side of the front and rear panels to make the hem fold less bulky.

Only the thigh measurement is used to calculate the width of the panels, so it is possible that when both sides of the chaps are laced together, the chaps may not fit around the waist. You can fix this problem by shortening or lengthening the upper part of the front panel (and the corresponding part of each inside panel), or by adding an expansion panel. To make an expansion panel, take two panels of the same leather with 15mm (⅝") folds on all sides, big enough to hold six grommets. Mark the grommets in two vertical rows of three to match the grommets on the front panels. Glue the panels, flesh sides together, let them dry overnight, sew around the perimeter 2mm (¹⁄₁₆") from the edge, punch the holes and insert and set the grommets. The expansion panel can then be laced over the front panels so that their ends meet, or in between the ends of the front panels.

Tools

- Sewing machine (leather needle)
- Shears
- Hobby knife
- Drive punch
- Rivet setter and anvil
- Snap setter and anvil
- 6mm (¼") grommet setter and anvil
- Cutting board
- Hammer
- Pliers
- Measuring tape
- Pencil and ruler
- Water pencil
- Lighter

Materials

- Garment leather
- Matching thread
- 300mm (12") of 5mm (³⁄₁₆") matching leather lace
- 10 x medium rivets
- 6 x short snaps
- 19 x 6mm (¼") grommets
- 1 x 38mm (1½") roller buckle
- 2 x 650mm (26") separable zippers
- Paper

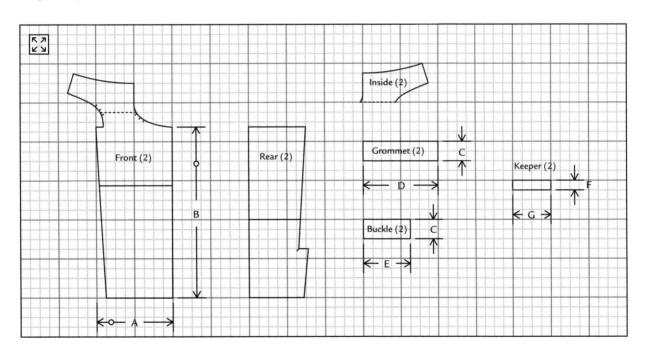

$A = 0.57[\phi + 110mm\ (4½")]$

$B = \tau + 65mm\ (2½")$

$C = 80mm\ (3⅛")$

$D = 0.40\theta + 15mm\ (⅝")$

$E = 0.15\theta + 65mm\ (2½")$

$F = 30mm\ (1¼")$

$G = 100mm\ (4")$

Instructions

- Draft the pattern as shown.

- Trace, mark and cut out all pieces, taking care to make each pair of panels mirror images of each other. Cut the incisions along the curves of the front panels and at the protrusions on the rear panels. Each rear panel incision is made at a 45° angle, starting from the corner of the protrusion, deep enough to allow 15mm (⅝") folds along the zipper edge and top edge of the protrusion.

- Apply contact cement to the flesh side of each keeper panel and fold the long edges in to the center.

- Apply contact cement to the flesh side of the grommet and buckle panels and fold the long edges in to the center. Then, apply contact cement to the inside of each panel and align each pair of panels, insides together. Press all edges firmly and let dry overnight.

- Sew the keeper folds in place 3mm (⅛") from each fold edge.

- Sew each pair of grommet and buckle straps together 2mm (¹⁄₁₆") from each fold edge.

- Trim both ends of the buckle strap and one side of the grommet strap right and flat, then sew across each 3mm (⅛") from the edge. Sketch a curve on the other side of the grommet strap, sew along this line, then trim to 3mm (⅛") from the seam.

- Apply contact cement to the flesh side of the outer 30mm (1 ¼") of the top, back and bottom edges of the top section of each front panel, and the outer 20mm (¾") of the top front edge of each front panel. The front edge curve runs all the way down to the inseam, and the inseam must be sewn before that fold is made, so leave the area below the incisions unglued for now. Make 15mm (⅝") folds along the top, back and bottom edges of the top section of each front panel, and 10mm (⅜") folds along the top front edge of each front panel.

- Apply contact cement in the same manner and make identical folds on each inside panel.

- Apply contact cement to the flesh side, as well as the insides of the folds of each inside panel and the area above the dashed line on the flesh side of each front panel.

- Place the buckle strap 20mm (¾") below the top edge and 20mm (¾") inside the front edge of the left front panel (fig 3.15). Place the grommet strap similarly on the right front panel.

- Align each inside panel over the corresponding front panel. First align the edges precisely, then press the center of the panels in place. Press all edges firmly and let dry overnight.

- Sew around the perimeter of the inside panel (including the bottom) 2mm (¹⁄₁₆") from the edge and down the remaining back edge of the top section of the front panel 10mm (⅜") from the edge. There are many layers of leather to be sewn through over the straps. If the machine will not sew through them, simply end the seam just above the strap and begin it again just below it.

- Mark and punch two rivet holes over where the buckle and eyelet straps are sandwiched between the front and inside panels, 15mm (⅝") from the front edge (fig 3.15). Insert and set the rivets.

- Mark and punch the rivet holes and cut the buckle pin slot in the buckle strap (fig 3.15).

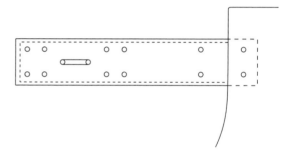

fig 3.15

- Mark and punch two rivet holes in each keeper, 10mm (⅜") from each end.

- Fix the buckle in place with rivets through the holes closest to the buckle.

- Fix the first keeper in place with rivets behind the buckle, sandwiching it between the layers of the buckle strap, and the second keeper using the remaining holes.

- Mark and punch six grommet holes in two vertical rows of three spaced approximately 25mm (1") apart, 15mm (⅝") from the back edge of the top section of the front panels.

- Mark and punch seven evenly spaced grommet holes in the grommet strap.

- Insert and set the grommets.

- Apply contact cement to the outer 100mm (4") of the flesh side of the zipper edge on each front panel and make 50mm (2") folds.

- Apply contact cement to the outer 30mm (1¼") of the flesh side of the zipper edge and the outer 100mm (4") of the area from the protrusion to the bottom on each rear panel. Make 15mm (⅝") folds along each zipper edge, 15mm (⅝") folds along the top of each protrusion (facilitated by the diagonal incision at the corner of each protrusion), and 50mm (2") folds from the protrusion down to the bottom.

- Adjust each zipper length to match the zipper edges on the rear panels less 10mm (⅜"). Turn the slider on one of the zippers around front to back before you reattach the stop.

- Apply contact cement to the zipper edge fold allowance on each rear panel and press the pin side of a zipper in place so that the backs of the teeth are flush with the fold edge and the pin is 10mm (⅜") from the top. Press firmly and let dry overnight.

- Sew the pin sides of the zippers in place from the inside, with the seam running down the center of the zipper tape. Reinforce this seam by sewing a second 30mm (1¼") seam at the top and 4mm (³⁄₁₆") inside the first (fig 3.10, page 64).

- Sew the protrusion fold in place, from the inside, 15mm (⅝") from the inside raw edge of the fold and 3mm (⅛") from the top edge.

- Zip the slider sides of the zippers onto the pin sides. Align the front and rear panels, flesh sides up and bottoms together, so that the slider side of the zipper tape is 10mm (⅜") from the inside raw edge of the fold on the front panel's zipper edge. Mark where the zippers start and stop on the front panels.

- Apply an 8mm (⁵⁄₁₆") wide strip of contact cement to the inside of each front panel between the marks, 10mm (⅜") from the inside raw edge of the fold. Press the slider side of each zipper in place, pull tab side down, 10mm (⅜") from the edge and teeth facing out, with the zipper box at the top marking. Press firmly and let dry overnight.

- Sew the slider sides of the zippers in place from the inside, with the seam running down the center of the zipper tape. Reinforce this seam by sewing a second 30mm (1¼") seam at the top and 4mm (³⁄₁₆") inside the first (fig 3.10, page 64).

- Sew each front panel to the corresponding rear panel along the inseam, grain sides together, 15mm (⅝") from the edge.

- Trim the top and bottom 20mm (¾") of the inseam allowances down to 5mm.

- Topstitch the inseams in place, from the inside, 10mm (⅜") from the seam, folding the seam allowance towards the rear panel.

- Apply contact cement to the top 20mm (¾") of each rear panel and the remaining portion of the curve of the top section of the front panel. Make 10mm (⅜") folds and press firmly.

- Place the sides of the chaps together so that the grommets overlap. Lace them together using the 5mm (³⁄₁₆") leather lace.

- Try on the chaps and check for length, keeping the 20mm (¾") fold allowances in mind. Mark and trim if necessary.

- Apply contact cement to the bottom 40mm (1½") of the flesh side of both sides of the chaps and make 20mm (¾") folds. Press all edges firmly and let dry overnight.

- Sew each top fold in place from the zipper edge all the way up to the inside panel, 7mm (¼") from the edge.

- Sew the bottom folds in place from the inside, 15mm (⅝") from the edge.

- Mark holes for the snaps at the top, bottom and middle of each rear panel protrusion, 20mm (¾") from the edge.

- Mark matching holes on the front panels using the rear panels as guides.

- Punch all holes where marked.

- Insert and set the male halves of the snaps in the rear panels, and the female halves of the snaps in the front panels.

Gloves

The difficulty of this project cannot be overstated. Glovers apprentice for many years to learn their craft. You cannot hope to approach their level of competence without years of training and practice. There is unfortunately very little literature currently available on this subject, so hopefully this book will serve in some small way to keep the glover's craft alive.

Before beginning, please consider that pursuing this project may not initially be economical. Because of errors and practice runs, you may initially spend more than you would on high-quality store-bought gloves. That said, you can make bare leather gloves in whatever style you can imagine, and to fit any hand (the techniques in this section can also be used to alter store-bought gloves to irregular sizes). Once you've acquired this skill, you can use it fairly painlessly over and over again.

Gloves can be made from a wide variety of materials. Generally, you can use any flexible material that doesn't fray easily and is thin enough to be hand-sewn. If you want leather gloves, you can use cow, calf, sheep, lamb, pig, goat, deer and more. Deer skins are particularly suitable, due to their weight, strength and availability.

The techniques described in this section will produce machine-sewn gloves, though you'll do a lot of hand-sewing while basting the fourchettes and thumb panels. The seams are sewn with the gloves inside out and the grain sides together. For a more traditional approach, you can try hand-sewing the gloves in their entirety. When hand-sewing, the seams lie 2mm (¹⁄₁₆") from the

edge, on the outside of the glove, with the flesh sides together, though the fourchettes should still be sewn grain sides together with this seam lying on the inside of the gloves. This approach allows for the use of a slightly heavier skin, as the gloves will not need to be turned right side out when finished. When sewing outside-seam gloves, consider using an overcast stitch, or even sewing the seams with a machine.

The side entry and clasp differ from tradition as well, and are more the style of a sports glove. Traditionally, the width of the glove runs straight from the knuckles down to the wrist edge, or flares out slightly. With that design, you may need to gather the leather with fabric elastic on the palm or back side of each glove. It is possible to cut both the palm and back panels in one piece when using this kind of design, which eliminates the side seams on the inside (see the zentai glove pattern on page 41). To make this kind of panel, overlap the palm and back pattern panels at the index finger by twice the seam allowance. And, as in the zentai glove pattern, the thumb measurements are not used as the relationship between the thumb panel and the thumb opening is precise. The length, and to a lesser degree the width, of the upper portion of the panel (to the left of the protrusion and slit on the pattern) can be adjusted to match if necessary, taking the allowances into consideration.

Fingerless gloves can also be made using this pattern. Simply clip off the ends of the fingers at the desired length on the back panel pattern. Then flip it over, line it up with the palm panel pattern, mark the finger lengths on it and clip them off as well. The fourchette patterns will then have to be trimmed, one side at a time, using the matching clipped-off fingertips as guides. This style of glove is typically sewn down both sides and has an open section on the back panel to allow entry. This raw edge can be finished in the same way as the side entry, then straps with snaps or hook-and-loop can be sewn on to each side of the opening.

To practice hand-stitching for hand-sewn gloves, trim a straight edge on two pieces of scrap leather and hold them

flesh sides together with the straight edges even. Binder clips, readily available at stationery and department stores, make this process easier. Push the needle through both layers of leather perpendicularly, approximately 2mm ($\frac{1}{16}$") from the edge. A glover's needle and sailor's palm can make this process easier on the fingers. Use a saddle stitch (fig 3.3 on page 54), and make the stitches quite close together and as even as possible. The thread should be pulled firm, but not so tight that the leather begins to pucker. Practice this stitch well before you attempt to hand-sew a pair of gloves.

Tools

- Sewing machine
- Glover's needle and sailor's palm
- Shears
- Snips
- Snap setter and anvil
- Cutting board
- Measuring tape
- Pencil and ruler
- Water pencil

Materials

- Leather (see project description)
- Matching thread
- 4 x short snaps
- Contact cement
- Paper

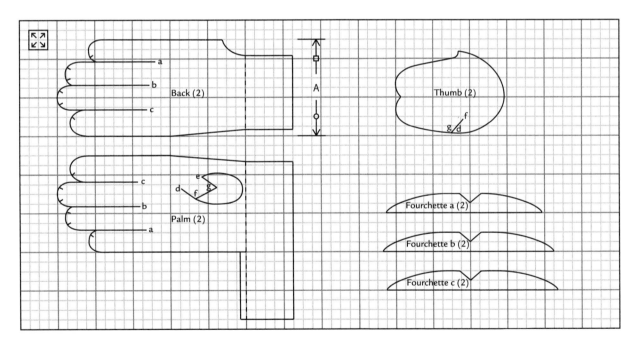

A = [0 + 12mm (½")]/2

2 x 150mm (6") of 15mm (⅝") matching garment leather binding

Instructions

- Draft the pattern as shown. Note that only one measurement is needed and the grid cells will be of equal height and width for all panels. When sewing inside-seam gloves, the basting seams lie 2mm (¹⁄₁₆") from the edge and the machine-sewn seams 3mm (¹⁄₈") from the edge.

- Place the wearer's hand over the palm panel of the pattern, lining up the ends of the finger division lines, and check for finger length fit. Alter if necessary, and transpose the alterations on to the back panel. The length of the affected fourchettes will need to be altered as well. Add or remove length at the widest portion of any fourchette sides that need to be modified, preserving the gentle curve to the tip of the finger.

- Trace, mark and cut out all the panels for the first glove, then flip the pattern pieces over and repeat for the second. The dashed line indicates the area where contact cement will be applied. Leave a small margin at the top of each palm and back panel and leave the finger tips and division lines uncut. Keep each glove's panels together to prevent mismatching.

- Sew around the end of each finger division line 2mm (¹⁄₁₆") from the line, up 10mm (³⁄₈") on each side of the line (fig 2.21, page 42). Omit this step if sewing outside-seam gloves.

- Cut out the fingers by first cutting down the finger division lines, then cutting the rounded tips of the fingers.

- Fold each thumb panel lengthwise, grain sides together, and sew from the folded edge up over the top to 3mm (¹⁄₈") away from the slit, 3mm (¹⁄₈") from the edge.

- The human thumb has a complex shape, so the thumb panels are also quite complex. For each glove, align point **g** on the opening with the end of the corresponding thumb seam, and baste from point **g** to point **f**, then from point **f** to point **d**, then from point **d** down to halfway around the opening. Start a new basting seam at the end of the thumb seam, and baste to point **e**, then around to meet the other basting seam (fig 3.16).

- Sew each thumb panel in place with the sewing machine. This step, particularly sewing the pointed protrusion in the thumb opening, can be very difficult. Have patience, and use snips, or even a pair of tweezers, to help maneuver the material through the machine. Practice this on scrap before attempting it with leather. If this proves to be too difficult or even impossible with your machine, hand-sewing the protrusion seams is an option. If going that route, ensure that the stitches are close together and evenly spaced, and that you keep a precise constant seam allowance.

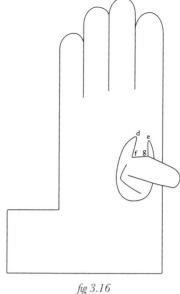

fig 3.16

- Sew each palm panel to the corresponding back panel, grain sides together, from the mark at the tip of the index finger down to the cuff 3mm (¹⁄₈") from the edge.

- Sew the other side of each glove, grain sides together, from the mark at the tip of the little finger down to the opening 3mm (¹⁄₈") from the edge.

- Sew the tops of the middle and ring fingers between the marks, 3mm (¹⁄₈") from the edge.

- Sew each fourchette by folding it widthwise grain sides together at the notch, and sewing along the line of the notch 3mm (¹⁄₈") from the edge. The seam will not run right to the corner, but will rather run off the edge of the fold a few millimeters from the long edge. Trim the seam allowances down to 2mm (¹⁄₁₆").

- Baste each of the fourchettes in place, grain sides together, by first lining up the center of the fourchette with the end of the appropriate finger slot and sewing from there up to each tip. Note that the longer sides of the fourchettes are sewn to the back sides of the gloves.

- Machine-sew the fourchette seams on the palm side of each glove in three seams: one from the seam at the top of the index finger to the middle finger seam, the second from other side of the middle finger seam to the ring finger seam, and the third from the other side of the ring finger seam to the seam at the top of the little finger.

- Machine-sew the fourchette seams on the back side of each glove in one seam, going from the tip of the little finger to the tip of the index finger for the left glove, and from the tip of the index finger to the tip of the little finger for the right glove. Sew over the tops of each finger in a fairly round seam, and fold the fourchettes in to the middle of the fingers so that they lay flat. This seam can be rather difficult, especially at the end of the finger division lines, so use snips to maneuver the fabric through the machine.

- Remove the basting.

- Trim the seam allowances below the glue line and around the fingers and thumb of each glove down to 2mm (1/16"). This includes all of the fourchette seams, the tips of the fingers, the outer seams around the index and little fingers, and the thumb panel seams (though not the seams attaching the thumb panels to the palm panels).

- Apply contact cement to the flesh side of each strap protrusion and to the areas below the glue lines.

- Fold each strap section so that the bottom edge of the glove meets up with the glue line. Then, fold each section on the protrusion that has the glue still exposed over the top raw edge of the strap section. Press all edges firmly and let dry overnight.

- Cut the end of the straps straight if necessary, then cut the end of the strap to match the curvature of the snap.

- Sew each strap in place from the underside, starting from the bottom of the entry on the back panel, 2mm (1/16") from the fold, going around the end of the strap,

then 2mm (1/16") from the inside edge of the leather and back to the entry on the back panel.

- Baste each binding strip to an entry, grain sides together, 2mm (1/16") from the edge. Start sewing at the top of the strap of each glove, then trim the strip to fit when the bottom edge is reached.

- Machine-sew each binding strip in place, 3mm (1/8") from the edge.

- Remove the basting.

- Apply contact cement to the flesh side of each binding strip, fold it over the entry edge, and press the flesh side of the strip to the underside of the glove. Press all edges firmly and let dry overnight.

- Sew the binding strips in place 3mm (1/8") from the edge.

- Mark and punch holes for the female halves of the snaps, one at the beginning of the strap protrusion and one at the tip.

- Try each glove on, tighten the strap, and mark holes for the male halves of the snaps through the existing holes.

- Punch all holes where marked.

- Insert and set the snaps.

EYE MASKS

This style of mask, sometimes called a domino, has its roots in the molded leather half masks used in the Commedia Dell'Arte theatre of the Italian renaissance (Nunley, 1999). This was only the beginning of the eye mask's cultural significance, though, as this style was then often a part of the costume worn to masquerades and Carnival.

The use of black eye masks was prevalent in the media of days gone by as part of the attire of robbers and other crooks, and still is common in cartoons. On the other hand, many comic book heroes also don eye masks in order to hide their identity. The effectiveness of this disguise is debatable, but they were nonetheless the mask of choice of Zorro, The Lone Ranger, Robin, and many others.

This is another project with a lot of room for creativity. Two example patterns are given here, and two more complex masks are described in the succeeding sections. Generally, the only rule you need to follow is that the eye openings should be 30-35mm (1³⁄₁₆"-1³⁄₈") apart before molding.

In the first examples, leather laces keep the mask in place. Alternatively, you could use a length of 6mm (¼") fabric elastic or leather straps with a buckle closure. If opting for a buckle closure, fix the straps to the mask with medium rivets. (The main buckle and main eyelet straps of the head harness gag on page 159 are a close approximation.) When making larger masks of this type, it is advisable to use several lengths of fabric elastic, as in the female eye mask variation on page 99.

Tools

- Shears
- Hobby knife
- Drive punch
- Eyelet setter and anvil
- Cutting board
- Hammer
- Needle files
- Measuring tape
- Small foam brush
- Pen
- Pencil and ruler
- Small clean rag

Materials

- Heavy vegetable-tanned leather
- 500mm (20") of 6mm (¼") matching leather lace
- 2 x short eyelets
- Dye
- Leather conditioner
- Paper

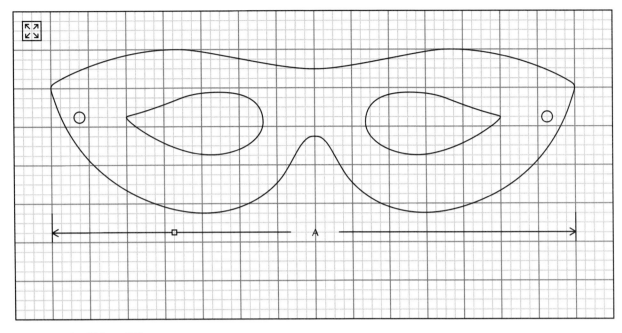

A = 205mm (8")

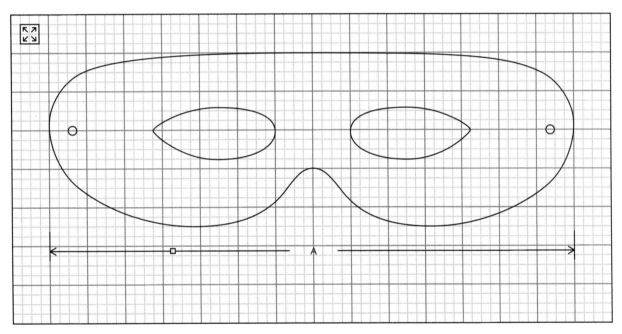

A = 225mm (9")

Instructions

- Draft the pattern as shown.

- Trace and cut out the mask.

- Cut the eye openings out with a hobby knife.

- Round all the inside and outside edges with needle files.

- Soak the mask in hot water for fifteen minutes.

- Remove the mask from the water and mold it into the desired shape as it dries. Pinch the eye openings from the back of the mask with the right hand, and the nose and top of the mask from the front with the left (fig 3.17).

- As the mask begins to harden, curve it into a symmetrical crescent shape.

- Let the mask dry overnight.

- Punch the eyelet holes where marked.

- Apply a coat of dye, let the mask dry for a few hours, dye again, then let dry overnight.

- Apply leather conditioner to the mask and polish well.

- Insert and set the eyelets.

- Cut the lace in two and make a 10mm (³/₈") long cut in the center of each 5mm (³/₁₆") from the end. Thread the other end of each lace through an eyelet and then through the cut, and pull tight.

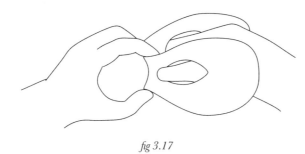

fig 3.17

98

FEMALE EYE MASK VARIATION

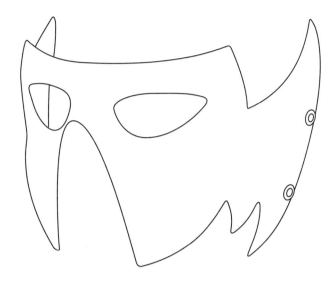

Tools

- Sewing needle
- Shears
- Hobby knife
- Stitch chisel (optional)
- Drive punch
- Eyelet setter and anvil
- Cutting board
- Hammer
- Needle files
- Measuring tape
- Small foam brush
- Pen
- Pencil and ruler
- Small clean rag
- Lighter

Materials

- Heavy vegetable-tanned leather
- Matching thread
- 10 x small studs (optional)
- 2 x large studs (optional)
- 4 x short eyelets
- 500mm (20") of 6mm (¼") fabric elastic
- Dye
- Leather conditioner
- Paper

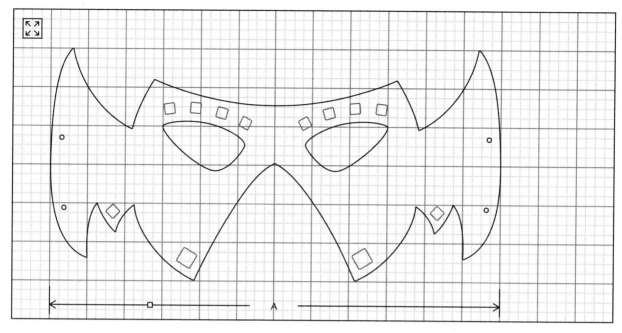

A = 260mm (10¼")

Instructions

- Draft the pattern as shown.

- Trace, mark and cut out the mask.

- Cut the eye openings out with a hobby knife.

- Round all of the inside and outside edges with needle files.

- Use a stud to make indentations in the mask where the studs will be set, if desired. Stud placement suggestions are marked in gray on the pattern.

- Punch slots with a stitch chisel centered on each indentation.

- Soak the mask in hot water for fifteen minutes.

- Remove the mask from the water and mold it into the desired shape as it dries. Pinch the eye openings from the back of the mask with the right hand, and the nose and top of the mask from the front with the left (fig 3.17, page 98).

- Curve the mask into a symmetrical crescent shape, curving each of the points slightly inward.

- Let the mask dry overnight.

- Punch the eyelet holes where marked.

- Apply a coat of dye, let the mask dry for a few hours, dye again, then let dry overnight.

- Apply leather conditioner to the mask and polish well.

- Insert and set the eyelets.

- Push studs through each set of slots and fold in place.

- Cut the fabric elastic in two and melt the ends.

- Thread each length of fabric elastic through an eyelet on one side of the mask and sew or tie in place.

- Try the mask on, and pull each length of fabric elastic around to the corresponding eyelet on the other side. Mark.

- Cut the fabric elastic at the marks and melt the ends.

- Thread the other ends of the fabric elastic through the other set of eyelets and sew or tie in place.

MALE EYE MASK VARIATION

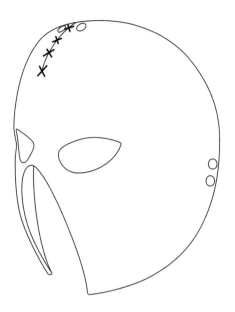

Tools

- Leather needle
- Shears
- Hobby knife
- Awl
- Stitch chisel
- Drive punch
- Rivet setter and anvil
- Cutting board
- Hammer
- Needle files
- Measuring tape
- Small foam brush
- Pen
- Pencil and ruler
- Small clean rag
- Lighter

Materials

- Heavy vegetable-tanned leather
- Black chap leather
- Black waxed cotton
- 12 x medium rivets
- 1 x 38mm (1 ½") ring
- 300mm (12") of 25mm (1") black fabric elastic
- Black leather dye
- Leather conditioner
- Paper

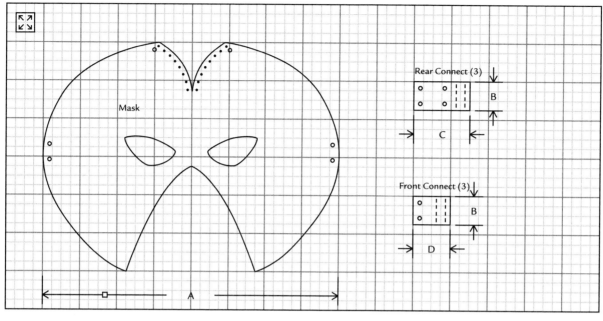

A = 280mm (11")
B = 25mm (1")

C = 60mm (2⅜")
D = 35mm (1⅜")

Instructions

- Draft the pattern as shown.

- Trace, mark and cut out the mask and connector panels. (Use a pen to mark up the mask, as pencil marks may disappear when immersed in hot water later in the project.) Cut the mask from vegetable-tanned leather, and the connector panels from chap leather.

- Cut the eye openings out with a hobby knife.

- Round all the inside and outside edges with needle files.

- Punch the holes and stitch slots where marked on the connector panels. Do not punch the holes in the mask at this time.

- Mark eight evenly spaced holes along the length of each side of the forehead seam. The distance from the edge should be half the distance between the markings.

- Use an awl to make stitch holes where marked.

- Hand-sew the forehead seam (fig 3.18).

- Soak the mask in hot water for fifteen minutes.

- Remove the mask from the water and mold it to the intended wearer's face as it dries. Pinch the eye openings from the back of the mask with the right hand, and push the nose up from the front with the thumb of the left.

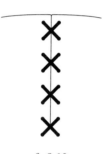

fig 3.18

- Curve the cheeks slightly inwards while keeping the overall shape symmetrical.

- Let the mask dry overnight.

- Check the hole markings on the mask for symmetry and fit with the connector panels. Adjust if necessary, and punch.

- Apply a coat of dye, let the mask dry for a few hours, dye again, then let dry overnight.

- Apply leather conditioner to the mask and polish well.

- Cut the length of fabric elastic in half, then cut one half of that in half and melt the ends.

- Hand-sew one end of each length of fabric elastic to a rear connector panel.

- Fix the rear connector panels to the ring with medium rivets.

- Fix the front connector panels to the mask with medium rivets.

- Check the mask for fit. Trim and melt the fabric elastic if necessary.

- Hand-sew the other end of each length of fabric elastic to the front connector panels.

MASKS

"I can't explain myself, I'm afraid, Sir, because I'm not myself, you see."

- Alice, *Alice in Wonderland*

We experience a certain excitement when we don a mask. In social contexts, masks are worn to become anonymous, which can serve a number of purposes – not least the pleasure involved in being unrecognized. Masks have been and still are a part of celebration and revelry across cultures; one need only look as far as masquerades, Mardi Gras celebrations or even the party supply section of most department stores.

It is a part of our nature to want to change who we are and how we appear, to want to experience ourselves in myriad forms. This urge, perhaps even need, to transform ourselves probably grew initially from our spiritual capacity. Masks can facilitate this transformation, and help us play out our deepest images of ourselves.

Since the majority of our identifiable features are located above the neck, it is not surprising that covering them with a mask has such a powerful effect. We associate our faces with our identity, so covering them can actually suppress the ego, resulting in a marked change in behavior. Paradoxically, masks can actually expose more than they cover – framing the eyes (the windows to the soul) and the mouth (with which we communicate), drawing attention to them, intensifying them.

The revelatory nature of masks can allow us to expose our hidden selves and share thoughts and desires that we would not normally be able to express. Wearing a mask can generate feelings of freedom and safety because the wearer's identity is hidden. Masks can also help to open up new avenues of communication; with egos somewhat subdued, partners can more readily converse with each other's true selves.

There is nothing quite like a personally tailored leather mask. It is the perfect finishing touch to any leather ensemble, and can certainly be the defining piece. As was discussed on page 51, being completely enclosed in a second skin of leather can generate intense, often transformative sensations that are difficult to describe. The mask is an integral part of this experience.

Masks are especially powerful devices when it comes to fetishism, bondage, dominance and submission. For the submissive, the mask comes with a feeling of depersonalization, sometimes of being reduced to the status of a object or toy, rather than a person or partner. For many, donning a mask also comes with a feeling of humility.

This feeling can be used to enforce dominance, but humility in itself has been said to be "a dark valley in which flowers can be found." For the dominant, the mask can project an image of power and superiority, helping them appear more impersonal and intimidating.

When introducing both the zentai mask and the eye mask projects, I pointed out that there is a lot of room for creativity in mask making. I cannot emphasize this point enough. Mask-making is a very personal undertaking. From the material, to the style, to the options, to the feel, you can choose who or what you want to be, and how you want to appear.

With regard to the overall style of the mask, there is much to consider. Your first choice is how much of the wearer's head the mask will conceal: it can cover the entire head and neck, or just the head from the base of the skull and jawbone up. It can cover the head and neck leaving the lower half of the face exposed, or it can cover only the top half of the head, from the base of the skull and the nose up.

Most daily routines can be performed in a half mask, whereas a full mask makes eating difficult. Meditation is easier when the nose is left exposed, which makes half masks a better choice for that activity as well. Half masks also allow for the use of a small gag, whereas full masks generally make gagging uncomfortable if not impossible.

You must also decide how the mask will close. The best-fitting masks have lace closures. The lace closure allows for a precise fit, as tight or as slack as you like. Also, as the leather stretches, the mask can be tightened to provide a correct fit. The only drawback is that it is difficult to thread and tighten laces on the back of one's own head. So, if it is imperative that the wearer be able to get in and out of the mask alone, a zipper closure may be a better idea.

Making a mask with a zipper closure fit well is considerably more difficult than making one with a lace closure. if a tight fit is desired, I suggest making the mask slightly too tight to allow for stretch in the leather. It is also worth noting that half masks and open-face hoods cannot be tightened as much as full masks, so zipper closures can be a good choice for those.

If the intended wearer has long hair, consider whether to install a ponytail retainer at the top of the lacing or zipper. It is often more comfortable to have the hair fall outside the mask through a ponytail retainer than inside and out the bottom of the mask, and allows for a tighter fit. Long hair is also less prone to get tangled in whatever restraints may be used when tied in a ponytail.

Then, of course there are the mask's defining characteristics, the shape of the eye and mouth appliqués. These can be made in almost any shape and size, conforming to the guidelines set out on page 44. See fig 2.22 on page 43 for examples of eye and mouth appliqués.

The final decision you must make is whether or not to punch holes over the ears and under the nose. Depending on the leather, the closure and the fit, the mask may only slightly impair the hearing, or not allow the wearer to hear much of anything at all. Although impaired hearing is often one of the desired effects of a bondage hood, there are many situations in which the wearer may want to have full hearing capacity. This desire can be met by making one or more small holes in the sides of the mask over the ear canals. Holes can also be punched under the nose to allow for easier breathing, which is a good idea with most leather. Whether or not these holes are reinforced with eyelets is at the discretion of the designer, but I suggest it when you're working with lighter skins.

Because the nose in the full mask is created by sewing the two front panels grain sides together, it really only has two dimensions. This style works surprisingly well for most face shapes, although for some irregular shapes you must make allowances. The easiest way is to replace the panels of this pattern with the front, rear, neck, and nose panels of the hood pattern on page 168. Another option, more in keeping with the style of this project, is to trim the 10mm (⅜") seam allowance off the front edges of the front panels and include a 20mm (¾") strip of leather between them, using a 5mm (³⁄₁₆") seam allowance. This has the effect of giving the nose a third dimension, with the expansion panel running down the bridge and tip of the nose, and the front panels covering the sides. I suggest basting this panel in place prior to machine-sewing. Before you join the rear panels to the front, first join the rear panels together from the apex down to the

opening mark, then join the front panels to the rear. The seam running over the top of the mask runs from one side seam to the other, rather than from the front panels to the rear panels. Alternatively, have the expansion panel run all the way to the opening, joining each set of front and rear panels together at the sides before basting in the strip. This technique can be used anytime its style or fit is preferred.

If making a half mask that covers the wearer from the base of the skull and the nose up, you may wish to alter the pattern so that the line from the nose to the back of the head is a gentler curve. Alternatively, you can keep the original shape of the front panel, and add a 25mm (1") strap that goes from one side of the rear closure around the neck to the other side of the closure and is held in place with a center-bar buckle. Sew the strap to the bottom of the mask with two seams on the buckle side. Finish the bottom of the other side of the mask by covering it with a length of the same width of strapping, with two 10mm (⅜") wide strap keepers on either end, one at the throat and one at the closure, with everything sewn in place with two seams.

Attractive and useful open-faced hoods can also be made using the techniques in this section. The modifications to the pattern are discussed on page 44.

Something else to consider is the use of vinyl instead of leather. You could do this for a number of reasons, including, significantly, cost. Some upholstery-grade vinyl can be used to make many of the garment leather projects in this book, but it must be of the type with a fabric backing. Although vinyl will not take the shape of the wearer's head the way leather does, most vinyl can be molded to form with the aid of a hair dryer.

Describing each of the many combinations of styles and options would be lengthy and redundant, so two example masks will be presented to illustrate the techniques used in making these projects: first, a full mask covering just the head with a lace closure and a pony tail retainer; then a half mask covering the head and neck with a zipper closure. The methods used to construct the masks are very similar to those described in Chapter II.

LACE-UP MASK

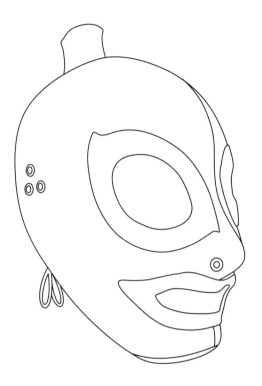

Tools

- Sewing machine (leather needle)
- Shears
- Small scissors
- Drive punch
- Snap setter and anvil
- Eyelet setter and anvil
- Cutting board
- Hammer
- Measuring tape
- Pencil and ruler
- Water pencil

Materials

- Garment leather
- Matching thread
- 910mm (36") shoelace
- 2 x short snaps
- 22 x medium eyelets
- Contact cement
- Paper

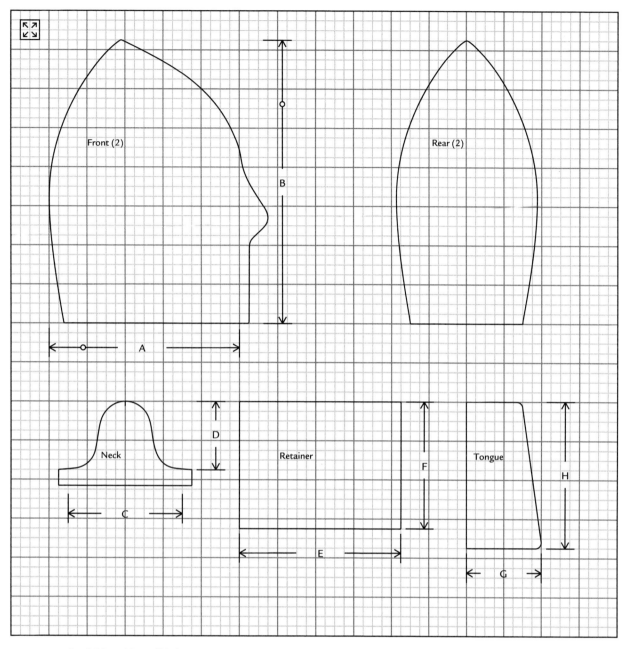

A = 0.30α + 10mm (³⁄₈")

B = 0.50γ + 10mm (³⁄₈")

C = 1.50[δ + 10mm (³⁄₈")]

D = δ + 10mm (³⁄₈")

E = 150mm (6")

F = 110mm (4³⁄₈")

G = 70mm (2³⁄₄")

H = B - 105mm (4¹⁄₈")

Instructions

- Draft the pattern as shown. The drafting method is described on page 47. Since this mask covers the whole face but not the neck, only the tongue-shaped protrusion with a 15mm (⅝") fold allowance on the bottom is needed for the neck panel.

- Trace, mark and cut out all panels, taking care to make the front panels mirror images of each other.

- Sew the front panels, grain sides together, 5mm (³⁄₁₆") from the front edge.

- Trim the bottom 10mm (⅜") of the front seam allowance down to 2mm (¹⁄₁₆").

- Align each rear panel with a front panel, grain sides together, so the tip extends 5mm (³⁄₁₆") above the front seam. Sew the panels together 5mm (³⁄₁₆") from the edge.

- Trim the top and bottom 10mm (⅜") of the side seam allowances down to 2mm (¹⁄₁₆").

- Mark the top of the opening on the rear panels 60mm (2⅜") from the apex.

- Sew the top of the rear panels, grain sides together, 5mm (³⁄₁₆") from the edge, starting from the opening mark and going over the top of the mask.

- Align the center of the neck panel with the bottom of the front seam, grain sides together. Sew in place 5mm (³⁄₁₆") from the edge in two seams, each starting from 20mm (¾") to the far side of the center. Basting the neck panel to the front panels before sewing can make this step easier.

- Check these seams for quality and straightness, and re-sew if necessary

- Trim 30mm (1¼") of each end of the neck panel seam allowance down to 2mm (¹⁄₁₆").

- Try on the mask, still inside out, and check for fit. If it is too big, keeping the 15mm (⅝") meeting edge folds in mind, pinch, mark up and trim.

- Clip off 15mm (⅝") square sections from the bottom corners of the meeting edges. This is to minimize the layers to be sewn through once the meeting and bottom edges have been folded.

- Apply contact cement to the flesh side of the retainer panel. Make 10mm (⅜") folds on the short sides, then fold it in half lengthwise, press firmly and let dry overnight.

- Sew the sides and folded edge of the retainer 5mm (³⁄₁₆") from the edge.

- Mark the center of the retainer on the raw edge.

- Align the center marking on the retainer with the opening of the mask, grain sides together, and sew in place 10mm (⅜") from the edge, starting and stopping 25mm (1") from the sides of the retainer.

- Apply contact cement to the outer 30mm (1¼") of the flesh side of the meeting edges and make 15mm (⅝") folds.

- Apply contact cement to the bottom 30mm (1¼") of the flesh side of the bottom edge. Make a 15mm (⅝") fold.

- Apply contact cement to the left 5mm (³⁄₁₆") of the grain side of the tongue and fix it to the inside of the left meeting edge, over the fold allowance. Press all edges firmly and let dry overnight.

- Sew the meeting edges from the grain side, 10mm (⅜") from the edge, taking care not to sew through the tongue on the right side.

- Sew the bottom edge from the grain side 10mm (⅜") from the edge.

- Mark seven evenly spaced eyelet holes on each meeting edge, starting 15mm (⅝") from the top and ending 10mm (⅜") from the bottom, taking care to ensure symmetry.

- Punch all holes where marked, taking care not to damage the tongue.

- Mark holes for the retainer snaps 12mm (½") from each corner of the retainer. Punch.

- Set the snaps in the retainer (fig 3.19).

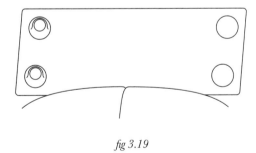

fig 3.19

- Turn the mask right side out and try it on again. Make small dots over the eyes, the corners of the mouth, and the ear canals.

- Mark three dots in an equilateral triangle with 15mm (⅝") sides, centered around each ear marking, keeping the triangles symmetrical with each other. Punch all holes where marked, taking care not to damage the other side of the mask.

- With the mask inside out, mark and punch the nostril holes (fig 3.20).

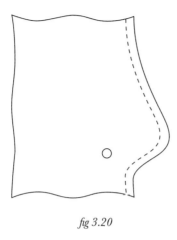

fig 3.20

- Insert and set the eyelets in the ear and nostril holes and meeting edges.

- Trace and cut out the eye and mouth appliqués, taking care to make the eye appliqués mirror images of each other.

- Place a cardboard template inside the mask and lace it shut (see page 48).

- Apply contact cement to the flesh side of the right eye appliqué. Place it on the right side of the mask while the contact cement is still wet, taking care to place it around the marking and sufficiently close to the center seam, and press firmly (fig 2.25, page 49).

- Repeat with the left eye appliqué, taking care to place it in symmetry with the right one. Before pressing, remove the cardboard from the mask and check it for symmetry. If it is a bit off, remove it, replace the cardboard, and try again. Once satisfied, replace the cardboard and press firmly.

- Apply contact cement to the flesh side of the mouth appliqué and place a little less than half of it on the right side of the mask (fig 2.25, page 49). Place the appliqué around the markings and sufficiently close to the eye appliqués, usually no further than 10-30mm (³⁄₈"-1¼"). Remove the cardboard from the mask and check to be sure the center seam runs through the center of the mouth appliqué. If it is a bit off, try again. Once it is centered, press firmly and let the mask dry overnight.

- Sew the eye and mouth appliqués in place with two seams, one 2mm (¹⁄₁₆") from the outside edge and another 2mm (¹⁄₁₆") from the inside edge. This is intricate work and must be done slowly and with care. It is often useful to adjust the needle position so that the edge of the appliqué can be seen through the presser foot, or you can use a transparent presser foot.

- With the stitches firmly in place, pull the leather inside the openings away from the appliqués and clip it from underneath with small scissors.

HALF MASK

Tools

- Sewing machine (leather needle)
- Shears
- Small scissors
- Drive punch
- Cutting board
- Hammer
- Pliers
- Measuring tape
- Pencil and ruler
- Water pencil
- Lighter

Materials

- Garment leather
- Matching thread
- 300mm (12") metal zipper
- Contact cement
- Paper

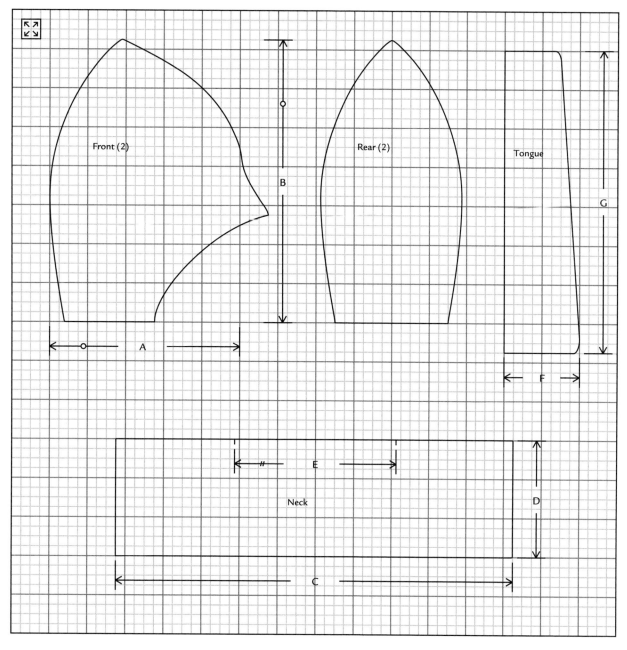

$A = 0.30\alpha + 15mm\ (^5/_8")$

$B = 0.50\gamma + 10mm\ (^3/_8")$

$C = \varepsilon + 40mm\ (1\frac{1}{2}")$

$D = 110mm\ (4^3/_8")$

$E = 2.20[\delta + 10mm\ (^3/_8")]$

$F = 70mm\ (2^3/_4")$

$G = B + D - 75mm\ (3")$

Instructions

- Draft the pattern as shown. The drafting method is described on page 47. Note that the curved line running from the tip of the nose to the bottom of the front panel should end a quarter cell further from the front edge. This is done to allow for a larger opening, which is necessary for leather half masks.

- Trace, mark and cut out all panels, taking care to make the front panels mirror images of each other.

- Sew the front panels, grain sides together, 5mm ($^3/_{16}$") from the upper front edge.

- Trim the bottom 10mm ($^3/_8$") of the front seam allowance down to 2mm ($^1/_{16}$").

- Align each rear panel with a front panel, grain sides together, so the tip extends 5mm (3/16") above the front seam. Sew the panels together 5mm (3/16") from the edge.

- Trim the top and bottom 10mm (3/8") of the side seam allowances down to 2mm (1/16").

- Mark the top of the opening on the rear panels 60mm (2 3/8") from the apex.

- Sew the top of the rear panels, grain sides together, 5mm (3/16") from the edge, starting from the opening mark and going over the top of the mask.

- Align each join mark on the neck panel with the corner of the corresponding front panel, grain sides together, and sew in place all the way to the meeting edge, 5mm (3/16") from the edge.

- Trim 30mm (1 1/4") of the meeting edge end of each circumferential seam allowance down to 2mm (1/16").

- Try on the mask, still inside out, and check for fit. If it is too big, keeping the 15mm (5/8") meeting edge folds in mind, pinch, mark up and trim.

- Clip off 15mm (5/8") square sections from the bottom corners of the meeting edges. This is to minimize the layers to be sewn through once the meeting and bottom edges have been folded.

- Apply contact cement to the outer 30mm (1 1/4") of the flesh side of the meeting edges. Make 15mm (5/8") folds.

- Apply contact cement to the bottom 30mm (1 1/4") of the flesh side of the bottom edge. Make a 15mm (5/8") fold.

- Adjust the zipper length to match the meeting edges. If using an open-ended zipper, sew the base of the zipper together with heavy thread (fig 3.21). (Note: When using a zipper closure on a mask with a ponytail retainer, you'll need a open-ended zipper which has not been sewn together.)

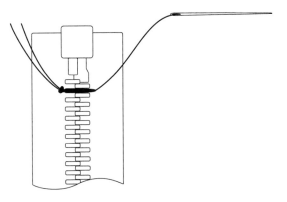

fig 3.21

- Apply contact cement to the meeting edge fold allowances. Press the zipper in place so the tips of the teeth are flush with the meeting edges.

- Apply contact cement to the left 5mm (3/16") of the grain side of the tongue, and fix it to the inside of the left meeting edge over the zipper. Press all edges firmly and let dry overnight.

- Sew the meeting edges from the grain side, 5mm (3/16") from the edge, taking care not to sew through the tongue on the right side.

- Sew the bottom from the grain side, 10mm (3/8") from the edge.

- Pull the zipper back from the mask and tongue, and rub off the contact cement. Use contact cement thinner very sparingly and only if necessary.

- Turn the mask right side out, try it on again, and mark dots over the eyes and the ear canals.

- Mark three dots in an equilateral triangle with 15mm (5/8") sides, centered around each ear marking, keeping the triangles symmetrical with each other. Punch, taking care not to damage the other side of the mask.

- Trace and cut out the eye appliqués, taking care to make them mirror images of each other.

- Cut a 10mm (3/8") x 450mm (18") strip of garment leather for the liner.

- Place a cardboard template inside the mask and zip it shut (see page 48).

- Apply contact cement to the flesh side of the right eye appliqué. Place it on the right side of the mask while the contact cement is still wet, taking care to place it around the marking and sufficiently close the center seam. Press firmly (fig 2.25, page 49).

- Repeat with the left eye appliqué, taking care to place it in symmetry with the right one. Before pressing, remove the cardboard from the mask and check for symmetry. If it is a bit off, remove it, replace the cardboard, and try again.

- Apply contact cement to the flesh side of the liner and press it down around the perimeter of the opening, starting at the base. The liner should touch the eye appliqués, and if aligning it this way leaves a section of the leather exposed outside the liner, the excess can be trimmed off. Overlap the liner at the base by 15mm (5/8"), and trim any excess.

- Press all edges firmly and let the mask dry overnight.

- Sew the eye appliqués and liner in place with two seams, one 2mm (¹⁄₁₆") from the outside edge and another 2mm (¹⁄₁₆") from the inside edge. This is intricate work and must be done slowly and with care. It is often useful to adjust the needle position so that the edge of the appliqués and liner can be seen through the presser foot, or to use a transparent presser foot.

- With the stitches firmly in place, pull the leather inside the eye openings away from the appliqués and clip it from underneath with small scissors.

CHAPTER IV

Restraints

The projects in this chapter are used to control the movement of the wearer. They can be used in restrictive bondage, or to lead a submissive around. Although they are designed to be functional, simply having a submissive wear these items can cause a shift in consciousness. The body harnesses in particular can generate unique physical sensations, and just wearing a collar can have a profound psychological effect.

Freedom cannot be fully experienced or appreciated without the experience of captivity – but bondage has much to offer beyond contrast. It is said that the only way to be truly free is to surrender to another. Without choices to occupy the mind, the spirit is free to soar: this is why bondage can be an effective meditational aid. When one is bound, the conscious mind often mimics the body's predicament and acts as if it too was restrained. Thoughts of past and future cease, and inner chatter quiets to a whisper, or stops altogether. This effect intensifies with the addition of the sensory deprivation projects in Chapter V.

Strapping

All of the projects in this chapter are made of leather straps and assembled with rivets. They can all be made with either latigo or medium to heavy vegetable-tanned leather, though chap can be used for some projects.

Restraints made with chap leather are soft, comfortable, and luxurious, but have a degree of stretch and are not very durable. Latigo and vegetable-tanned leather are harder and not as flexible, but produce a sturdier product. Working with latigo and vegetable-tanned leather can be more time consuming than chap, but if the restraints will be under any amount of stress, I suggest using these.

Some vegetable-tanned leather can be cut with shears, but when cutting lengths of strapping, use a rotary cutter. The cut should first be marked on the skin with a pen, or a pencil if the leather will not later be dyed. Align a ruler with the marking, and make a cut, using the ruler as a guide while pressing firmly to keep it in place. If the strap is longer than the ruler, as it often will be, stop the cut just before the end of the ruler. Leaving the blade in the leather, move the ruler up to the next section of the marking and continue. If there are any width changes in the strap, use a rotary cutter to approach the inside corner, then finish the cut off with a hobby knife. This is also the most efficient way to cut strapping from chap leather.

After cutting your strapping from a vegetable-tanned or latigo skin, round off the grain-side edges with a beveler. If you want to color a vegetable-tanned skin, apply a couple of coats of dye to both sides and all edges of the strapping after you've made all the holes, slots, and notches. Let the project dry overnight, then apply a small amount of plaiting soap (see page 188) or leather conditioner to soften it, and wipe it clean. With latigo, you just have to color the cut edges to match.

Locking buckles

All of the restraints in this chapter attach with buckles. Regular heel-bar or center-bar buckles will suffice, but cuffs and collars can be made more effective both psychologically and practically by using locking buckles. These ingenious little devices are simply center-bar buckles with loops at the end of the pins. They can sometimes be purchased at leather stores, but you may have to acquire them from a specialty store. Some locking buckles have rollers, and it is worth mentioning that strapping made with vegetable-tanned leather will move much more freely through a roller buckle than a regular one.

Locking buckles are installed the same way other buckles are, but the pin loops require slots to fit through rather than regular holes made with a drive punch. These slots should be just longer than the loop is wide, spaced at least 5mm (³⁄₁₆") apart, and made in the same manner as a buckle pin slot (fig 3.4 on page 56).

If you want a locking buckle but can't find one, a regular heel-bar or center-bar buckle can be made lockable by punching a hole through the center of the keeper. Reinforce this hole and the buckle pin holes with eyelets. After you fasten the buckle, you can slip a small padlock through the keeper hole and the appropriate buckle pin hole, locking it in place (fig 4.1). Regular keepers are required any time you use a heel-bar buckle, but you can add one to any kind of buckle closure.

To make smaller straps lockable, use a center-bar buckle and simply reinforce the last buckle pin hole on the strap with an eyelet. Slip a small padlock through the eyelet after fastening the buckle, and as long as the eyelet is one or two buckle pin holes away from the one in use, the strap will be locked in place.

Since the width of strapping is often determined by the size of the buckle or D-ring it will run through, strapping will often be 13mm (½"), 19mm (¾"), 25mm (1") , 38mm (1½") or 51mm (2") wide. (Please note that most buckles and rings are made in imperial units. I'm listing the metric measurement first for consistency.)

When riveting a strap, it is very important to use the correct number of rivets and to choose a cap diameter that covers enough of the strap, but not so much that it encroaches on other rivets. Using an inappropriate number or size of rivets will impact both the strength and visual appeal of the restraint. How many and what kind of rivets you use depends entirely on the width of the strap. Generally, the following guidelines should be observed:

6mm (¼") - One small rivet

13mm (½") - One medium or large rivet

19mm (¾") - Two small or one medium or large rivet

25mm (1") - Two medium or large rivets

38mm (1½") - Two medium or large rivets

51mm (2") - Three medium or large rivets

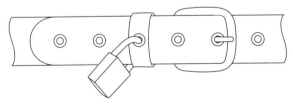

fig 4.1

COLLAR

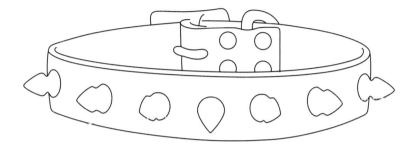

This basic collar is a simple buckling leather strap. The D-ring behind the buckle makes a hidden attachment point, and is optional. More rings can be added to the front and sides of the collar to provide additional attachment points if desired.

Simple cuffs can be made in the same manner by using the wrist circumference ξ and ankle circumference χ in place of the neck circumference ε.

Embellishing the collar with spikes or studs can do much for its visual appeal. These can be purchased from leather stores and are easy to install.

To install spikes or studs, complete the collar, then draw a line bisecting the collar lengthwise. For spikes, mark and punch evenly spaced holes along this line and fix the spikes in place with a screwdriver. For studs, use a spare stud to mark evenly spaced indentations along the line. For a continuous line of studs or a stud's width between each one, stick the left stud leg into the last right leg indentation and proceed along the line. Slots are then cut at each indentation with a stitch chisel and the studs pressed into place (fig 3.8 on page 57).

Tools

- Hobby knife
- Rotary cutter and ruler
- Drive punch
- Rivet setter and anvil
- Cutting board
- Hammer
- Measuring tape
- Water pencil

Materials

- Chap, heavy vegetable-tanned leather, or latigo
- 4 x medium rivets
- 1 x 19mm (¾") D-ring
- 1 x 19mm (¾") center-bar or locking buckle

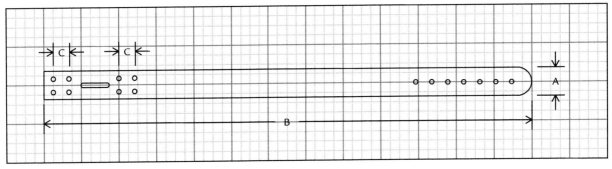

A = 20mm (¾")

B = ε + 100mm (4")

C = 15mm (⅝")

Instructions

- Mark and cut the strap as shown.

- Punch all holes where marked and cut the slot.

- Bevel the grain side of all edges if using vegetable-tanned leather or latigo. Dye and condition if using vegetable-tanned leather, dye the edges if using latigo.

- Fix the buckle in place with medium rivets through the holes closest to the buckle.

- Fix the D-ring in place behind the buckle with medium rivets.

CHAIN COLLAR

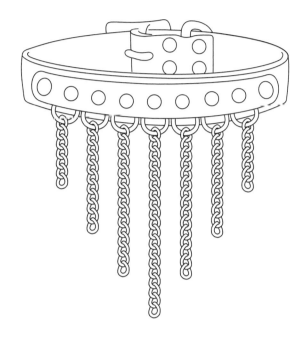

Adding draped lengths of twist-link chain is a beautiful way of embellishing a collar, imparting a classic leather look. This project describes how to use D-rings to attach the chains to the collar described in the previous section.

The chains can also be fixed to the collar with small rivets, if rivets small enough to fit through the chain links can be found.

Tools

- Shears
- Rotary cutter and ruler
- Drive punch
- Rivet setter and anvil
- Cutting board
- Hammer
- Pliers
- Locking pliers
- Wire cutter
- Measuring tape
- Water pencil

Materials

- Chap, heavy vegetable-tanned leather or latigo
- Matching garment leather
- ¾" collar from page 118
- 2 x 40mm (1 ½") of 5mm (³⁄₁₆") twist link chain
- 2 x 60mm (2 ¼") of 5mm (³⁄₁₆") twist link chain
- 2 x 80mm (3") of 5mm (³⁄₁₆") twist link chain
- 1 x 100mm (3 ¾") of 5mm (³⁄₁₆") twist link chain
- 7 x small rivets
- 2 x medium rivets
- 7 x 13mm (½") D-rings

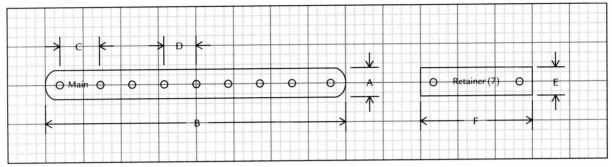

A = 14mm (½")

B = 170mm (6¾")

C = 23mm (⅞")

*Distance between holes = outside width of D-ring

D = 18mm (¾")*

E = 13mm (½")

F = 40mm (1½")

Instructions

- Construct the collar described on page 118.

- Mark and cut the strapping as shown. The main strap is cut from the same skin as the base collar, and the retainer panels from matching garment leather.

- Punch all holes where marked.

- Bevel the grain side of all edges if using vegetable-tanned leather or latigo. Dye and condition if using vegetable-tanned leather, dye the edges if using latigo.

- Cut the twist link chain to the prescribed lengths, taking care to leave each pair of chains with the same number of links.

- Twist each D-ring open, using locking and regular pliers. It is important that the D-rings be twisted open rather than pulled apart, as once pulled apart they are be very difficult to squeeze back together. Do not open the D-ring too much – just enough to slip on a chain link. Depending on the D-rings and the locking pliers, it may be a good idea to use a piece of scrap leather between the D-rings and the locking pliers to avoid damaging them.

- Thread a D-ring through an end link of each length of chain, then twist it closed. This can be difficult if the D-ring is made of thicker wire. Try both sides of both ends of the chain. Failing that, try to acquire some new D-rings.

- Mark the center between the buckle rivets and the first buckle pin hole on the collar base, centered widthwise as well.

- Lay the main strap over the collar centered on the center mark, and make marks through the holes in the main strap.

- Punch all holes where marked on the collar base.

- Assemble the collar, but do not set the rivets until assembly is complete. Medium rivets are used in the outside holes on the main strap, then the 40mm (1½") lengths are fixed to the next holes on each side with retainer straps and small rivets (fig 4.2), then the 60mm (2¼"), then the 80mm (3"), and finally the 100mm (3¾") length is fixed to the center hole. With the collar assembled, set the rivets in place.

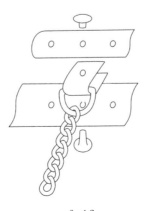

fig 4.2

CHAIN COLLAR VARIATION

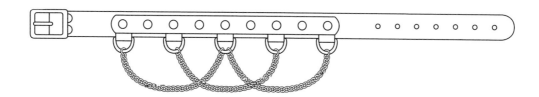

Another way of embellishing a collar with twist link chain, this variation drapes three lengths of chain, each attached at both ends to the collar. Like the previous project, this one also uses the collar described on page 118 as a base. To assemble the collar, use the techniques described on page 120, but attach a D-ring to both ends of each length of chain, and assemble the collar as shown above.

Tools

- Shears
- Rotary cutter and ruler
- Drive punch
- Rivet setter and anvil
- Cutting board
- Hammer
- Pliers
- Locking pliers
- Wire cutter
- Measuring tape
- Water pencil

Materials

- Chap, heavy vegetable-tanned leather or latigo
- Matching garment leather
- ¾" collar from page 118
- 3 x 120mm (4¾") of 5mm (³⁄₁₆") twist link chain
- 9 x medium rivets
- 5 x 13mm (½") D-rings

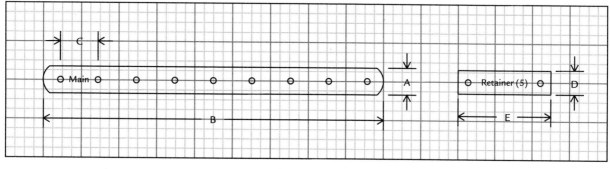

A = 14mm (½")

B = 175mm (6¾")

C = 20mm (¾")

D = 13mm (½")

E = 40mm (1½")

HEAVY COLLAR

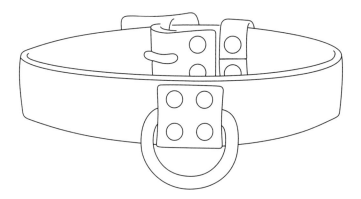

The strapping for this collar must be cut from heavy vegetable-tanned leather or latigo, as chap leather is too supple for this construction method. Sometimes you can purchase small sections of heavy vegetable-tanned sides, which is great, since a whole side can be expensive and is not necessary for most of the projects in this book. When working with a piece of leather that is not long enough to cut a strap of the required length, a collar can be built in two straps, as shown in this project.

Tools

- Hobby knife
- Rotary cutter and ruler
- Drive punch
- Rivet setter and anvil
- Cutting board
- Hammer
- Measuring tape
- Small foam brush
- Pen
- Small clean rag

Materials

- Heavy vegetable-tanned leather or latigo
- 4 x small rivets
- 4 x medium rivets for 1", small rivets for ¾"
- 1 x 25mm (1") or 19mm (¾") D-ring
- 1 x 25mm (1") or 19mm (¾") center-bar roller buckle
- Dye
- Plaiting soap or leather conditioner

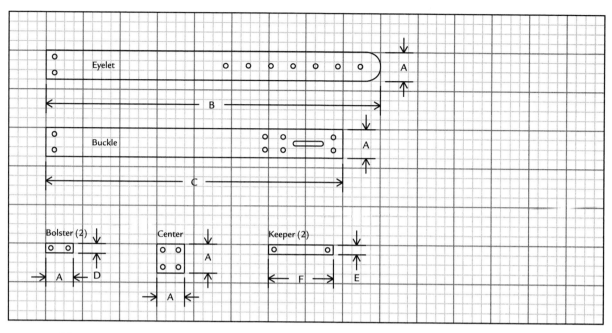

1"

A = 26mm (1")
B = 0.50ε + 80mm (3⅛")
C = 0.50ε + 40mm (1½")
D = 9mm (⅜")
E = 12mm (½")
F = 90mm (3½")

¾"

A = 20mm (¾")
B = 0.50ε + 80mm (3⅛")
C = 0.50ε + 40mm (1½")
D = 7mm (¼")
E = 10mm (⅜")
F = 75mm (3")

Instructions:

- Mark and cut the strapping as shown.

- Bevel the grain side of all edges.

- Punch all holes where marked and cut the slot.

- Apply a coat of dye, let the pieces dry for a few hours, dye again, then let them dry overnight.

- Join the halves of the collar with the D-ring assembly and small rivets, as shown in fig 4.3.

- Fix the buckle in place with medium or small rivets through the holes closest to the buckle.

- Fix the keeper in place with medium or small rivets.

- Apply and rub in a small amount of plaiting soap or leather conditioner, then wipe clean.

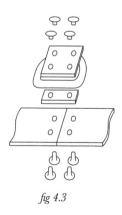

fig 4.3

POSTURE COLLAR

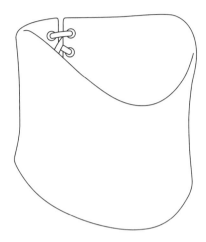

This collar is a made with a pair of wide leather panels cut to fit around the neck. It is reinforced with boning, and has a lace closure. The boning greatly restricts any movement of the head. Posture collars can be a valuable addition to many bondage positions, but cannot generally be worn comfortably while moving about.

A simpler version can be made with a single panel of chap leather. This provides the look and some of the restriction of the original, but can be worn reasonably comfortably for longer periods of time. For a slightly more restrictive fit, it can be made with a single panel of medium to heavy vegetable-tanned leather or latigo instead.

Another option is to sandwich a layer of padding between garment leather panels in the style of the padded cuffs on page 128. The padding can be held in place with the boning stitching, though you should take care not to make the padding large enough that it is caught by the circumferential stitching: doing so will make the top and bottom edges difficult to bind.

Tools

- Shears
- Drive punch
- Eyelet setter and anvil
- Cutting board
- Hammer
- Measuring tape
- Pencil and ruler
- Water pencil

Materials

- Chap leather
- Matching garment leather
- Matching thread
- 1830mm (72") shoelace
- 12 x medium eyelets
- 1m (40") boning
- Contact cement
- Paper

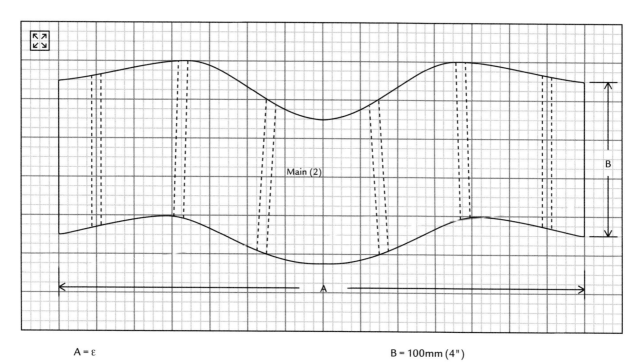

A = ε   B = 100mm (4")

1m (40") x 22mm (⅞") matching garment leather binding

Instructions

- Draft the pattern as shown, taking care to make it symmetrical.

- Trace and cut out the first main panel from chap leather, then flip it over, trace it and cut out the second panel.

- Use the pattern to mark the boning lines on the grain side of the outside panel.

- Flip over the pattern and mark the same lines on the flesh side of the outside panel.

- Cut the boning to match the length of each pair of boning lines.

- Apply contact cement to the flesh sides of both panels, then place each piece of boning centered on a pair of boning lines. Press the panels together from one side to the other, taking care to align all the edges. Press firmly, paying special attention to the areas surrounding the boning, and let dry overnight.

- Use the zipper foot to sew seams on both sides of each piece of boning, keeping as close to the boning as possible while maintaining a straight seam.

- Cut binding strips to match the meeting edges. Apply contact cement to the flesh side of each and then fold the binding over these edges.

- Cut the binding strips to match the top and bottom edges. Apply contact cement to the flesh side of each and fold them over these edges. Press all edges firmly and let dry overnight.

- Sew the binding in place 2mm (¹⁄₁₆") from the edge of the binding.

- Mark five evenly spaced eyelet holes on each meeting edge, starting 10mm (⅜") from the top and ending 10mm (⅜") from the bottom, taking care to ensure symmetry between the meeting edges.

- Punch all holes where marked.

- Insert and set the eyelets along the meeting edges.

ARM BANDS

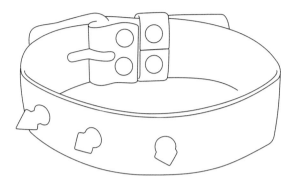

These simple restraints can be a valuable addition to many positions. They can be used to keep the upper arms behind the back, spread them apart, or can be buckled together to make a larger restraint for both arms. You can also make multipurpose restraints, using the same pattern and varying the length of **B**. Roller buckles can make this type of restraint easier to use.

You can add D-rings to the arm bands or to multipurpose restraints (to be used on the thighs, for example), or you could make the arm bands with three spikes in place of the D-ring, as pictured above. Alternatively, you can cut the band in between the marked D-ring holes and fasten the two halves around a 32mm (1 ¼") ring. Use only heel-bar buckles, as center-bar buckles protrude, causing discomfort.

Tools

- Shears
- Hobby knife
- Rotary cutter and ruler
- Drive punch
- Rivet setter and anvil
- Cutting board
- Hammer
- Measuring tape
- Water pencil

Materials

- Chap, heavy vegetable-tanned leather or latigo
- 12 x medium rivets
- 2 x 19mm (¾") D-rings
- 2 x 25mm (1") heel-bar buckles

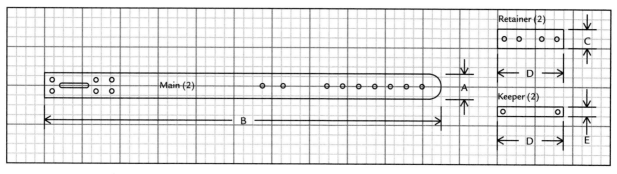

A = 26mm (1")
B = λ + 100mm (4")
C = 20mm (¾")

D = 75mm (3")
E = 12mm (½")

Instructions

- Mark and cut the strapping as shown.

- Punch all holes where marked and cut the slots.

- Bevel the grain side of all edges if using vegetable-tanned leather or latigo. Dye and condition if using vegetable-tanned leather, dye the edges if using latigo.

- Fix a D-ring to each band with a retainer strap and medium rivets.

- Fix each buckle in place with medium rivets through the holes closest to the buckle.

- Fix each keeper in place with medium rivets.

PADDED CUFFS

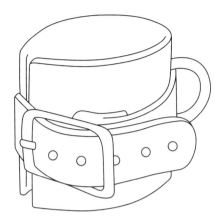

These classic leather cuffs are an essential: durable, attractive, and quite comfortable. They consist of an outer layer of chap, vegetable-tanned leather or latigo, with padding made of quilted cotton (or a 15mm ($^5/_8$") slab of polyurethane foam, see page 12), covered by an inner layer of garment leather.

The padding and inner layer of garment leather can be replaced with real or artificial sheepskin if desired. The outer perimeter of the cuffs can be stitched with a machine if the leather is thin enough, and can be hand-stitched otherwise, although hand-stitching through fleece can be difficult. Sheepskin will actually adhere quite well to the outer layer with glue alone, though with vegetable-tanned and latigo skins, the flesh side should first be ruffled up with a rasp. The length of the pile on most sheepskins may be longer than ideal for this project – see page 52 for trimming instructions.

If the buckle strap is cut from leather thick enough that the strap will not twist laterally, the four rivets around the D-ring will be sufficient to fix it to the outer panel. With lighter or softer leather, though, you'll need to sew the buckle strap to the outer panel on both sides of the D-ring before mounting the padding (fig 4.5, page 130). Using a heavier leather for the buckle strap and a lighter one for the outer panel can be a good idea, as it makes for a sturdy restraint and allows the perimeter seams to be sewn on a machine.

The same pattern is used for both wrist and ankle cuffs, using the appropriate set of measurements. Human wrists and ankles are not cylindrical, though, so the stiffer the leather is, the longer the cuffs will need to be in order to fit properly. The same goes for piling and padding: the thicker it is, the longer the cuffs will need to be.

Tools

- Sewing machine (leather needle/universal needle)
- Shears
- Hobby knife
- Rotary cutter and ruler
- Drive punch
- Rivet setter and anvil
- Cutting board
- Hammer
- Measuring tape
- Water pencil

Materials

- Chap, vegetable-tanned leather or latigo
- Matching garment leather
- Matching thread
- 4 x 250mm (10") scrap cotton cloth for padding
- 12 x medium rivets
- 12 x small rivets
- 2 x 25mm (1") D-rings
- 2 x 19mm ($^3/_4$") D-rings
- 2 x 25mm (1") center-bar or locking buckles
- 2 x 19mm ($^3/_4$") center-bar or locking buckles
- Contact cement

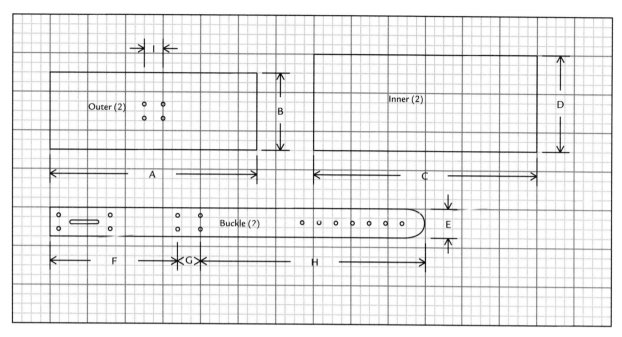

Wrist cuffs

A = ξ + 30mm (1¼")

B = 50mm (2")

C = ξ + 50mm (2")

D = 70mm (2¾")

E = 20mm (¾")

F = 0.50ξ + 30mm (1¼")

G = 25mm (1")

H = 0.50ξ + 110mm (4½")

I = 20mm (¾")

Ankle cuffs

A = χ + 20mm (¾")

B = 70mm (2¾")

C = χ + 40mm (1½")

D = 90mm (3½")

E = 26mm (1")

F = 0.50χ + 25mm (1")

G = 25mm (1")

H = 0.50χ + 110mm (4½")

I = 20mm (¾")

Instructions

- Mark and cut all pieces as shown. Cut the outer panels and buckle straps from the chap, vegetable-tanned leather or latigo, and the inner panels from garment leather.

- Punch all holes where marked, and cut the slots.

- Bevel the grain side of all edges if using vegetable-tanned leather or latigo. Dye and condition if using vegetable-tanned leather, dye the edges if using latigo.

- Fold each piece of scrap cloth in half widthwise, lengthwise, then widthwise to make eight layers. Press.

- Trim each piece of padding so that it is 20mm (¾") less the length and width of the outer panels.

- Make quarter, half and three-quarter marks on the long sides and halfway marks on the short sides of each piece of padding. Sew each piece together as shown in fig 4.4, using a universal machine needle.

- Clip off 20mm (¾") isosceles triangles from the corners of each inner panel (see page 60).

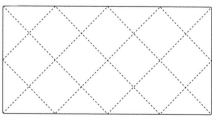

fig 4.4

- Apply contact cement to the outer 20mm (¾") of the flesh sides of each inner panel. Make 10mm (⅜") folds and press firmly.

- Fix each buckle strap to an outer panel with medium rivets around a D-ring.

- If using lighter leather for the buckle straps, sew each buckle strap to the outer panel from the grain side as shown in fig 4.5, using a leather machine needle.

- Apply contact cement to the fold allowances on each inner panel.

- Place a piece of padding in the center of each inner panel.

- Place each outer panel over an inner panel with the padding in between, taking care to align all of the edges. Press firmly and let dry overnight.

- Sew the perimeter of each cuff from the outer panel, 4mm (³⁄₁₆") from the edge, using a leather machine needle or hand-sewing, taking care not to sew through the buckle straps.

- Fix the buckles in place with medium rivets.

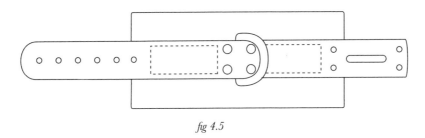

fig 4.5

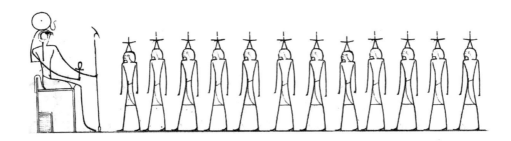

WRAP AROUND CUFFS

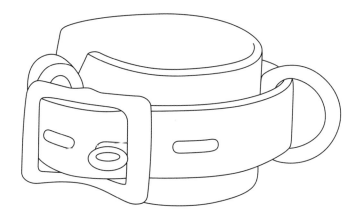

These cuffs are simple to make, and are a bit sturdier than the padded cuffs. Very soft cuffs can be made with this pattern using chap leather, but soft leather tends to stretch, and thus can reduce the utility of the cuffs.

Tools

- Hobby knife
- Rotary cutter and ruler
- Beveler
- Drive punch
- Rivet setter and anvil
- Cutting board
- Hammer
- Measuring tape
- Small foam brush
- Pen
- Small clean rag

Materials

- Medium-heavy vegetable-tanned leather or latigo
- 16 x small rivets
- 16 x medium rivets
- 2 x 19mm (¾") D-rings
- 2 x 25mm (1") D-rings
- 2 x 19mm (¾") locking or center-bar buckles
- 2 x 25mm (1") locking or center-bar buckles
- Dye
- Plaiting soap (or leather conditioner)

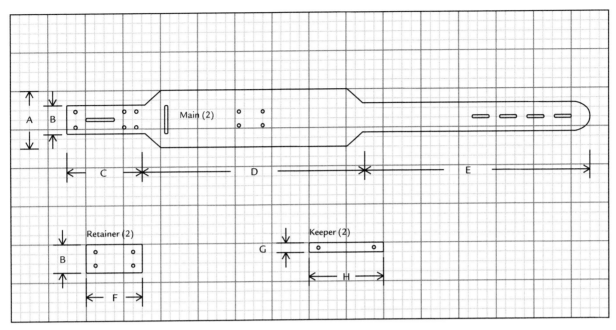

Wrist Cuffs

A = 40mm (1½")

B = 20mm (¾")

C = 70mm (2¾")

D = ξ + 20mm (¾")

E = ξ + 80mm (3¼")

F = 45mm (1¾")

G = 10mm (⅜")

H = 75mm (3")

Ankle Cuffs

A = 50mm (2")

B = 26mm (1")

C = 70mm (2¾")

D = χ + 20mm (¾")

E = χ + 80mm (3¼")

F = 45mm (1¾")

G = 10mm (⅜")

H = 90mm (3½")

Instructions

- Draft the pattern as shown.

- Mark and cut the strapping.

- Bevel the grain side of all edges.

- Punch all holes where marked, and cut the slots.

- Apply a coat of dye if using vegetable-tanned leather, let the pieces dry for a few hours, dye again, then let them dry overnight. Dye the edges if using latigo.

- Fix each buckle in place on the wrist cuffs with small rivets, and on the ankle cuffs with medium rivets, through the holes closest to the buckles.

- Fix each keeper in place on the wrist cuffs with small rivets and on the ankle cuffs with medium rivets.

- Fix each D-ring in place with its retainer strap and small rivets on the wrist cuffs and medium rivets on the ankle cuffs.

- Apply and rub in a small amount of plaiting soap or leather conditioner if using vegetable-tanned leather. Wipe clean.

FOUR-WAY CLIP

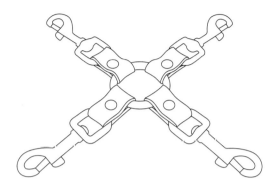

This simple device makes getting a submissive into a hog-tie position easier, and allows the submissive to be more comfortable while there. It is not completely secure because of the use of spring clips, so it may be possible for some submissives to get in and out of the position themselves.

Tools

- Rotary cutter and ruler
- Drive punch
- Rivet setter and anvil
- Cutting board
- Hammer
- Water pencil

Materials

- Chap, medium-heavy vegetable-tanned leather or latigo
- 4 x medium rivets
- 1 x 32mm (1¼") ring
- 4 x spring clips

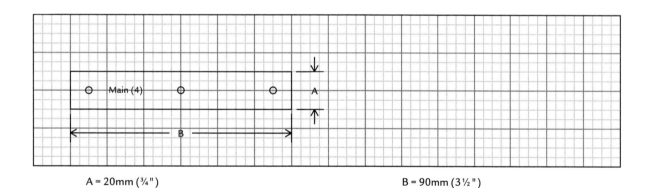

A = 20mm (¾")   B = 90mm (3½")

Instructions

- Mark and cut the strapping as shown.

- Punch all holes where marked.

- Bevel the grain side of all edges if using vegetable-tanned leather or latigo. Dye and condition if using vegetable-tanned leather, dye the edges if using latigo.

- Thread one end of each main strap through a spring clip and the other end through the ring. Fix each strap in place with a medium rivet.

LEASH

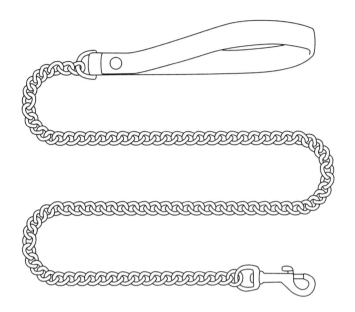

The leash design presented here is simply a length of twist link chain with a leather strap fixed to one end and a spring clip to the other. Chap leather is suggested for the strap, but medium to heavy vegetable-tanned leather or latigo can also be used. Any size or type of chain can be used for this project, cut to whatever length is desired. Having a couple of different lengths as well as some small padlocks on hand can be useful for moderate movement restriction and many bondage positions.

Tools

- Rotary cutter and ruler
- Drive punch
- Rivet setter and anvil
- Cutting board
- Hammer
- Pliers
- Locking pliers
- Wire cutter
- Measuring tape
- Water pencil

Materials

- Chap, medium-heavy vegetable-tanned leather or latigo
- 1m (39") of 10mm (³⁄₈") twist link chain
- 1 x medium rivet
- 1 x 13mm (½") D-ring
- 1 x connector ring
- 1 x spring clip

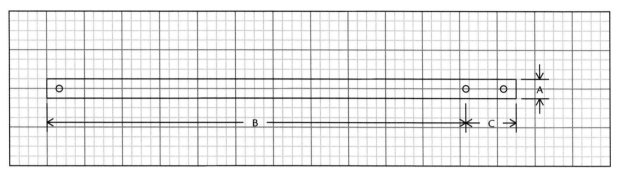

A = 13mm (½")   C = 40mm (1⅝")

B = 300mm (12")

Instructions

- Cut the chain to the desired length with a wire cutter.

- Mark and cut the strap as shown.

- Punch the holes where marked.

- Bevel the grain side of all edges if using vegetable-tanned leather or latigo. Dye and condition if using vegetable-tanned leather, dye the edges if using latigo.

- Twist the D-ring open with the regular and locking pliers, thread it through one of the end links of the chain, then twist it closed.

- Thread the strap through the D-ring and form a loop with the other end. Fix in place with the medium rivet.

- Attach the spring clip to the other end of the chain with the connector ring.

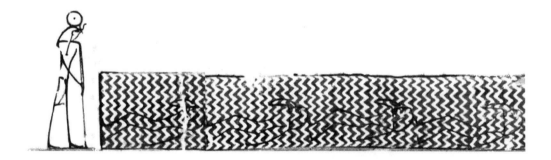

REINS

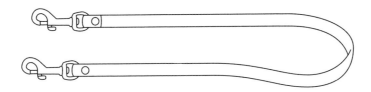

This simple project can be clipped on to the rings on the gag projects in Chapter V or any restraint with symmetrical side attachment points. It can be used to direct or restrict the motion of the submissive, and works well in conjunction with the head harness on page 137.

Tools

- Rotary cutter and ruler
- Drive punch
- Rivet setter and anvil
- Cutting board
- Hammer
- Measuring tape
- Water pencil

Materials

- Chap, medium-heavy vegetable-tanned leather or latigo
- 2 x spring clips
- 2 x medium rivets

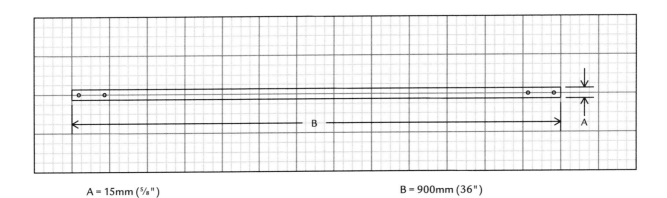

A = 15mm (⁵⁄₈")   B = 900mm (36")

Instructions

- Mark and cut the strap as shown.

- Punch all holes where marked.

- Bevel the grain side of all edges if using vegetable-tanned leather or latigo. Dye and condition if using vegetable-tanned leather, dye the edges if using latigo.

- Fix a spring clip to each end of the strap with a medium rivet.

HEAD HARNESS

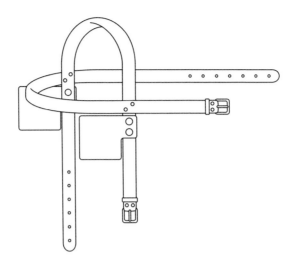

This simple head harness can have a unique and surprisingly dehumanizing effect. It is presented here in its most basic form, but can be altered to suit its intended use. Snap-on blinders are included in this design, but these can be riveted in place or omitted if desired.

Changing the shape of the strapping is an easy way to produce a more decorative visual effect. Equine, canine or feline ears can also be added by riveting folded tapered leather panels between the horizontal and vertical straps.

If the intention is to use the harness for bondage, D-rings can be fixed anywhere you like. Although chap leather will make a much more comfortable harness, medium vegetable-tanned leather may be more suitable for a harness designed for bondage. Also, although the blinders are cut from vegetable-tanned leather, chap leather could be used if two layers are glued and sewn together.

The harness can also be used as a frame on which to mount a mask or muzzle. The male eye mask pattern on page 97 is an ideal base upon which to expand, as its upper edge runs straight and can be riveted under the horizontal strap. Its upper corners should be made square, and the sides may need to be shortened or extended so that they can be riveted under the vertical strap.

A muzzle can be made of three panels of vegetable-tanned or chap leather: two side panels with slightly curved front edges and curved lower corners, and a front expansion panel that tapers at the top over the bridge of the nose, hooks under the chin, and flares out slightly at the base, like the chin protrusion in the mask neck panel (see page 107). Alternatively, the muzzle could be made of a single piece of vegetable-tanned leather molded to the desired shape. With either option, though, the muzzle should hook under the chin at the base, attach to the vertical strap at the sides, and rest on the bridge of the nose at the top. It can even be joined to the mask if one is included.

Tools

- Shears
- Hobby knife
- Rotary cutter and ruler
- Drive punch
- Rivet setter and anvil
- Snap setter and anvil
- Cutting board
- Hammer
- Small foam brush
- Water pencil
- Small clean rag

Materials

- Chap, medium-heavy vegetable-tanned leather or latigo
- Medium vegetable-tanned leather
- 12 x small rivets
- 4 x short snaps
- 2 x 19mm (¾") heel-bar buckles
- Dye
- Leather conditioner

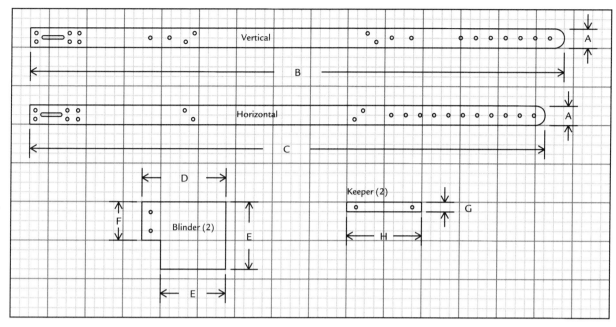

A = 20mm (¾")
B = 1.33γ + 120mm (4¾")
C = α + 150mm (6")
D = 90mm (3½")

E = 70mm (2¾")
F = 40mm (1⅝")
G = 10mm (⅜")
H = 65mm (2½")

Instructions

- Mark and cut the strapping from chap, medium-heavy vegetable-tanned leather or latigo. Mark and cut the blinder panels from medium vegetable-tanned leather, taking care to make them mirror images of each other.

- Bevel the grain sides of all edges of the blinder panels. If using vegetable-tanned leather or latigo, bevel the grain sides of all edges of the strapping as well.

- Punch the holes in the blinder panels and keepers, as well as the buckle rivet and pin holes where marked, and cut the slots.

- Fix the buckles in place with small rivets through the holes closest to the buckles.

- Fix the keepers in place with small rivets.

- Try the harness on and mark where the straps should intersect on both sides of both straps.

- Mark and punch the intersection rivet holes in the horizontal strap.

- Mark the intersection rivet holes on the vertical strap through the holes in the horizontal strap and punch.

- Assemble the harness with small rivets.

- Apply a coat of dye to the blinder panels, let the pieces dry for a few hours, dye again, then let them dry overnight. Dye the strapping if using vegetable-tanned leather, dye the edges if using latigo.

- Apply leather conditioner to the blinder panels (and the strapping if using vegetable-tanned leather). Polish well.

- Lay each blinder on the appropriate side of the vertical strap so that the top of the blinder is flush with the horizontal strap. Mark holes through the holes in the binder.

- Set the female halves of the snaps in the blinders and the male halves in the vertical strap.

CHASTITY BELT

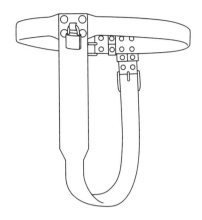

Chastity belts are devices designed to prevent sexual contact, protecting the wearer from rape or temptation. They are often associated with the Middle Ages, but no evidence exists for their use before the Renaissance. Although they are historically more closely associated with females, devices have been created for both males and females.

The female chastity belt presented here follows the Florentine design, with a band around the waist and a shield running between the legs. Chastity devices typically lock, and although locks are not functionally necessary in this design, it can be locked in place with one padlock in the front and one slipped through a buckle pin hole in each of the straps in the rear, or two padlocks through locking buckles. This design is generally intended for short-term wear, in a scene where the wearer is restrained and supervised by a dominant.

This design allows the chastity belt to be unlocked from the front, allowing access when the wearer is seated, against a wall, or lying down. The staple from a small padlock hasp or barrel bolt is the ideal hardware through which to slip the padlock. A fitting hole or slot is cut in one half of the main strap, then the staple is mounted between the two halves of the main strap and fixed in place with the appropriate size rivets. A simpler version of the chastity belt can be made with a ring instead of the front locking assembly, in the style of the ring harness on page 174. Also, 19mm (¾") D-rings added to the sides of the belt can make useful restraint points.

With regard to materials, chap leather will produce soft and supple strapping, but heavy vegetable-tanned leather or latigo will produce a functional chastity device.

Tools

- Rotary cutter and ruler
- Drive punch
- Rivet setter and anvil
- Snap setter and anvil
- Cutting board
- Hammer
- Needle files
- Measuring tape
- Water pencil

Materials

- Chap, medium-heavy vegetable-tanned leather or latigo
- 12 x medium rivets
- 2 x large rivets (optional)
- 2 x 25mm (1") heel-bar buckles
- Padlock hasp or barrel bolt (optional)

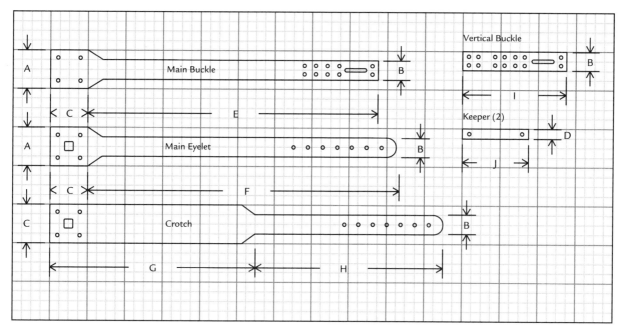

A = 45mm (1¾")

B = 26mm (1")

C = 50mm (2")

D = 12mm (½")

E = 0.50θ + 40mm (1½")

F = 0.50θ + 70mm (2¾")

G = 0.45σ

H = 0.33σ + 100mm (4")

I = 125mm (5")

J = 80mm (3⅛")

Instructions

- Mark and cut the strapping as shown.

- Cut the openings in the center of the main eyelet and crotch straps to match the staple being used. Punch the four surrounding holes in the eyelet strap and use these to mark the holes on the main buckle and crotch straps. Keep the diameter of the snaps in mind when determining the location of these holes. Punch the remainder of the holes where marked, and cut the slots.

- Bevel the grain side of all edges if using vegetable-tanned leather or latigo. Dye and condition if using vegetable-tanned leather, dye the edges if using latigo.

- Place the staple on the wide section of the main buckle strap, lay the eyelet strap on top, and align the edges.

- Remove the eyelet strap, mark holes through the holes in the staple, and punch. Use these holes to mark matching holes in the eyelet strap and punch.

- Fix the staple in between the buckle and eyelet straps with large (or appropriate size) rivets.

- Set the male halves of the snaps in the holes surrounding the staple in the buckle and eyelet straps.

- Set the female halves of the snaps in the crotch strap.

- Fix the buckles in place with medium rivets through the holes closest to the buckles.

- Fix the keepers in place with medium rivets.

- Fold the vertical buckle strap over the horizontal buckle strap so that all the holes line up. Fix in place with medium rivets.

PRISON

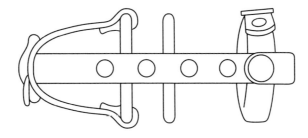

This unique apparatus functions somewhat like a chastity device, as it will prevent the penis from becoming fully erect. Partial erections are not only possible, but highly likely. This device can be so stimulating, in fact, that it may have to be put on very quickly in order to be put on at all. First, the balls are pulled through the opening between the strap and the first ring, then the penis is slid through the rings so the head is entirely past the second ring. The strap is then done up. The device will be at its most effective when fastened to a harness ring, which will need to be put on first.

Since this is a restrictive device, it is designed to be one size fits all, but it can be lengthened or shortened if desired. The ring diameter can also be adjusted – if the wearer is not sure about his size, some experimentation can establish a baseline. Whichever ring size you choose, it should touch the erect penis but not constrict it: overconstricting the genitals during an erection can make a ring difficult or impossible to remove, a situation which can be both dangerous and embarrassing.

Tools

- Leather needle
- Shears
- Hobby knife
- Rotary cutter
- Awl
- Drive punch
- Rivet setter and anvil
- Snap setter and anvil
- Cutting board
- Hammer
- Needle files
- Measuring tape
- Water pencil

Materials

- Chap, medium-heavy vegetable-tanned leather or latigo
- Matching waxed cotton
- 2 x small rivets
- 11 x medium rivets
- 2 x tall snaps
- 6 x short eyelets
- 2 x 44mm (1¾") rings
- 1 x 13mm (½") D-ring
- 1 x 13mm (½") center-bar buckle

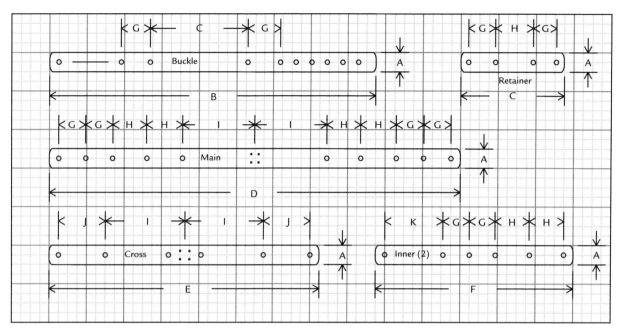

A = 15mm (⅝")
B = 240mm (9½")
C = 75mm (3")
D = 300mm (11¾")
E = 200mm (8")
F = 145mm (5¾")

G = 20mm (¾")
H = 25mm (1")
I = 55mm (2⅛")
J = 40mm (1⅝")
K = 45mm (1¾")

Instructions

- Mark and cut the strapping as shown.

- Smooth out the welds on both rings with needle files.

- Use an awl to make four small holes in a square in the center of the main and cross straps. Punch all remaining holes where marked, and cut the slot.

- Bevel the grain side of all edges if using vegetable-tanned leather or latigo. Dye and condition if using vegetable-tanned leather, dye the edges if using latigo.

- Hand-sew the cross strap over the main strap, going around the square three times, then tying off on top of the cross strap (fig 4.6).

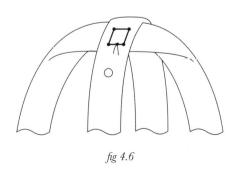

fig 4.6

- Fold in the edges of the D-ring retainer strap so that the holes line up. Fix the D-ring to the cross strap with small rivets.

- Place an inner strap on each side of the main strap, flesh sides together, so that the holes line up. Fix in place with medium rivets through the holes closest to the D-ring.

- Fix the first ring on both sides of the main strap between it and the inner straps, using medium rivets. Fix the second ring on both sides of the main strap between it and the inner straps, using medium rivets.

- Insert and set medium rivets in the next set of holes in the main and inner straps.

- Wrap each end of the cross strap around the first ring, and fix in place with a medium rivet.

- Fix the buckle in place with a medium rivet. Insert and set the eyelets in the buckle pin holes.

- Fix the buckle strap between the ends of the main and inner strap straps with the male halves of the snaps from the main strap side.

- Fix the female halves of the snaps to the ends of the inner straps.

142

FEMALE HARNESS

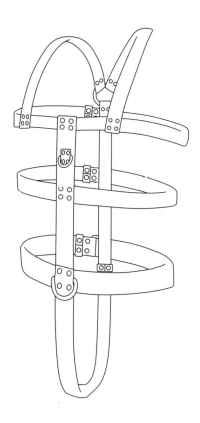

Two body harness designs are presented in this book, this one better suited to the female anatomy, and the other to the male – though elements of either can be used to create a custom design.

Medium to heavy vegetable-tanned leather can be used instead of chap leather, which will make a stiffer, sturdier harness, rather than a soft and supple one.

Tools

- Shears
- Rotary cutter and ruler
- Drive punch
- Rivet setter and anvil
- Cutting board
- Hammer
- Measuring tape
- Water pencil

Materials

- Chap, medium to heavy vegetable-tanned leather or latigo
- 12 x small rivets
- 34 x medium rivets
- 1 x 44mm (1¾") ring
- 1 x 19mm (¾") D-ring
- 1 x 38mm (1½") D-ring
- 3 x 25mm (1") heel-bar buckles
- 1 x 38mm (1½") heel-bar buckle

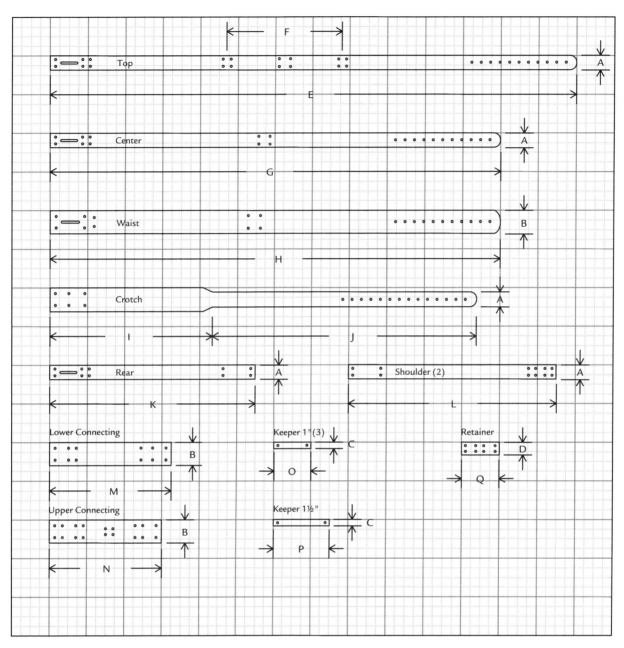

A = 26mm (1")

B = 40mm (1½")

C = 12mm (½")

D = 20mm (¾")

E = ζ + 140mm (5½")

F = 0.25ζ

G = η + 90mm (3½")

H = θ + 90mm (3½")

I = 0.33σ + 110mm (4⅜")

J = 0.50σ + 160mm (6¼")

K = 0.50σ + 100mm (4")

L = 0.66σ

M = 0.30σ + 50mm (2")

N = 0.25σ + 50mm (2")

O = 80mm (3⅛")

P = 100mm (4")

Q = 75mm (3")

Instructions

- Mark and cut the strapping as shown.

- Punch all holes where marked and cut the slots. Note that the values for M and N should work for most body types but can be adjusted if necessary.

- Bevel the grain side of all edges if using vegetable-tanned leather or latigo. Dye and condition if using vegetable-tanned leather, dye the edges if using latigo.

- Fix the buckles in place with medium rivets through the holes closest to the buckles.

- Fix the keepers in place with medium rivets.

- Mount the 19mm (¾") D-ring on the upper connecting strap with the retainer strap and small rivets.

- Fold the upper connecting strap, flesh sides together, over the top strap, so that all eight holes match up with the four center holes on the top strap. Fix in place with medium rivets.

- Fold the other side of the upper connecting strap, grain sides together, so the two outside holes match up with the next row of holes. Fold the side of the lower connecting strap (the one whose second and third rows of holes are closer together), flesh sides together, in the same manner as before. Lay it over the upper connecting strap so that all the holes line up. Finally, lay this piece over the four holes in the center strap and fix in place with medium rivets.

- Fold the other side of the lower connecting strap, grain sides together, so the two outside holes match up with the next row of holes. Fold the top side of the crotch strap, flesh sides together, in the same manner. Lay it over the lower connecting strap so that all the holes line up. Finally, slip the 38mm (1½") D-ring through the crotch strap so it lies between the two rows of holes. Align this piece over the four holes in the waist strap, and fix in place with medium rivets.

- Fold each of the shoulder straps, flesh sides together, over a set of holes on the top strap so that all eight holes match up with the four holes in the top strap. Fix in place with small rivets.

- Fix the ends of the shoulder straps and the rear strap around the 44mm (1¾") ring, using medium rivets.

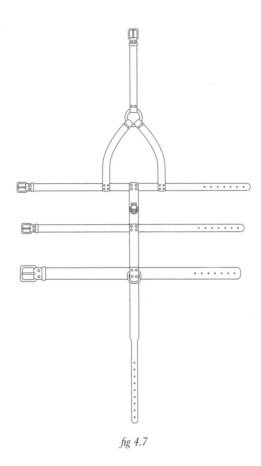

fig 4.7

Male harness

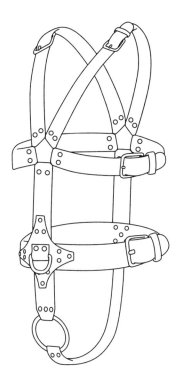

The male harness design presented here buckles at the sides, which allows the wearer to put the harness on easily without assistance, and also allows him to lie comfortably on his back or front.

Medium to heavy vegetable-tanned leather can be used instead of chap leather, which will make a stiffer, sturdier harness, rather than a soft and supple one.

Tools

- Shears
- Rotary cutter and ruler
- Drive punch
- Rivet setter and anvil
- Cutting board
- Hammer
- Needle files
- Measuring tape
- Pencil and ruler
- Water pencil

Materials

- Chap, medium-heavy vegetable-tanned leather or latigo
- 12 x small rivets
- 64 x medium rivets
- 2 x large rivets
- 3 x 51mm (2") ring
- 1 x 44mm (1¾") D-ring
- 1 x 25mm (1") heel-bar buckle
- 4 x 38mm (1½") heel-bar buckles
- 2 x 51mm (2") heel-bar buckles
- Paper

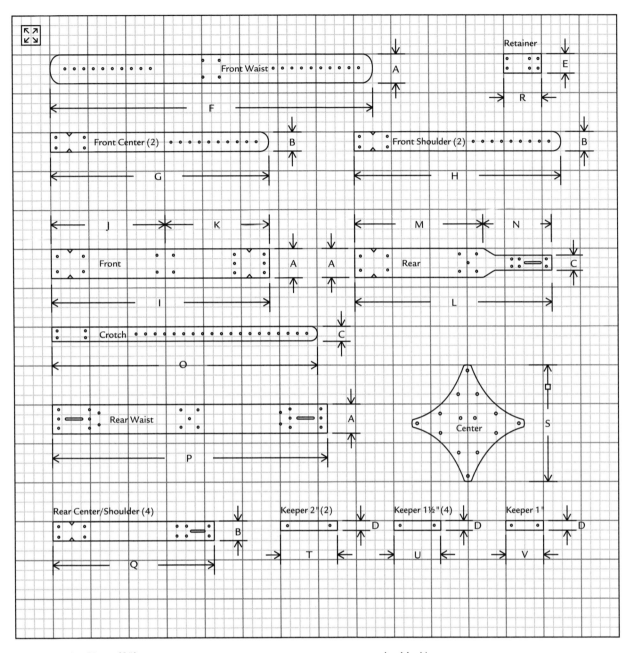

A = 51mm (2")

B = 40mm (1½")

C = 26mm (1")

D = 12mm (½")

E = 45mm (1¾")

F = 0.50θ + 200mm (8")

G = 0.25η + 200mm (8")

H = 0.30σ + 200mm (8")

I = 0.50σ + 70mm (2¾")

J = 0.53I

K = 0.47I

L = M + N

M = 0.30σ + 40mm (1½")

N = 120mm (4¾")

O = 0.50σ + 160mm (6¼")

P = 0.50θ + 40mm (1½")

Q = 0.25η + 70mm (2¾")

R = 100mm (4")

S = 160mm (6¼")

T = 140mm (5½")

U = 100mm (4")

V = 80mm (3⅛")

Instructions

- Mark and cut the strapping and the center panel as shown.

- Punch all the holes where marked and cut the slots.

- Bevel the grain side of all edges if using vegetable-tanned leather or latigo. Dye and condition if using vegetable-tanned leather, dye the edges if using latigo.

- Make ring notches where indicated by folding the end of the straps, aligning the rivet holes and clipping 10mm (³⁄₈") equilateral triangles off each corner of the folds.

- Fix the buckles in place with medium rivets through the holes closest to the buckles.

- Fix the keepers in place with medium rivets.

- Assemble the front and rear of the harness around two of the 51mm (2") rings with medium rivets.

- Fix the rear waist strap over the rear strap with medium rivets.

- Fix the front waist strap over the front strap with medium rivets.

- Place the center panel over the intersection of the front and front waist straps. Mark rivet holes through the holes in the center panel.

- Punch the holes where marked.

- Fix the center panel in place with small rivets, leaving the center holes empty.

- Thread the retainer through the D-ring and fix in place with large rivets through the center holes.

- Smooth out the weld on the remaining 51mm (2") ring with a needle file. Attach it to the base of the front strap with medium rivets.

- Attach the crotch strap to the ring with medium rivets.

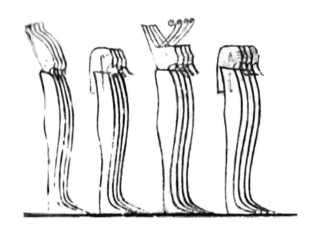

CHAPTER V

Sensory Deprivation

Most of us are born with five senses. If one is lost, the remainder are heightened. Temporarily losing a sense isolates the mind and propels us further into our own inner space, and this effect is amplified with each sense lost. Depriving someone of most or all of their senses can bind their conscious mind in the same way restraints bind their body.

Being relieved of our senses loosens our connection to the physical world. The projects in this chapter provide the means to dampen the senses as much as is safely possible.

It is easy enough to deprive someone of the sense of sight, but the remaining four senses are more difficult. Hearing can be dampened with a pair of earplugs; their effect can be increased when used in conjunction with a leather mask with a lace closure. The hood presented in this chapter has padded sections over the ears, and when laced tightly reduces the wearer's hearing to almost nothing, practically eliminating the need for earplugs. If the hood is used in conjunction with earplugs, even those last few decibels can be silenced.

Taste is a difficult sense to subdue. The majority of the taste buds are located on the tongue, so isolating the tongue would seem to be the most efficient way of diminishing this sense. However, it could also be argued that simply depriving a person of the ability to put

anything in their mouth deprives the mouth of any real taste. Either of these goals can be accomplished by using a gag, which is a small object inserted into the mouth and held in place with a strap or harness. A gag, by removing the capacity of speech, can also enforce the feeling of helplessness. (A non-verbal signal should be established ahead of time – a pattern of sounds made with the gag in place, or dropping a held object.) However, gags are not generally comfortable for long periods of time.

Depriving someone of their sense of smell is not easy to accomplish in the context of a scene. Plugging the nose is easy enough, but unsafe if a gag is also being used. The safest way to diminish smell is to overwhelm it. While wearing a leather mask, one smells little else but leather. Alternatively, incense can be burned, or essential oils deployed near the submissive's nose.

The most difficult sense to subdue is certainly the sense of touch. There really is no way to induce a complete loss of touch without using an anesthetic, which is both unsafe and counterproductive. Taking away the capacity for movement and physical stimulus is probably as close as we can go. Covering the entire body – depriving the skin of direct contact with anything else – can be one effective method. However, most of us experience touch primarily through our hands. Thus, bondage mitts will be presented in this chapter.

PADDED BLINDFOLD

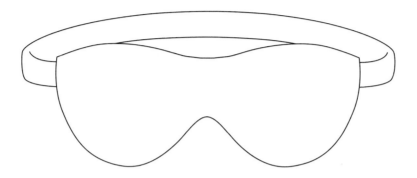

This first design is a simple padded leather blindfold in the shape of a sleep mask. It is easy to make and quite effective.

This design is held in place with a length of fabric elastic, and can be made adjustable with the addition of a slide buckle and rectangular ring (fig 3.14, page 75). A second length of fabric elastic can be mounted below the first for a more secure fit if desired.

Tools

- Sewing machine (leather needle/universal needle)
- Shears
- Measuring tape
- Pencil and ruler
- Water pencil
- Iron
- Lighter

Materials

- Chap leather
- Matching garment leather
- Matching thread
- 250mm (10") scrap cotton cloth for padding
- 400mm (16") of 25mm (1") fabric elastic
- Contact cement
- Paper

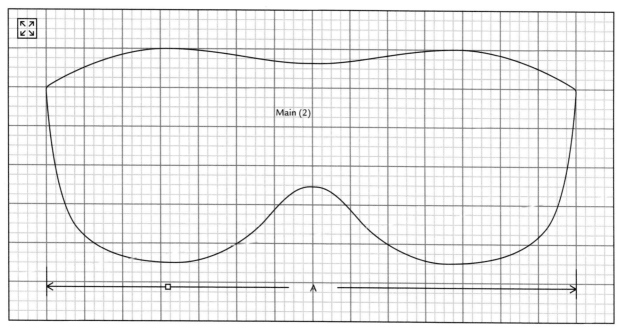

A = 220mm (8⅝")

Instructions

- Draft the pattern as shown.

- Trace and cut out one panel from chap leather. Trace it on the garment leather, flesh sides together, and cut out.

- Place one panel over the eyes and check the fabric elastic length for fit.

- Cut the fabric elastic if necessary and melt the ends.

- Fold the scrap cloth in half widthwise, lengthwise, then widthwise to make eight layers. Press.

- Sew the folded fabric together with a universal needle (fig 4.4, page 129).

- Lay the panel pattern on the padding and trace.

- Sew a perimeter seam 10mm (⅜") inside the trace.

- Cut around the perimeter seam, leaving a 5mm (³⁄₁₆") seam allowance.

- Apply contact cement to the outer 15mm (⅝") of the flesh sides of both panels.

- Place each end of the fabric elastic just below a top corner and 10mm (⅜") inside the edge of the flesh side of the chap leather panel. Press firmly.

- Place the padding in the center of the chap leather panel, then place the garment leather panel on top, taking care to align all of the edges. Press the perimeter firmly and let it dry overnight.

- Sew around perimeter of the blindfold, 3mm (⅛") from the edge, with a leather needle.

EYES OPEN BLINDFOLD

This project is a variation on the padded blindfold on page 150, using polyurethane foam fixed to a layer of vegetable-tanned leather or latigo. Circular openings are cut from the foam to prevent any material from touching the eyes. This style has become popular with meditators and those with difficulty sleeping, as it can produce total darkness while allowing the eyes to remain open and untouched by the blindfold.

Cutting the foam to size can be difficult without the proper equipment. A band saw with an appropriate blade is ideal for cutting the foam to the required width and the outer contour, and a hole saw of the appropriate diameter is the best way of cutting out the openings. Even with a hole saw, this can be difficult with some foam, which can twist under the rotation of the saw. You can make the process easier and cleaner by compressing the foam between a couple of pieces of plywood when cutting the hole. Upholstery stores, in addition to being a great source of foam, can often assist with cutting. Having said all of that, though, most foam can be cut very nicely with an electric knife, or even a sharp bread knife and some patience.

Most polyurethane foam is colorless, so you may wish to paint it, after cutting it, to match the leather. A single coat of acrylic paint should be sufficient. Depending on the thickness of the paint, you may find that it works better if you dilute it with a bit of water or an acrylic paint additive, as doing so prevents the paint from forming a hard layer over the foam. Experiment on some scrap foam first. Be sure not to use a solvent-based paint, as it will melt the foam. Contact cement, also solvent-based, cannot be used on foam either. A foaming polyurethane glue is ideal for this project.

Tools:

- Leather needle
- Utility knife
- Beveler
- Stitch chisel
- Cutting board
- Hammer
- Measuring tape
- Small foam brush
- Pen
- Pencil and ruler
- Lighter

Materials:

- Medium-heavy vegetable-tanned leather or latigo
- Matching waxed cotton
- Matching acrylic paint
- 25mm (1") polyurethane foam
- Polyurethane glue
- 400mm (16") of 25mm (1") fabric elastic
- Dye
- Leather conditioner
- Paper

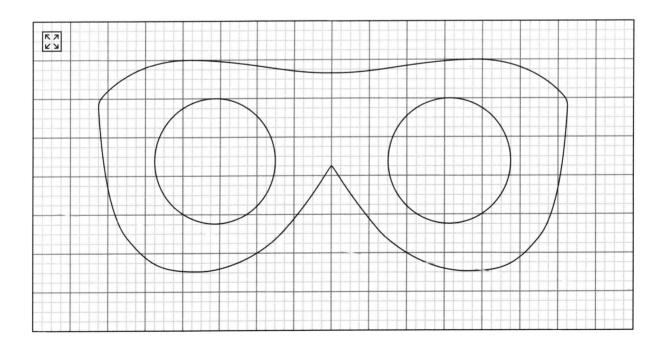

Instructions:

- Draft the padded blindfold pattern as shown on page 151.

- Trace the pattern on the leather, and cut out the panel.

- Bevel the grain side of the panel. It may be necessary to bevel the tight curve over the bridge of the nose free-hand, with a utility knife.

- Place the panel on the foam and trace with a pen that will mark the foam. Use the panel, rather than the pattern, for this step, so that the outer contours of both panels will match up. (Because the patterns are drafted separately, small inconsistencies may exist between them.)

- Draft the pattern on page 152, using the cell size calculated for the padded blindfold on page 151.

- Center the pattern over the tracing on the foam. Trace.

- Cut out the foam panel, using the first tracing for the top edge and bottom sections where the foam will be flush with the leather, and the second tracing for everything else.

- Apply a coat of paint to the top and sides of the foam panel.

- Dye and condition the leather panel if using vegetable-tanned leather, dye the edges if using latigo. Let both pieces dry overnight.

- Punch a row of six stitch slots on each side of the leather panel just below the top corners.

- Place the foam panel pattern on the flesh side of the leather panel and trace with a pencil.

- Apply polyurethane glue to the flesh side of the leather panel inside the traced lines.

- Moisten the unpainted side of the foam panel and fix it to the flesh side of the leather panel, matching it up with the traced lines. Compress it by placing something flat and heavy over the foam for several hours.

- Melt one end of the fabric elastic, make a 7mm (¼") fold, and hand-sew it to a set of stitch slots.

- Try on the blindfold to ensure a good fit. Trim the fabric elastic if necessary.

- Melt the other end of the fabric elastic, make another 7mm (¼") fold, and hand-sew it to the other set of stitch slots.

DISC BLINDFOLD

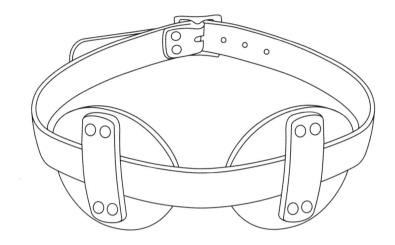

This blindfold is comprised of two discs held snugly over the eyes with a leather strap. The discs can be adjusted to fit the wearer, and the buckle can be placed anywhere around the head, allowing the wearer to lie down comfortably. The entire blindfold can be made with chap leather, but when using vegetable-tanned leather or latigo, its effectiveness can be increased greatly by using a piled material such as sheepskin for the inner panels. The length of the pile on most sheepskins may be longer than ideal for this project – see page 52 for trimming instructions.

Tools

- Sewing machine (leather needle)
- Utility knife
- Rotary cutter and ruler
- Drive punch
- Rivet setter and anvil
- Cutting board
- Hammer
- Measuring tape
- Water pencil

Materials

- Chap, medium-heavy vegetable-tanned leather or latigo
- Genuine or synthetic sheepskin (optional)
- Matching thread
- 10 x small rivets
- 1 x 19mm (¾") center-bar buckle
- Contact cement

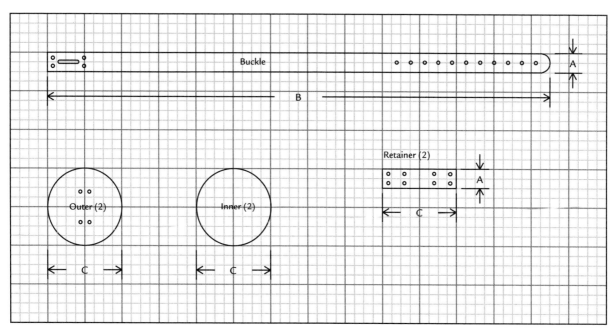

A = 20mm (¾")

B = α + 120mm (4¾")

C = 70mm (2¾")

Instructions

- Draft the pattern as shown. Note that if using heavy vegetable-tanned leather or latigo, the strap retainers can be shortened to exclude the areas with the outer pairs of holes, as the folds will not be necessary.

- Trace, mark and cut out all pieces.

- Punch all holes where marked and cut the slot.

- Bevel the grain side of all edges if using vegetable-tanned leather or latigo. Dye and condition if using vegetable-tanned leather, dye the edges if using latigo.

- Fix the buckle in place with small rivets.

- Fix the strap retainers to the outer panels with small rivets.

- Apply contact cement to the flesh side of the inner and outer panels.

- Align each outer panel with an inner panel, press firmly and let dry overnight.

- Sew around the perimeter of the discs, 3mm (⅛") from the edge, if using chap leather

- Thread the buckle strap through the strap retainers.

BASIC BALL GAG

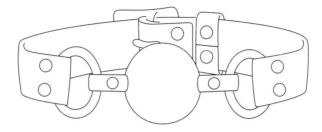

Producing a quality gag is difficult without specialized equipment. Making the insertable part of the gag out of leather is possible, but not generally a good idea, as the leather will decompose over time. Ideally, the ball should be made from a non-reactive material such as non-toxic silicone rubber or latex.

Since injection molding is beyond the scope of this book, the gags presented in this section will be made with rubber balls, which can then be dipped in latex if desired. The kinds of balls that work best can be purchased at most toy stores and are generally made with non-toxic material, though they should be thoroughly washed before use. Any rubber ball 38mm-51mm (1 ½" to 2") in diameter, with a surface that cannot be punctured with your thumbnail, should be suitable.

You will have to bore a hole through the ball. The easiest way to do this is with a drill and a 6mm-10mm (¼"-⅜") drill bit, although with a little patience this can be accomplished with a hobby knife or chisel. For wider straps, you can cut a slot through the ball by first drilling two smaller holes through it, then connecting them with a square needle file, a coping saw, or a length of waxed cotton or wire threaded through both holes and pulled through.

To pull the strap through the hole, use a leather needle to draw a doubled-over length of artificial sinew or waxed cotton through the hole in the ball, then through the end of the strap, then back through the hole in the ball. Then, slowly pull the ends of the thread and guide the strap through the hole. This process can be made easier by clipping the corners of the end of the strap to be pulled through.

If no suitable rubber ball can be found, a plastic practice golf ball can be used in its place. These are usually white and about the size of a golf ball, but hollow and perforated, making for easy breathing. They can be purchased at sporting equipment stores. A wooden ball can also be used, but only a well-sanded sphere of a tight-grained

wood. Neither of these alternatives are suitable for dipping in latex.

The first design presented here is simply a small center strap threaded through a ball and held in place with two rings and a buckling leather strap. The rings and center strap can be omitted and a single ¾" buckling strap used to hold the ball in place if desired. This would necessitate cutting a ¾" slot through the ball, and it is critical that the slot be perfectly centered. If you don't use liquid latex, this alternative allows for easy cleaning, as the ball can be slid right off the strap.

Latex

Dipping the ball and center strap in liquid latex prior to assembly can make the gag easy to clean and can give it a professional look. Liquid latex can often be purchased at sculpture supply and hobby stores, as it is used to build molds. It usually comes white and dries colorless, but can be colored with a small amount of universal colorant. A 500ml (16 oz.) wide-mouth canning jar is an ideal vessel to use to prepare the latex and for dipping, and it also makes a good storage container. If adding color, add a little at a time and stir thoroughly to mix, but do not shake. Keep in mind that the latex will dry a much darker color than it appears in its liquid state. When the latex is approaching the correct tone, let your stirring stick dry completely and check its color. If necessary, add more color and repeat.

Once the center strap has been threaded through the ball and centered (but prior to punching the rivet holes), remove the needle from the thread and tie the ends together. Holding it by the knot at the end of the thread, slowly dip the strap and ball into the liquid latex at a rate of about 5mm (¼") per second. Once it is completely immersed, slowly remove the strap and ball at the same rate, taking care not to bump the edges of the jar. Use a needle to pop any bubbles that appear, and allow the ball and strap to dry for about an hour, or until the latex is almost dry but still somewhat tacky. Repeat this process three times, or until a sufficient size and covering is achieved. Leave the ball to dry completely, preferably for several days.

Once the ball is dry, it can be vulcanized. Most liquid latex is pre-vulcanized, meaning there is some sulfur added to the latex to strengthen it. When you heat the latex, the sulfur is fixed in place, adding to the strength of the finished product. Vulcanization can be performed in a regular oven heated to 77°C (170°F). Remove the bottom rack from the oven, move the top rack to the highest position and hang the ball from it with a binder clip. Bake for ten minutes.

Once the ball is vulcanized and cool, it should be coated in baby powder and left overnight to remove any remaining moisture from the latex. Once the ball is rinsed and dried, the process is complete, though baby powder can be applied a second time if required. Clip the threads from the end of the strap.

Before you insert this or any gag, ensure that the wearer's nasal pssages are clear: if they are inclined to sinus problems, they might wish to use a decongestant nasal spray.

Tools

- Leather needle
- Rotary cutter and ruler
- Hobby knife
- Drive punch
- Rivet setter and anvil
- Cutting board
- Hammer
- Measuring tape
- Water pencil

Materials

- Chap, medium-heavy vegetable-tanned leather or latigo
- 38mm-51mm (1½"-2") ball, with a hole or slot
- 8 x small rivets
- 2 x 25mm (1") rings
- 1 x 19mm (¾") center-bar buckle
- Artificial sinew or waxed cotton
- Dye
- Leather conditioner

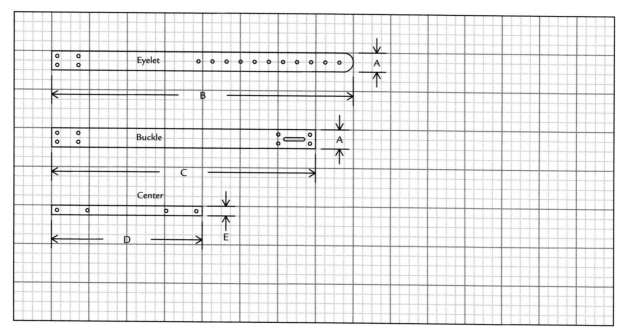

A = 20mm (¾")
B = 0.50β + 60mm (2½")
C = 0.50β - 10mm (⅜")

D = 150mm (6")
E = 10mm (⅜") [8mm (⁵⁄₁₆") if using liquid latex]

Instructions

- Mark and cut the strapping as shown.

- Punch all holes where marked and cut the slot.

- Bevel the grain side of all edges if using vegetable-tanned leather or latigo. Dye and condition if using vegetable-tanned leather, dye the edges if using latigo.

- Thread the center strap through the ball, using one of the options on page 156.

- Fix the buckle in place with small rivets.

- Assemble the gag around the rings using small rivets.

HEAD HARNESS GAG

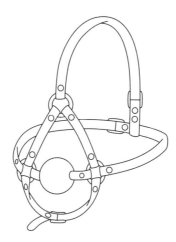

This gag design is similar to the first, but in addition to the main straps there are two straps going under the chin and two connecting straps running from the side rings to a third ring just below the forehead, which is connected to a strap running over the top of the head.

In this configuration, the connecting straps should meet at the bridge of the nose and can obstruct vision. The connecting straps can be extended to meet above the forehead if desired, though to achieve this configuration the center strap must be extended as well. How much

length should be added to achieve a comfortable and functional fit can vary between wearers and can be a very narrow range. First, estimate the lengths of the strapping, but cut the connecting straps a little long and do not punch the top sets of rivet holes. Assemble the gag, try it on the intended user, bring connecting straps up to the top of the forehead and mark. Mark and punch the rivet holes on both sides of the markings, then finish the assembly.

Because the strapping is narrow, latigo or vegetable-tanned leather can generally be used without sacrificing comfort.

Tools

- Leather needle
- Rotary cutter and ruler
- Hobby knife
- Drive punch
- Rivet setter and anvil
- Cutting board
- Hammer
- Measuring tape
- Water pencil

Materials

- Chap, medium-heavy vegetable-tanned leather or latigo
- 38mm-51mm (1½"-2") ball with a hole or slot
- 13 x medium rivets
- 2 x small rivets
- 3 x 25mm (1") rings
- 3 x 13mm (½") center-bar buckles
- Artificial sinew or waxed cotton

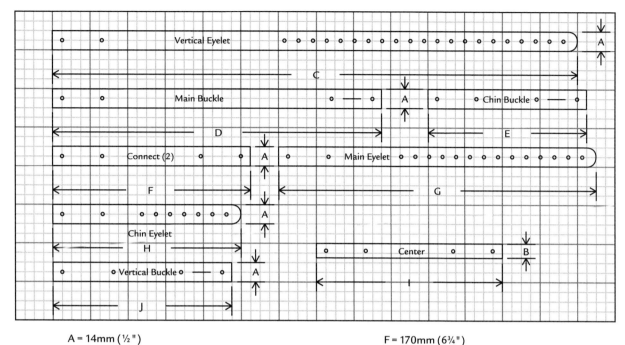

A = 14mm (½")

B = 10mm (⅜") [8mm (⁵⁄₁₆") if using liquid latex]

C = 0.66γ + 100mm (4")

D = 0.50β + 20mm (¾")

E = 130mm (5")

F = 170mm (6¾")

G = 0.50β

H = 160mm (6¼")

I = 150mm (6")

J = 140mm (5½")

Instructions

- Mark and cut the strapping as shown.

- Punch all holes where marked and cut the slots.

- Bevel the grain side of all edges if using vegetable-tanned leather or latigo. Dye and condition if using vegetable-tanned leather, dye the edges if using latigo.

- Thread the center strap through the ball, using one of the options on page 156.

- Fix the buckles in place with medium rivets.

- Fold the vertical buckle strap around the main buckle strap and fix it in place with a medium rivet.

- Fix the center strap to the rings with small rivets.

- Assemble the gag around the rings using medium rivets (fig 5.1).

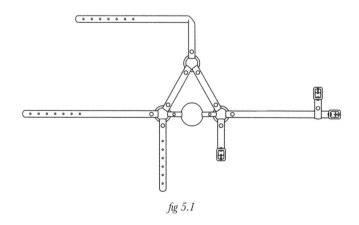

fig 5.1

MUZZLE

This project functions in more or less the same manner as a gag, but does not have an insertable component. The muzzle is designed to fit around the human head, preventing anything from going in or coming out of the mouth, and it also keeps the jaw shut fairly effectively. It can be used in conjunction with the basic ball gag to prevent the wearer from dripping or making any sound whatsoever, or with an athletic mouth guard to provide the wearer with a comfortable surface to bite down on. The muzzle makes a perfect alternative to an insertable gag all on its own, and is also an ideal choice when the user is also wearing a full face mask, as it does not require anything to go through the mouth opening.

The muzzle can be made even more versatile by fixing the horizontal straps to the vertical straps with the male halves of four snaps, omitting the rivet holes in the area between the snaps and sewing some hook velcro over these areas. The female halves of the snaps are mounted on the corners of the front panel, and hook velcro sewn between the snaps to match the strapping. This not only allows access to the mouth without removing the muzzle, but also allows other front panels with gags mounted on them to be attached to the muzzle.

Tools

- Rotary cutter and ruler
- Hobby knife
- Drive punch
- Rivet setter and anvil
- Cutting board
- Hammer
- Measuring tape
- Water pencil

Materials

- Chap leather
- 26 x small rivets
- 14 x medium rivets
- 3 x 25mm (1") rings
- 1 x 13mm (½") D-ring
- 3 x 19mm (¾") center-bar buckles

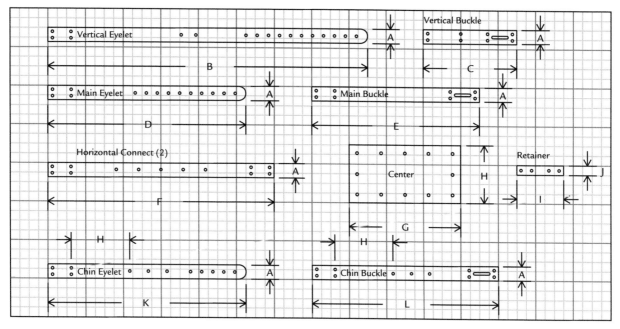

A = 20mm (¾")

B = 0.66γ + 120mm (4¾")

C = 150mm (6")

D = 0.50β + 40mm (1½")

E = 0.50β - 40mm (1½")

F = 310mm (12¼")

G = 140mm (5½")

H = 65mm (2½")

I = 75mm (3")

J = 14mm (½")

K = 250mm (10")

L = 240mm (9½")

Instructions

- Mark and cut the strapping and center panel as shown.

- Punch all holes where marked and cut the slots. The holes in the center panel should be used to mark the center three holes in the chin straps and the center five holes in the horizontal connecting straps.

- Fix the D-ring in place on the vertical eyelet strap with the retainer strap and medium rivets.

- Fix the buckles in place with small rivets.

- Fold the rear vertical buckle strap around the main buckle strap and fix it in place with small rivets.

- Attach the chin and horizontal connecting straps to the front panel with medium rivets (fig 5.2).

- Assemble the muzzle around the rings with small rivets (fig 5.2).

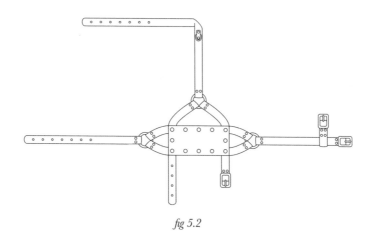

fig 5.2

LEATHER MITTS

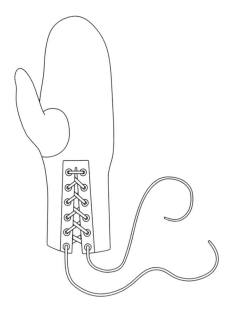

These mitts are of a fairly ordinary design, with the addition of a lace closure for a tight fit. When made of high-quality garment leather, they can turn the wearer's hands in to a source of intense or subtle sensation.

This design includes thumbs, which enable the wearer to perform some basic functions while wearing them. The thumbs can be omitted to make a more typical bondage mitt, if desired. If the thumbs are to be omitted, you may wish to decrease the vertical cell size of the palm and back panels and increase the depth of the lace closure to allow for a tighter fit. The measurements provided will

make a very snug mitt, so if a looser fit is desired, or if the mitts will be lined (winterizing them), the vertical cell size should be increased.

The vertical cell size should be decreased by 10% if stretch material is used. In order to make attached mitts for the zentai on page 31, line up the dashed line on the pattern with the wrist edge of the arm panel. The mitts will have a fold on the thumb side of the mitt rather than a seam, and when tracing out the pattern the palm and back panels should be drawn so that the thumb side edges overlap by 10mm (³⁄₈") to account for no seam allowance on that side.

Tools

- Sewing machine (leather needle)
- Glover's needle and sailor's palm
- Shears
- Drive punch
- Eyelet setter and anvil
- Cutting board
- Hammer
- Measuring tape
- Pencil and ruler
- Water pencil

Materials

- Garment leather
- Matching thread
- 2 x 760mm (30") shoelaces
- 24 x medium eyelets
- Paper

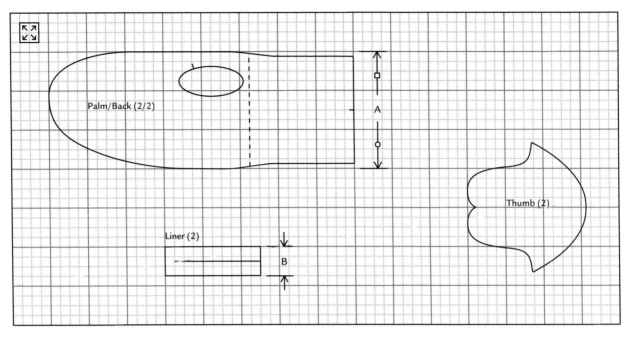

Palm/Back (2/2)

A

Thumb (2)

Liner (2)

B

A = 0.50o + 15mm (⅝")   B = 25mm (1")

Instructions

- Draft the pattern as shown. Place a hand over the pattern to ensure a good fit, and adjust if necessary.

- Trace, mark and cut out all pieces. For the first mitt, trace out the first panel with no thumb opening, then flip the pattern over for the second panel and mark a thumb opening in this one. Then, for the second mitt, flip the panel over again, trace and include a thumb opening, then flip the pattern over a final time, trace and omit the thumb opening.

- Sew each pair of panels, grain sides together, from the top down the side with the thumb opening, 5mm (³⁄₁₆") from the edge.

- Fold each thumb panel lengthwise, grain sides together. Sew from the folded edge up over the top and down to the point 5mm (³⁄₁₆") from the edge.

- Turn the thumb panels right side out, and insert each into a thumb opening in a mitt. Line the seam up with the marking on the thumb opening grain sides together, and baste each in place.

- Sew each thumb panel in place, 5mm (³⁄₁₆") from the edge.

- Remove the basting.

- Apply contact cement to the flesh side of the liner panels and place each one centered on a palm panel so that the bottom of the liner is 10mm (³⁄₈") above the bottom of the panel. Press firmly and let dry overnight.

- Sew each liner in place 3mm (⅛") from the inside and outside edges.

- Pull the center of each liner away from the palm panel and make a cut in the palm panel to match the liner.

- Mark and punch six evenly spaced holes on both sides of each liner.

- Insert the top five eyelets in both sides of each liner and set in place.

- Sew around the remaining perimeter of each mitt, 5mm (³⁄₁₆") from the edge.

- Trim the lower 20mm (¾") of the seam allowances on each mitt down to 2mm (¹⁄₁₆").

- Apply contact cement to the bottom 20mm (¾") of the flesh side of each mitt and make 10mm (³⁄₈") folds. Press firmly and let dry overnight.

- Sew each cuff from the top side, 7mm (¼") from the edge.

- Punch through the bottom holes of each liner and insert and set the eyelets.

FIST MITTS

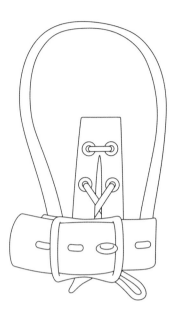

Fist mitts can render the wearer unable to perform the most basic of functions, which can quite effectively enforce dependence on the dominant. They can restrain without restricting movement, so they can be used to enforce submission over longer periods of time. They can also make a worthwhile addition to animal role-play scenes.

Fist mitts are simply cuffs attached to leather pouches just large enough for a fist. They restrict the sense of touch and can also be used in place of wrist restraints. For maximum effectiveness, they must fit the wearer's hand very snugly. With this in mind, it may be helpful to make a scrap cloth prototype to test the pattern before cutting out the project.

Tools

- Sewing machine (leather needle)
- Shears
- Drive punch
- Rivet setter and anvil
- Eyelet setter and anvil
- Cutting board
- Hammer
- Measuring tape
- Pencil and ruler
- Water pencil

Materials

- Chap leather
- Matching thread
- 2 x 690mm (27") shoelaces
- 12 x medium rivets
- 16 x tall eyelets
- 2 x 25mm (1") D-rings
- 2 x 25mm (1") locking or center-bar buckles
- Paper

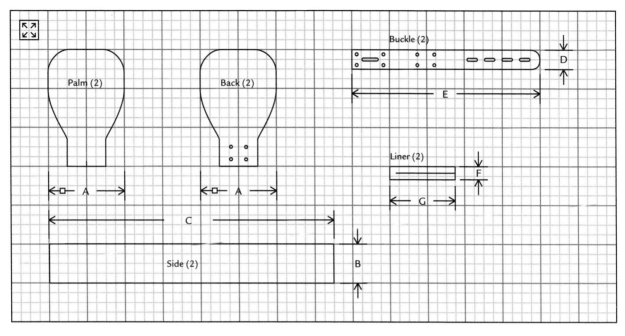

A = 0.50o

B = 0.30ξ + 10mm (⅜")

C = 2o

D = 26mm (1")

E = ξ + 130mm (5")

F = 25mm (1")

G = 85mm (3⅜")

Instructions

- Draft the pattern as shown.

- Trace, mark and cut out all pieces.

- Align each palm panel with a side panel, grain sides together. Sew around the entire curved edge of the palm panel 5mm (³⁄₁₆") from the edge.

- Apply contact cement to the flesh side of each liner and place it centered on the base of a palm panel. Press firmly and let dry overnight.

- Sew each liner to the palm panel with seams 2mm (¹⁄₁₆") from the inside and outside edges.

- Pull the center of each liner away from the palm panel. Make a cut in the palm panel to match the liner.

- Mark four evenly spaced eyelet holes on both sides of each liner.

- Punch the eyelet holes where marked and insert and set the eyelets.

- Punch the holes in the back panels and buckle straps where marked. Cut the slots.

- Align each back panel with the other edge of a side panel, grain sides together. Sew around the entire curved edge of the back panel 5mm (³⁄₁₆") from the edge, taking care that this seam starts from the same side of the side panel as the palm panel seam.

- Trim each cuff edge straight if necessary.

- Turn the mitts right side out.

- Fix the buckles in place with medium rivets.

- Thread each buckle strap through a D-ring and align the holes in the straps with the holes in the back panels, with a D-ring in between. Insert medium rivets and set in place.

BONDAGE HOOD

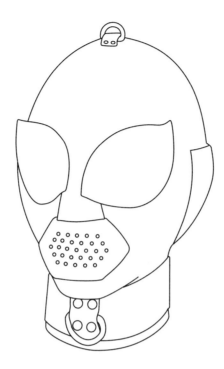

Whether the hood is used for sensory deprivation, punishment, or regular submissive attire, it can be one of the most effective tools in this book. It can be made in a number of ways with various optional attachments, but the design of the hood will depend on what it is to be used for. This is yet another project that screams for personal customization.

The base design is similar to the one used for the masks in Chapters I and III, but the face of the hood is made in one piece rather than two. If the look or feel of the previous masks is preferred for this project as well, it is not difficult to modify the hood to use those construction methods.

The base of the hood is made of garment leather, with chap leather for the collar. The entire hood can be made of chap leather if a heavier hood is desired. The thickness of the leather will make sewing it together and finishing the edges more difficult, and taller eyelets will be required for the meeting edges. But, when done correctly, the heavier leather will be well worth the effort.

When leather is laced around one's head, hearing is muffled but still marginally functional, which is why the hood has padded sections over the ears that reduce hearing to almost nothing. Although scrap cloth can be used for the padding (see page 129), the ideal material to use is polyurethane foam.

This hood also has detachable eye and mouth covers, which means that it deprives the wearer of three senses all on its own. Many other detachable options are possible, using the eye and mouth covers as templates. One option that works particularly well with this project is the perforated covers (see fig 2.22 on page 43 for templates). Note that in order to achieve the hole pattern in that template, you'll need a slightly smaller drive punch than the 3mm (⅛") typically used. Alternatively, you can sandwich a layer of transparent PVC or wire mesh between a regular appliqué with an opening, and a matching layer of loop from hook-and-loop fastener.

Detachable gags are not discussed in this project, simply because of the project's very tight fit and small mouth opening. Do not use an unattached mouth filling that could potentially drift to the back of the wearer's throat – an extremely dangerous practice, especially in conjunction with this hood.

These attachments are typically fixed to the hood with snaps, but greater flexibility can be achieved with the use of hook-and-loop fastener. Very wide strips are required for this method: 100mm (4") is ideal, and can sometimes be found at upholstery and canvas stores. The hook side is glued to the grain side of each of the eye and mouth appliqués, then the excess is trimmed off. The appliqués are then glued and sewn to the hood as usual. With these in place, any number of eye and mouth coverings can be made, using the appliqués as templates. After the attachment is made, a piece of the loop side is cut to match the inner curve of the appliqué, and then glued to

the flesh side of the attachment and sewn in place. Then the excess loop can be trimmed from the attachment.

Though hook-and-loop does have a lifespan, it is a long one, especially in a product like this that won't involve excessive use. But it is for this reason that the hook side is used for the hood and the loop side for the attachments. The loop side will wear faster than the hook side, and it is easier to replace the loop on the attachments than on the hood itself. Of course, replacing the hook-and-loop attachment design with the more traditional snaps or buckles is possible if the attachments are altered to accommodate these kinds of fasteners.

Tools

- Sewing machine (leather needle/universal needle)
- Glover's needle and sailor's palm
- Shears
- Small scissors
- Drive punch
- Rivet setter and anvil
- Eyelet setter and anvil
- Cutting board
- Hammer
- Measuring tape
- Pencil and ruler
- Water pencil

Materials

- Garment leather
- Chap leather
- Matching thread
- Polyurethane foam or scrap cotton cloth for padding
- 1830mm (72") shoelace
- 10 x medium rivets
- 22 x short eyelets
- 1 x 19mm (¾") D-ring
- 1 x 25mm (1") D-ring
- 1 x 25mm (1") center-bar buckle
- 300mm (12") of 100mm (4") hook-and-loop
- Contact cement
- Paper

Legend for pattern on page 168

$A = 0.30\alpha + 15\text{mm} \ (⅝")$

$B = 0.50\gamma + 10\text{mm} \ (⅜")$

$C = 1.50[\delta + 10\text{mm} \ (⅜")]$

$D = \delta + 10\text{mm} \ (⅜")$

$E = \varepsilon + 40\text{mm} \ (1½")$

$F = 110\text{mm} \ (4½")$

$G = 70\text{mm} \ (2¾")$

$H = B + F - 75\text{mm} \ (3")$

$I = 25\text{mm} \ (1")$

$J = 80\text{mm} \ (3⅛")$

$K = 50\text{mm} \ (2")$

$L = 26\text{mm} \ (1")$

$M = 70\text{mm} \ (2¾")$

$N = \varepsilon - 40\text{mm} \ (1½")$

$O = 100\text{mm} \ (4")$

$P = 60\text{mm} \ (2⅜")$

$Q = 45\text{mm} \ (1¾")$

$R = 20\text{mm} \ (¾")$

$S = 35\text{mm} \ (1⅜")$

$T = 40\text{mm} \ (1⅝")$

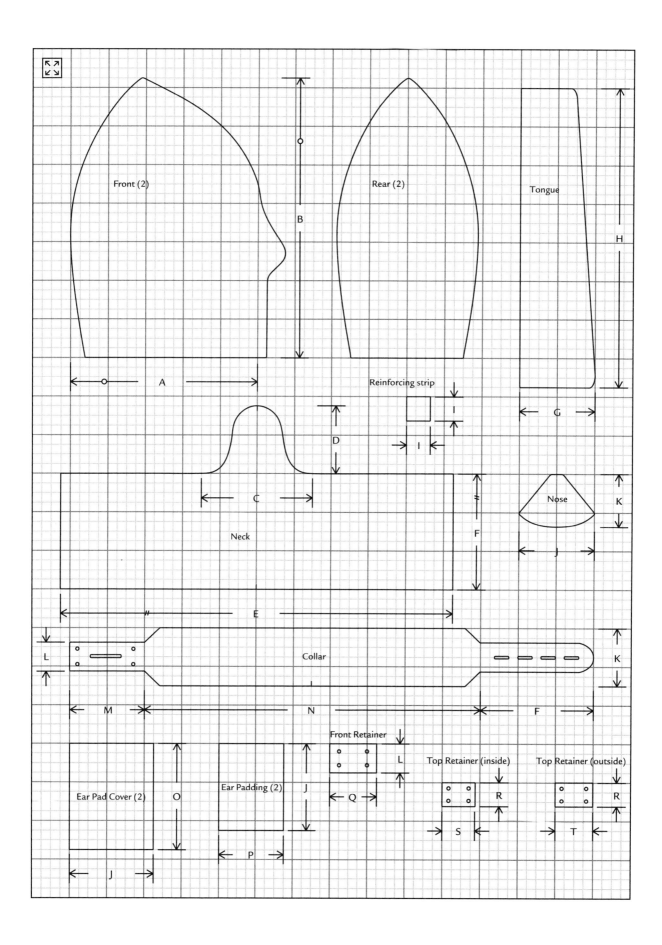

Front (2)

Rear (2)

Tongue

B

H

Reinforcing strip

A

I

I

D

G

C

Nose

Neck

F

K

J

E

Collar

L

K

M

N

F

Front Retainer

L

Ear Pad Cover (2)

O

Ear Padding (2)

J

Q

Top Retainer (inside)

Top Retainer (outside)

R

R

P

S

T

J

Instructions

- Draft the pattern as shown.

- To create the hood's front panel pattern, first draw a horizontal line at the base of a sheet of paper large enough to accommodate two front panels side by side.

- Place the original front panel on the left side of the sheet so that the face is pointing right, lining the bottom of the panel up with the bottom line drawn in the previous step, and trace.

- Make a mark on the bottom line 10mm (³⁄₈") inside the front edge of the traced panel.

- Flip the original front panel over and place it on the right side of the sheet so that the face is pointing left, lining the bottom of the panel up with the bottom line and the front of the panel up with the mark, and trace.

- Mark the center bottom of the complete front panel.

- Sketch the eye, nose, and mouth openings as shown below (fig 5.3).

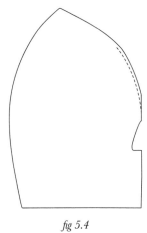

fig 5.4

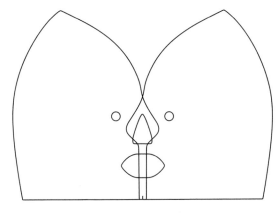

fig 5.3

- Cut out the pattern panel and all openings. The original front panel pattern will not be used further.

- Trace, mark and cut out all the panels and the nose opening. The collar strap and retainers are cut from chap leather, and the remainder from garment leather.

- Fold the front panel grain sides together and sew the front 50mm (2") of the center seam, starting 5mm (³⁄₁₆") from the edge and ending right next to the edge and parallel to the fold by the nose opening (fig 5.4).

- Baste the nose panel over the nose opening, overlapping it by 6mm (¼").

- Sew the nose panel in place 3mm (⅛") from the edge.

- Remove the basting.

- Trace and cut out the eye and mouth appliqués, taking care to make the eye appliqués mirror images of each other.

- Trace and cut out the eye and mouth coverings, taking care to make the eye coverings mirror images of each other. Use the same appliqué patterns as in the previous step, but without cutting the openings.

- Trace the appliqués, flesh side down, on the under side of the loop side of the 100mm (4") hook-and-loop. The hook-and-loop has a grid-like structure, and this should be taken into account when orienting the appliqués to ensure symmetry.

- Cut the openings out of the appliqué traces on the loop.

- Apply contact cement to the areas traced out on the loop, and place the coverings on to the traces, flesh sides down. Press firmly.

- Apply contact cement to the grain side of the appliqués, and stick them to the underside of the hook side of the 100mm (4") hook-and-loop, taking care to ensure symmetry. Press firmly and let all pieces dry overnight.

- Trim the excess hook-and-loop from the appliqués and coverings, and cut openings in the hook to match the appliqués.

- Sew the eye and mouth coverings in two seams, one 2mm (¹⁄₁₆") from the outside edge and another 2mm (¹⁄₁₆") from the inside edge of the loop. This is intricate work and must be done slowly and with care. It is often helpful to adjust the needle position so that the edge can be clearly seen through the presser foot, or a transparent presser foot can be used. The inside seam can be sewn from the grain side, using the trace as a guide, or from the underside of the covering.

- Arrange the appliqués on the front panel, using the eye and mouth markings from the pattern as guides. The mouth appliqué should be lined up with the bottom of the nose opening (and no wider than 10mm (³/₈") on the top side), and the eye appliqués will likely cover a portion of the nose panel. Mark each appliqué's position on the front panel, then apply contact cement to the flesh side of the appliqués and place them on the front panel, using the markings as guides. Press firmly and let dry overnight.

- Sew the eye and mouth appliqués in place with two seams, one 2mm (¹/₁₆") from the outside edge and another 2mm (¹/₁₆") from the inside edge. Again, do this slowly and with care.

- With the stitches firmly in place, pull the leather inside the openings away from the eye and mouth appliqués, and clip it from under the appliqués with small scissors.

- Sew the remainder of the front seam, 5mm (³/₁₆") from the edge.

- Align each rear panel with one side of the front panel, grain sides together, so that the tip extends 5mm (³/₁₆") above the front seam. Sew the panels together 5mm (³/₁₆") from the edge.

- Trim the top and bottom 10mm (³/₈") of the side seam allowances down to 2mm (¹/₁₆").

- Mark the top of the opening on the rear panels 60mm (2³/₈") from the apex.

- Sew the top of the rear panels, grain sides together, 5mm (³/₁₆") from the edge, starting from the opening mark and going over the top of the hood.

- Align the center of the neck panel with the center mark on the bottom of the hood front panel, grain sides together. Sew in place 5mm (³/₁₆") from the edge in two seams, each starting from 20mm (³/₄") to the far side of the center mark. Basting the tongue-shaped protrusion to the front panel prior to sewing can make this easier.

- Check these seams for quality and straightness. Re-sew if necessary.

- Trim 30mm (1¼") of each end of the circumferential seam allowance down to 2mm (¹/₁₆").

- Turn the hood right side out, try it on and check for fit. If it is too big, keeping the 15mm (⁵/₈") meeting edge folds in mind, pinch, mark up and trim. The finished hood's meeting edges should not quite meet, even when laced tightly, to allow for stretch in the leather. Make a mark over one of the ears. Turn the hood inside out again.

- Clip off 15mm (⁵/₈") square sections from the bottom corners of the meeting edges. This step minimizes the layers to be sewn through once the meeting and bottom edges have been folded.

- Apply contact cement to the outer 30mm (1¼") of the flesh side of the meeting edges and make 15mm (⁵/₈") folds.

- Apply contact cement to the bottom 30mm (1¼") of the flesh side of the bottom edge and make a 15mm (⁵/₈") fold.

- Apply contact cement to the flesh side of the reinforcing strip and fix it to the area just above the opening. The strip will be sewn in place when the meeting edge folds are sewn. This reinforcement is generally a good practice with this kind of unreinforced opening.

- Apply contact cement to the left 5mm (³/₁₆") of the grain side of the tongue, and fix it to the inside of the left meeting edge over the fold allowance. Press all edges firmly and let dry overnight.

- Sew the meeting edges from the grain side 10mm (³/₈") from the edge, taking care not to sew through the tongue on the right side.

- Sew the bottom from the grain side, 10mm (³/₈") from the edge.

- Mark eleven evenly spaced eyelet holes on each meeting edge, starting 30mm (1¼") from the top and ending 10mm (³/₈") from the bottom, taking care to ensure symmetry.

- Punch the holes where marked, taking care not to damage the tongue.

- Insert and set the eyelets.

- Transfer the ear marking from the outside of the hood to the inside.

- Place an ear pad cover on the inside of the hood centered on the ear marking, and so that the edges are parallel to the side seam and circumferential seam and mark. Make identical markings on the other side of the hood.

- Apply contact cement to the outer 5mm (³/₁₆") of the top, left and right edges of the flesh side of the ear pad covers and place them on the inside of the hood, using the markings as a guide. Press the edges firmly and let dry overnight.

- Sew the top, left and right edges of the ear covers in place from the inside of the hood 5mm (³/₁₆") from the edge.

- Cut two foam pads measuring 20mm (³/₄") x 60mm (2³/₈") x 80mm (3¹/₈") (see page 152 for foam cutting techniques).

- Inserting the foam pads can be difficult, as the foam will tend to stick to the flesh side of the leather. Try using a pair of needlenose or locking pliers to compress the foam when inserting it. Once the pads are inside the pockets, push the corners of the pads to the corners of the pockets and ensure each pad is lying flat.

- With the foam pads inserted and situated, push them into the pockets a bit further than they should be, apply contact cement to the outer 5mm (³⁄₁₆") of the bottom of the ear pad covers and press in place. Let dry overnight.

- Sew the bottom of the ear pad covers in place 5mm (³⁄₁₆") from the edge.

- Punch the holes in the retainers and collar strap where marked and cut the slots.

- Apply contact cement to the wide section of the collar strap. Place it on the hood's neck panel, centered vertically on the panel and aligning the center marks. Press firmly and let dry overnight.

- Sew the wide section of the collar strap in place in four seams, two running across the top and bottom of the wide section 3mm (¹⁄₈") from the edge, and two more joining the top and bottom seams on each end.

- Fix the buckle in place with medium rivets.

- Mark and punch holes in the center of the collar strap corresponding to the holes in the front retainer. The distance between the top and bottom pairs of holes should be reduced by 5mm (³⁄₁₆").

- Fix the 25mm (1") D-ring to the collar strap using the front retainer and medium rivets.

- Mark and punch four holes, centered on the apex of the hood, using the holes in the inside top retainer as guides.

- Thead the outside top retainer through the 19mm (¾") D-ring, then fix it to to the apex of the hood with medium rivets, sandwiching the hood between the inside top retainer and the outside top retainer.

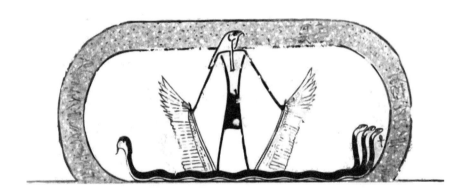

CHAPTER VI

Pleasure

It is said that our ability to experience mystical states grew out of our orgasmic capacity (Newberg, 2001). Just being kept at a heightened level of arousal for an extended period of time can certainly be enough to throw one into an altered state of consciousness.

The projects in this chapter are used to heighten and extend sexual arousal. When this kind of stimulation is combined with some of the of the other tools and techniques in this book, the result can be positively blissful.

The first project in this chapter, like the male harness in Chapter IV, is built around a cock ring. It can be difficult to put on, as one must be fully flaccid in order to get in to

a ring. First, the balls are pulled through the ring one after the other, then the head is pushed through, and then the rest of the penis can be pulled through the ring. The dilemma truly lies in the fact that arousal often occurs long before the ring can be put on. Complicating matters even further is that if any fetishwear is worn, it may have to be put on before the ring – a bodysuit before a body harness being a typical example. Sitting in quiet meditation and dissociating the mind from the body is usually the most efficient method of quelling physical arousal, although accomplishing this feat requires a mastery over one's body that can only be acquired over time. This practice can also serve to get one's lust under control, which if left unchecked can of course prematurely end the scene.

RING HARNESS

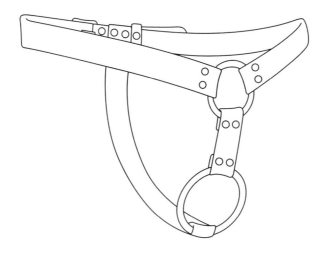

This simple harness has a variety of uses. It can be worn to prolong arousal, or simply because wearing it is arousing. A leash can be clipped to the top ring, which can then be threaded through a collar ring to intensify the sensations. When the leash is then fixed tightly to a restraint point, the harness turns every wriggle into a wave of pleasure, which can keep the wearer aroused for long periods of time, particularly when the harness is used with some of the other projects in this chapter. The cock ring can also be used as a base for the male chastity device presented in Chapter IV, and the harness can also be used in conjunction with the plug harness to keep a plug in place. A finger vibrator can also be clipped to the inside of the vertical eyelet strap.

This design will work on the female anatomy for the abovementioned applications with the cock ring in place, but the design can easily be altered to omit it. Also, reducing the size of the cock ring can turn this project into a strap-on harness.

Tools

- Rotary cutter and ruler
- Rivet setter and anvil
- Drive punch
- Cutting board
- Hammer
- Needle files
- Water pencil
- Measuring tape

Materials

- Chap, medium-heavy vegetable-tanned leather or latigo
- 22 x medium rivets
- 1 x 38mm (1½") ring
- 1 x 51mm (2") ring
- 2 x 25mm (1") heel-bar buckles

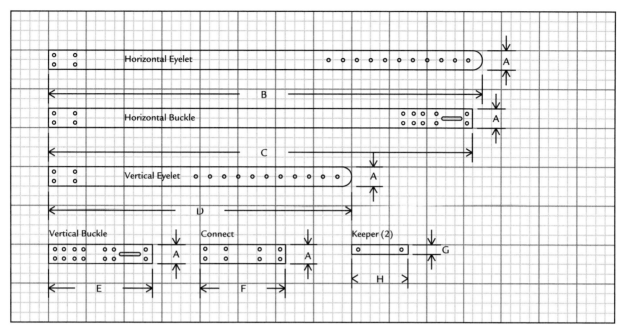

A = 26mm (1")
B = 0.50θ + 100mm (4")
C = 0.50θ + 60mm (2½")
D = 0.33σ + 120mm (4¾")

E = 150mm (6")
F = 130mm (5⅛")
G = 12mm (½")
H = 80mm (3⅛")

Instructions

- Mark and cut the strapping as shown.

- Punch all holes where marked and cut the slots.

- Bevel the grain side of all edges if using vegetable-tanned leather or latigo. Dye and condition if using vegetable-tanned leather, dye the edges if using latigo.

- Fix the buckles in place with medium rivets through the holes closest to the buckles.

- Fix the keepers in place with medium rivets.

- Smooth out the weld on the 51mm (2") ring with a needle file.

- Fold the vertical buckle strap over the horizontal buckle strap so that all of the holes line up and fix in place with medium rivets.

- Fix the horizontal straps to the 38mm (1½") ring with medium rivets.

- Fix the vertical eyelet and connecting straps to the 51mm (2") ring with medium rivets.

- Fix the connecting strap to the 38mm (1½") ring between and below the horizontal straps with medium rivets (fig 6.1).

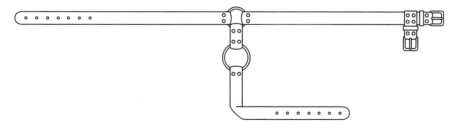

fig 6.1

PLUG HARNESS

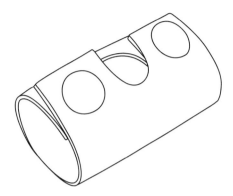

This project is simply a small piece of leather that is fitted around a plug. Once wrapped around the plug, a strap can be threaded through the harness to hold it in place. The harness described here was designed to fit a small plug. To make a custom harness, simply change the value of **A** to the circumference of the plug's base overlapping 20mm (¾"), and the value of **B** to the length of the base. The curved sections are then cut to match the plug.

Tools

- Shears
- Drive punch
- Snap setter and anvil
- Cutting board
- Hammer
- Pencil and ruler
- Water pencil

Materials

- Chap, medium-heavy vegetable-tanned leather or latigo
- 2 x short snaps
- Paper

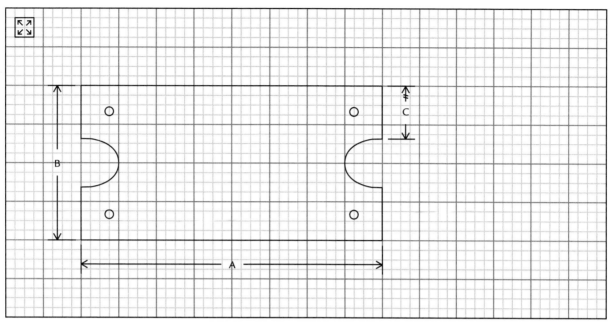

A = 125mm (5")
B = 65mm (2½")

C = 22mm (⁷⁄₈")

Instructions

- Draft the pattern as shown.

- Trace and cut out the harness.

- Use a snap cap to mark the holes by placing it on each of the desired spots and pressing it into the leather.

- Punch the holes where marked.

- Bevel the grain side of all edges if using vegetable-tanned leather or latigo. Dye and condition if using vegetable-tanned leather, dye the edges if using latigo.

- Set the male halves of the snaps in one side of the harness and the female halves in the other (fig 3.19 on page 108).

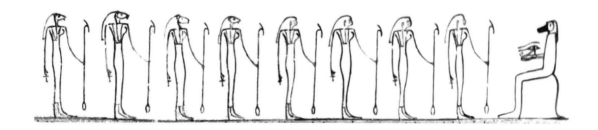

STRAP HARNESS

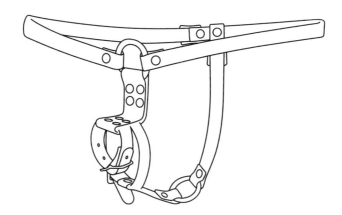

This harness is similar in functionality to the ring harness, but is comprised of a network of straps and buckles. This design is advantageous not only because of the harness's adjustability, but also because it is easier to get into when the wearer is aroused.

This harness is designed to be used in conjunction with the sheath on page 180. If the sheath will not be made, the snap can be replaced with a medium rivet. As discussed on page 174, sensation can be intensified and arousal prolonged when a leash is attached to the ring and threaded through a collar ring.

Tools

- Shears
- Rotary cutter
- Drive punch
- Rivet setter and anvil
- Snap setter and anvil
- Cutting board
- Hammer
- Measuring tape
- Water pencil

Materials

- Chap or light-medium vegetable-tanned leather
- 17 x medium rivets
- 1 x short snap (male half)
- 1 x 25mm (1") ring
- 1 x 32mm (1¼") ring
- 4 x 13mm (½") center-bar buckles

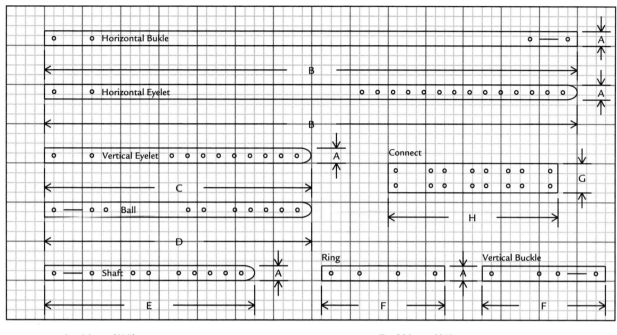

A = 14mm (½")   E = 200mm (8")
B = 0.50θ + 100mm (4")   F = 120mm (4¾")
C = 0.15σ +150mm (6")   G = 26mm (1")
D = 260mm (10")   H = 180mm (7")

Instructions

- Mark and cut the strapping as shown.

- Punch all holes where marked and cut the slots.

- Bevel the grain side of all edges, dye and condition if using vegetable-tanned leather.

- Assemble harness with medium rivets (fig 6.2). Note that the ring connecting strap is fixed to the ball strap with the snap.

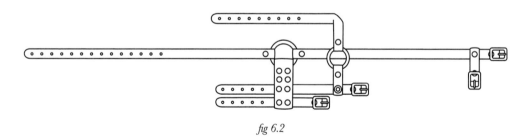

fig 6.2

Sheath

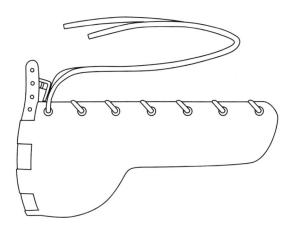

This device is designed to be used in conjunction with the strap harness on page 178. It works well during long periods to maintain arousal without any direct stimulation. The sheath can also allow the wearer to be brought to orgasm with a crop or other percussive means, and can produce intense stimulation when touched with a vibrator. If the wearer will be brought to orgasm while wearing the sheath, a condom should be fitted over the head of the penis inside the sheath.

Tools

- Sewing machine (leather needle)
- Shears
- Drive punch
- Rivet setter and anvil
- Snap setter and anvil
- Eyelet setter and anvil
- Cutting board
- Hammer
- Pencil and ruler
- Water pencil

Materials

- Garment leather
- Chap leather
- Matching thread
- 1200mm (47") shoelace
- 1 x medium rivets
- 1 x small snap (female half)
- 14 x short eyelets
- 1 x 13mm (½") center-bar buckle
- Contact cement
- Paper

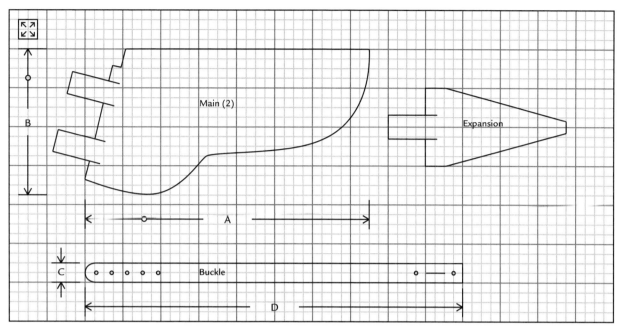

A = υ + 60mm (2⅜")   C = 14mm (½")

B = 125mm (5")   D = 350mm (14")

Instructions

- Draft the pattern as shown. The tabs extending from each panel should all be the same size, approximately 20mm (¾") wide, and should extend 30mm (1¼") from the panel and 10mm (⅜") inside the panel.

- Trace and cut out all pieces, taking care to make the two main panels mirror images of each other. The main and expansion panels are cut from garment leather, and the buckle strap from chap leather.

- Sew the two main panels, grain sides together, from the top of the curve down to the beginning of the next one, 5mm (³⁄₁₆") from the edge (fig 6.3).

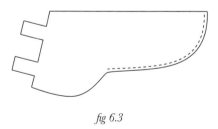

fig 6.3

- Sew the expansion panel to the curved portion of each main panel, grain sides together, 5mm (³⁄₁₆") from the edge (fig 6.4).

- Trim the top 30mm (1¼") of the main seam allowance and the bottom 20mm (¾") of the expansion seam allowances down to 2mm (¹⁄₁₆").

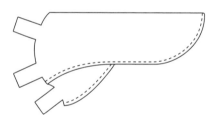

fig 6.4

- Apply contact cement to the outer 20mm (¾") of flesh side of the rear of the sheath and the tips of the tabs as shown (fig 6.5).

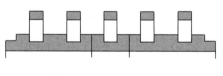

fig 6.5

- Fold each section of the rear to make 10mm (⅜") folds and 15mm (⅝") tabs.

- Apply contact cement to the outer 30mm (1¼") of the flesh side of the meeting edges, and make 15mm (⅝") folds. Press all edges firmly and let dry overnight.

- Sew the meeting edges from the grain side, 10mm (⅜") from the edge.

- Sew the rear in two seams from the flesh side, 2mm (¹⁄₁₆") from the inside edge and 2mm (¹⁄₁₆") from the fold.

- Mark seven evenly spaced eyelet holes on each meeting edge, starting 15mm (⁵⁄₈") from the tip and ending 10mm (³⁄₈") from the rear, taking care to ensure symmetry.

- Mark the holes and the slot on the buckle strap.

- Punch all holes where marked and cut the slot.

- Fix the buckle in place with a medium rivet.

- Insert and set all the eyelets in the meeting edges.

- Thread the strap through the tabs, using a lacing needle if necessary.

- With the strap positioned, punch a hole through the center tab and strap.

- Mount the female half of the snap with the cap on the grain side of this hole and set in place.

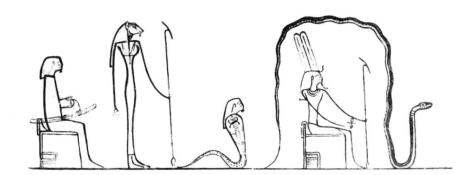

CORSET SHEATH

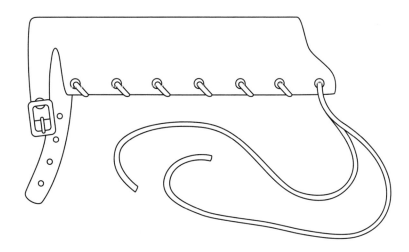

This simple sheath is made of a single piece of either medium vegetable-tanned or chap leather. It is designed to be slightly smaller than the circumference of the erect penis, to allow it to be laced tightly. This can be made easier by using a thicker round lace that barely fits through the eyelets of the sheath.

A finger vibrator can be fixed to the sensitive underside of the glans using the lace and the top three pairs of eyelets. This combination can allow the wearer to be gradually brought to orgasm without ever being touched.

Tools

- Shears
- Drive punch
- Rivet setter and anvil
- Eyelet setter and anvil
- Cutting board
- Hammer
- Measuring tape
- Small foam brush
- Pencil and ruler
- Water pencil
- Small clean rag

Materials

- Medium vegetable-tanned or chap leather
- 1200mm (47") shoelace (thick)
- 1 x medium rivet
- 12 x short eyelets
- 1 x 13mm (½") center-bar buckle
- Dye
- Leather conditioner
- Paper

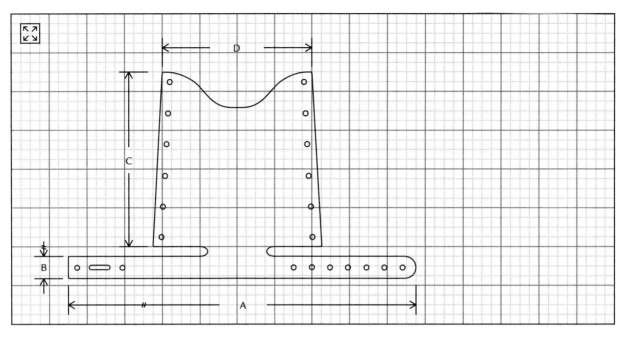

A = 260mm (10¼")

B = 14mm (½")

C = υ - 60mm (2⅜")

D = 115mm (4½")

Instructions

- Draft the pattern as shown.

- Trace, mark and cut out the sheath.

- Punch all holes where marked and cut the slot.

- Bevel the grain side of all edges. Dye and condition if using vegetable-tanned leather.

- Insert and set all eyelets.

- Fix the buckle in place with a medium rivet.

- Thread the shoelace through the eyelets so that the ends are at the top of the sheath. Make knots in them to prevent the lace from coming out.

CHAPTER VII

Pain

Pleasure intensifies when preceded or accompanied by pain. Beyond its contrasting and amplifying value, though, physical discipline can be an end in itself. Some crave the sheer intensity of the sensation, which can be experienced few other ways. Others prefer to be beaten into ecstasy. And pain can actually quiet the mind and enhance one's focus. Pain can help us truly and fully inhabit our bodies, allowing us to touch the essence of the physical world.

Using pain

Pain can be a versatile tool when it comes to play and submissive training. It can be used as punishment for transgressions (but for the masochist it is more aptly used as a reward). Pain can also be used to test and push the submissive's limits, and with respect to the play ritual forms discussed on page 211, pain could be considered a form of sacrifice.

Self-flagellation has been used in a spiritual context by a variety of cultures, including the Christian traditions. Priests and monks of some orders are known to flog their backs, ostensibly as a form of penance, though ultimately producing a change of consciousness.

Flagellation can have a variety of effects on the body and mind. Its best-known effect is triggering the release of endorphins and other endogenous opiates, as well as histamine and adrenaline. The kind of intense rhythmic stimulation one experiences while being flogged can cause a spillover effect in the autonomic nervous system, catapulting one to an ecstatic mystical state.

The spillover effect

The autonomic nervous system is composed of arousal (sympathetic) and quiescent (parasympathetic) subsystems. They are normally antagonistic to each other: increased activity in one tends to mean decreased activity in the other. However, if one system is driven to maximal activity, a spillover effect can activate rather than inhibit the other.

The brain states produced by the spillover effect have been experienced by meditators, shamans and religious mystics for centuries, and have been given names such as nirvana, samadhi, ecstasy, absorption and unity. Calming the mind sufficiently encourages the spillover effect by exploiting the quiescent subsystem, producing a paradoxical state of activated or energized serenity (Newberg, D'Aquili & Rause, 2001). On the other side of the coin, flagellation can drive the arousal subsystem to its maximum, activating the quiescent system to produce a state better experienced than described.

Putting it together

The stimulation inflicted by the projects in this chapter can be intensified with use of the restraints in Chapter IV and even more so with the sensory deprivation projects in Chapter V. The rhythm of the lashes can easily be kept from someone who can't see them coming, and an unexpected stroke after the submissive has been allowed to drift can feel extraordinary. In Chan Buddhism, the Chinese precursor to Zen, there is a tradition of unexpectedly "smacking" enlightenment in to the student. The master surprises the students with a slap from the palm of his hand, often as an answer to a question. Even today, Zen students whose posture or concentration wanes are brought back into focus by being struck on the back or shoulders with a keisaku, or encouragement stick – sometimes at the request of the student.

Plaited projects

Editor's note: U.S. readers may be more accustomed to hearing the process of whipmaking called "braiding." We have retained the author's "plaiting" as more elegant and universal.

With the exception of the easy flogger, the projects in this chapter tend to be quite time-consuming, requiring a great deal of dexterity and focus. However, if the patience can be found, crafting the plaited whips presented in this chapter can be a very rewarding experience.

Handles

The flogger and singletail handles are made of hardwood and covered with a 12-lace plait. The handle cores must be reduced to precise diameters, which will mean some hand-carving unless a lathe is available. It is imperative that you use a strong, dense hardwood, as the diameter of the holes bored into the length of the handles is not much smaller than the diameter of the handles themselves. Purchasing a replacement furniture leg from a hardware or building supply store is often a satisfactory and convenient way of obtaining a piece of hardwood close to the desired dimensions. Once the threaded metal post is unscrewed with a pair of locking pliers, these legs become even more convenient: the pre-drilled hole is in precisely the right place, and is often the right diameter and depth as well. If the hole is too narrow, it can be widened with a drill, or even with a round file.

The flogger's handle core is weighted with a lag screw and washers, a technique which could potentially be applied to the singletail as well. This proess improves the balance of the whip, and using a lag screw as a counterweight also allows for a unique way of mounting the laces on the handle core. The prescribed diameter of the holes in the handle cores is 9.5mm (³⁄₈"), to accommodate a lag screw

of the same diameter. Like many other materials called for in this book, lag screws are generally sold in imperial units. If metric lag screws are available and desired, use 9mm or 10mm and a matching drill bit, which should also suffice for the hole at the top to the singletail handle core, to accommodate the belly of the whip. The difficulty in counterweighting the singletail is that drilling a hole in the bottom of the handle core that nearly meets the hole in the top will weaken it significantly. If counterweighting the singletail, use a larger diameter handle core, a shorter lag screw, or a denser material.

After the hole for the lag screw has been bored, put the desired number of washers on the screw and turn it halfway into the core. If the fit is tight, you may wish first to wrap the core tightly, to guard against splitting. With this mounting method, the starts of the laces must be cut to a point forming a 45° angle and punctured with an awl (fig 7.1). The laces are then threaded on to a length of artificial sinew, using a leather needle, and tied snugly around the screw. After the laces have been arranged evenly around the end of the handle core, the screw is tightened the rest of the way.

fig 7.1

If you are not weighting the handle core you may omit the hole in the bottom and mount the laces using tacks. This process can be difficult, but can be made considerably easier by holding the tack in place with a pair of pliers when striking it with a hammer. The laces will generally have to overlap somewhat to achieve even spacing around the handle core.

Laces

Some of the finest whips are made from kangaroo leather. Due to the cost and difficulty of obtaining an appropriate skin, though, the plaited projects in this chapter use light vegetable-tanned cow leather. Once you've developed cutting, skiving and plaiting skills, investing in kangaroo leather is certainly an option. The principal difference to be taken into consideration when using kangaroo is that it is considerably thinner than cow. In this case, you'll want to increase the diameter of the handle, and probably add a second bolster to the singletail. Note that garment leather and suede are generally too soft to be skived (see below) and have too much stretch to be used for plaiting.

To get started, purchase a side of 1oz vegetable-tanned leather, taking care to check for too many marks and scars beforehand if possible, and then marking these with pen after the purchase. Once the back and belly are marked or cut from the skin (fig 3.1 on page 52), the laces can be marked and cut. Some of the laces required may be longer than the length of the skin, so they will have to start at one end and curve around the back of the other (fig 7.2). The radius of the curve should be as large as the skin will accommodate, as too small a radius will cause the laces to kink when they are plaited. This should also be kept in mind when cutting around scars. Working around each scar or mark should end up leaving a waste piece pointed on both ends, as wide as the scar, and 50-100mm (2"-4") long, depending on the width of the scar.

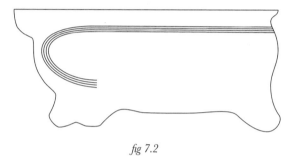

fig 7.2

Take notice of slight differences in the thickness of the skin before you mark and cut the laces. These variations typically occur at back and belly. A very small variation can mean a significant variation in the thickness over the plait, as the diameter of the plait is comprised of the core and four lace thicknesses. Special tools can be purchased to make the lace thickness uniform, and this task can also be performed with a wood plane, but you can often avoid having to splice the laces by carefully choosing what part of the skin to use for each part of the whip. The thickest skin at the back of the side is fine for cutting the belly laces.

Laces for plaiting whips are often cut to taper from one width down to another. Although whipmakers are known to cut laces freehand with a knife, tapering fractions of a millimeter at a time without measurement or a guide, a somewhat more structured method will be used here. Each lace is divided into several sections, each a millimeter thinner than the last. Although lace cutting can be accomplished by marking the lace width every 200mm (8") or so with a pen and then cutting with a sharp pair of shears, you may want to consider investing in an Australian strander (fig 1.13 on page 7). With this device, only the width change points must be marked on the leather. When

the markings are reached, you simply move the guide a millimeter and continue the process. Some, by preference or necessity, build stranding devices consisting of a blade fixed to a block of wood with an adjustable guide which approximate the function of the strander. This step-down tapering will not be noticed after the laces have been skived, which means to cut an approximately 45° angle on both sides of the lace (fig 7.3).

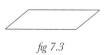

fig 7.3

Skiving

The laces are skived to help them fit together to form a round plait. Tools made specifically for skiving do exist, but the best way to skive leather for whipmaking is by hand, with a razor-sharp blade. Any knife that can be brought to a razor's edge will suffice for skiving, but it will likely need to be resharpened several times during the course of skiving the singletail. As soon as the edge gets the least bit dull it will become difficult to control, which will effectively make the edge of the lace uneven. I recommend using a good-quality utility knife with replaceable snap-off blades. As soon as you feel any resistance, snap off the blade and expose a new edge.

Before attempting to make any of the plaited whips, cut and skive four 7mm x 1.5m (¼" x 60") laces to practice the techniques used in this chapter. If they're not too badly mangled, you can use them later to make the belly of the singletail.

You must skive all laces that will be plaited, but not laces to be used for weaving knots. To skive a lace, first secure one end of a length of artificial sinew or waxed cotton to a fixed point around waist height (a table leg works well), and the other to the start of the lace. When skiving the singletail overlay, you'll need around three meters of open floor radiating away from the fixed point in one direction – less space for shorter laces. If nothing suitable can be found, you'll need to mount a hook somewhere with the required space, or take the task outdoors. Once the lace is fixed in place, wrap the base of the index finger of your non-dominant hand in tape: electrical, fabric, or duct. The blade rests on this area, and the tape will prevent it from getting cut. Begin by holding the lace taut in your non-dominant hand, between your thumb and index finger. With the knife in your dominant hand, place the blade over the lace with the tip resting on the taped finger (fig 7.4 on page 188). Begin skiving a few millimeters from the thread by cutting a slice running from the bottom corner of the lace to 1mm-2mm (¹/₃₂"-¹/₁₆") inside the top left edge, making a 45° angle. Holding the blade steady, feed

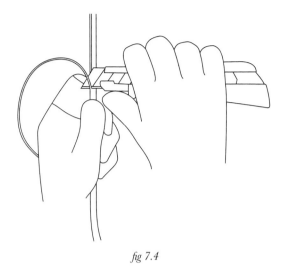

fig 7.4

the lace through your non-dominant hand as you slowly walk backward until you reach the end of the lace.

Once you've skived the first edge, flip the lace over and skive the other side.

Dyeing

After the laces have been skived, they are ready to be dyed. The plaited whip projects all include this step, although dyeing the laces is not strictly necessary: undyed whips can be quite attractive, and tend to get more so over time. If you're not dyeing the laces, mark them with a pencil or an awl instead of ink. As with the previous projects, the only tool required for dyeing is a small foam brush or dauber. When dyeing laces, though, it is easier to hold the brush stationary and draw the laces underneath it, rather than moving the brush along the laces. If a large amount of dye and a suitable vessel are available, the laces could also be dip-dyed. Be sure to wear gloves when dip-dyeing, and pull each lace through the thumb and index finger to wring out excess dye before drying. If using a brush or dauber, the laces will require two coats – vegetable-tanned leather is quite absorbent – although both coats can be put on one directly after the other. Once they have been dyed satisfactorily, they should be double-checked then left to dry overnight before plaiting.

Plaiting

To plait means to interweave, or braid. Once the laces are cut, skived, dyed, and dried, they are ready to be either bound together or mounted on the handle core and plaited. Once bound or mounted, tie a slipknot around the end of the work with a length of artificial sinew or waxed cotton, and tie the other end to a fixed point so that the work is around seated eye level. Whether you do your plaiting seated or standing is of course up

to you, but you will wish to be reasonably comfortable when taking on the larger projects.

When plaiting leather, the laces are first softened with plaiting soap to help them form a tight plait. Plaiting soap cannot generally be purchased, but you can make some fairly easily using the recipe below. This recipe will make enough soap for many whips, and can be scaled down if desired.

Plaiting soap

1 bar of plain soap (90g/3 oz)
300ml (10 oz) water
340g (12 oz) shortening

- Unwrap and grate the soap into a saucepan.

- Pour in the water and heat slowly while stirring.

- When all the soap has dissolved, add the shortening and bring the mixture to a gentle boil while stirring.

- After boiling the mixture for about ten minutes, take the saucepan off the stove and let it cool. Pour the plaiting soap into a wide-mouthed storage container before it hardens.

With the work mounted, apply the plaiting soap liberally to each lace and begin plaiting. When working with shorter laces, the entire length of each lace can be soaped up at once – but when plaiting the overlay of the singletail, only around a quarter of the overall length should be soaped up at a time. As you approach the end of the soaped-up laces, move the slipknot closer to the unplaited section and soap up the next quarter of the overlay.

Several different plaiting techniques are used in this chapter, though they are all round plaits, and very similar. The belly of the singletail is made of a 4-lace plait around a twisted leather core (fig 7.5 on page 189), which is the same plait used to make the crop. The flogger handle and the singletail overlay both begin with a 12-lace handle plait (fig 7.7 on page 190). On the singletail this switches to a 12-lace thong plait, then drops two laces to make a 10-lace plait, then eight, then finally six. The 12-lace handle plait is tighter and more decorative than the 12-lace thong plait. The handle plait pattern goes under two laces, over two, then under two, whereas the thong plait goes under three and over three. The transition from a 3-step plait to a 2-step is awkward, and will be covered with a turks-head knot.

The plaits are all basically comprised of two interwoven sets of laces running in opposite directions around a core, so that it is covered twice over (fig 7.6 on page 189).

Picturing how the sets of laces wrap around the core, or even wrapping a strip of leather (representing the set)

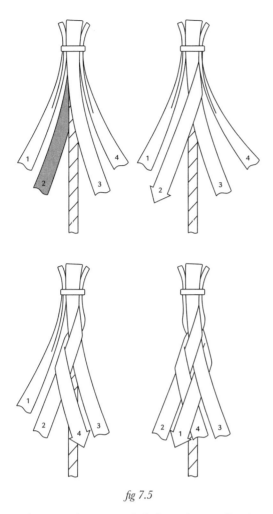

fig 7.5

around an actual core, can help in understanding how only certain combinations of lace widths and numbers of laces per set will work. In fig 7.6, the solid lines represent the strip of leather, the dashed lines represent how that strip would be divided into six laces (as in a 12-lace plait), and the gray lines represent the laces that would run in the other direction. Notice that the angle at which the laces exit, and therefore should be pulled, changes with the diameter of the core. In practice, of course, rather than laying one set of laces on top of the other, the two sets would be interwoven.

The weave pattern changes with the number of laces, and even with the same number many different patterns are possible (see Ron Edwards's book *How to Make Whips* for examples of how to plait complex patterns such as letters into your whips). Generally, though, the weave pattern is no more complicated than wrapping the top lace on the right around the core, going under x laces and over y, then wrapping the top left lace around the core, under x laces, over y, and repeating.

When the laces of the set are of different lengths, as in the singletail, the laces must be plaited from shortest to longest. The order should be checked periodically to ensure that an error has not been made: if the shortest laces are not plaited one after the other, some or all of the work will need to be backtracked and plaited again.

When you take a break from the work, make sure that the laces from the respective sets do not intermingle. Bind the laces from one of the sets together, either with a twist tie or bit of string, or tie the laces together in a loose knot.

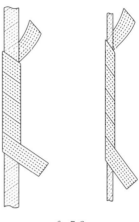

fig. 7.6

The example in fig 7.7 on page 190 describes a 12-lace handle plait, which is used in both the flogger and singletail projects. This is the only plaiting required on the flogger, and is the starting plait on the singletail from which the remainder of the singletail plaits will be reduced. The other plaits are woven in the same manner with different over and under patterns.

12-lace handle plait	. . .under 2, over 2, under 2
12-lace thong plait	. . . .under 3, over 3
10-lace plait	. . . . .under 3, over 2
8-lace plait	. . . . .under 2, over 2
6-lace plait	. . . . .under 2, over 1
4-lace plait	. . . . .under 1, over 1

When using fig 7.7 on page 190 to plait the handle on the singletail, the laces marked 1 correspond to the laces tagged overlay 1 in the pattern, laces marked 2 to overlay 2, laces marked 3 to overlay 3, and the laces marked 4, 5 and 6 to overlay 4.

To start the plait, first divide the laces into two groups, taking care to ensure that each group contains at least one of each lace length, and that they run from shortest to longest moving away from the division.

Although this is a round plait, meaning the laces are wrapped around the core as they are woven, the first steps in starting the plait are woven over the handle core.

1.

2. U1

3. U1

4. U2

5. U2

6. O1 U2

7. U2 O2 U2

8. U2 O2 U2

9. U2 O2 U2

10. U2 O2 U2

11. U2 O2 U2

12. U2 O2 U2

fig 7.7

Notice how the first three laces from each set are plaited in front, then the final three from each set are wrapped around the handle core as they are woven.

Once each lace has been plaited once, the process continues by taking the highest lace on the plait (fig 7.8), wrapping it around the core, and weaving it according to the "under two, over two, under two" pattern so that it ends up as the bottom lace on the same side. If you're not sure which lace is the next one to be plaited, remember: it's always the one highest up on the plait (respecting of course the right, left, right, left progression).

When you switch from one plait to the next, you will tie off the two shortest laces, the pattern will change, and the process will continue. The point at which the laces should be tied off is determined as the whip is plaited – usually when the plait becomes loose, or when there is only 100mm (4") of the laces left unplaited.

To tie off the laces, cross them over each other and pierce them with an awl. Then, run matching waxed cotton through the hole with a leather needle and around the belly and laces tightly several times, then tie off and clip the ends of the thread (fig 7.8). The ends of the laces should be cut to taper to a point, and should be pushed to opposite sides of the core, before being plaited over, to ensure as smooth a transition as possible.

It is very important that the laces be plaited as tightly as possible: a tight plait will make an excellent, long-lasting whip, whereas a loose plait will become even looser after rolling and will result in a shabby or even non-functioning whip. To achieve a tight plait, each lace must be pulled taut in the correct direction after it has been woven in place. Again, the direction in which the laces should be pulled relates to their width, the number of laces in the set, and the diameter of the core, and can be intuited by imagining how the set of laces wraps around the core (fig 7.6 on page 189). As the thickness of the core changes, so will the direction in which the laces are

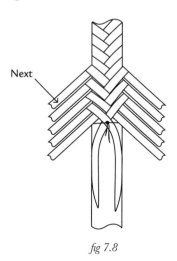

Next

fig 7.8

pulled. This guideline becomes particularly critical when transitioning from the handle core to the belly and bolster on the singletail. Also, if the laces are pulled directly to the side of the work, the weave of the plait will be much tighter in the front than the rear. For an even plait, each lace must be pulled in the direction in which it exits the plait: somewhat behind the plait as you look at it, rather than directly to the side. The laces should be pulled very hard, and it is advisable to give each lace an additional pull after each sequence. This can be tiring work, and is very hard on the hands. When you're plaiting large or complex projects, take regular breaks.

Rolling

After the laces have been plaited and the ends bound together or tacked in place, roll the plait between two boards to help the laces fit together better and give the plait a rounder shape (fig 7.9). A large cutting board will suffice for the bottom board, and the smaller board should be 250-300mm (10"-12") long and nearly as wide. Cover both boards with several layers of newspaper to provide traction and absorb excess plaiting soap (use packing or white paper if the whip is undyed, or dyed a color other than black). The paper may become saturated or tear, and thus may need to be replaced to complete one rolling.

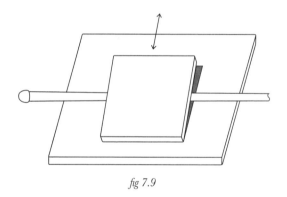

fig 7.9

Knots

In addition to the plaiting techniques, all the plaited whips use decorative turks-head knots to cover transitions and finish the knobs at the ends of the handles. You'll need an awl to weave a tight turks-head knot, and a lacing needle fixed to the working end of the lace will make the process a lot easier.

Before weaving the knots, you'll need to prepare the surface where the knot will be woven by removing any residual plaiting soap, as it will prevent the knot from adhering. Rub the area with some solvent, such as rubbing alcohol. Then you can build up a suitable base, or bolster, or the falls in the flogger project, for the knot to be woven over.

For handle knobs and flogger falls, apply contact cement to the flesh side of the bolster or base. Then tack it onto the handle core, wrap it around the core tightly, and tack the other end in place. You should add a few additional tacks around the circumference at this point. When you tack the bolster to the handle core, your tacks may encounter the tacks holding the laces in place underneath. So if you feel resistance or the tack bends, remove and discard the tack and choose a slightly different location for the next tack. Take care to choose tacks whose length is sufficient to adequately penetrate the core, but not so long as to be obstructed by the lag screw (if you're using one) at the center of the handle. If your core cannot be tacked, you must secure the bolster to the base some other way, such as the bolster on the crop, which is built up with artificial sinew and repeated dipping in contact cement.

If you've weighted the handle with a lag screw, you'll need to make a small leather cap for the bolt head. Cut a circular piece of vegetable-tanned leather with a diameter 5mm (³/₁₆") wider than the diameter of the core and bolster. Soak this in hot water for ten minutes, then form it into the shape of a dome as it dries. Let it dry overnight, then trim it to fit the core and bolster, dye it to match the laces, and fix it in place with a liberal amount of contact cement. Pressing the cap in place can be made easier with the use of a 1" ring. If you don't use a lag screw, a small disc of vegetable-tanned leather matching the diameter of the core and bolster and dyed to match the laces will suffice.

Once fixed in place, the bolster is then rounded by hand using a utility knife. If you're making a bolster for a cylindrical knot, only the edges need to be rounded, but for a spherical knot, the bolster should of course be rounded into a spherical shape. The degree to which the bolster will be rounded should be kept in mind when determining the placement of the tacks, as with a spherical knot they should be as close to the widthwise center as the handle structure will allow.

There is an infinite variety of turks-head knots, with the knot families classified by how many "parts" and "bights" they have (fig 7.10). The parts are the number

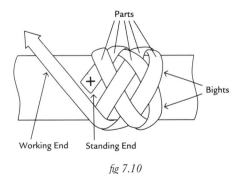

fig 7.10

of laces that would be cut through if a cut was made across the knot, and the bights are the loops or turn-around points at the top and bottom of the knot.

When making a spherical handle knob, you are rather limited in your knot options, as the bights all have to come together at the center of the end of the knot (if there are too many bights, the knot will not close). The 5-part, 4-bight knot is popular with whipmakers for this reason. Depending on the size of the bolster and the width of the laces, 6-bight knots can also work. The goal is to cover the bolster and cap completely, and one pass of a knot with a small number of parts and bights may not suffice. The solution is to add a second pass to the knot, essentially following the original lace around the knot so that the first and second passes lie side by side throughout the knot.

One might think that adding parts but not bights to the knot would eliminate the need for a second pass. Unfortunately, this strategy doesn't usually work: if the number of parts is much greater than the number of bights, the knot will be more of a cylinder than a sphere, and if tied around a spherical bolster will not cover the bolster or look right.

You can, however, give a spherical knot the illusion of having many parts by interweaving a third pass on the 5-part 4-bight knot, splitting the first two passes. There are two ways of going about this. You can cut the lace long enough for three passes, and simply split the first two passes with the third. I don't recommend this strategy, however, because the splitting pass should have actually been the second pass rather than the third, and will result in a small error at the base of the knot. The error-free alternative is to use two laces, one long enough only for two passes, and a second for the third pass. If you're using two laces, do not clip the ends of the first lace until the second is in place. Once both laces have been tightened, the ends can be clipped and colored.

There are many different ways of approaching most turks-head knots, some easier than others. Both the 5-part 4-bight and 7-part 6-bight knots are actually expanded from the 3-part 2-bight knot, which is one of their most interesting and useful properties. When tying them, start with the 3-part 2-bight, then expand it to a 5-part 4-bight. From there, the same technique can be used to augment the knot to 7-part 6-bight, 9-part 8-bight, ad infinitum.

The 3-part 2-bight knot is very simple to tie, and the expansion technique is also easy to understand. Armed with this information, you can tie very complex knots with relative ease. Using a cylindrical bolster rather than a spherical one allows for knots with dozens of parts and bights, all tied with these simple techniques.

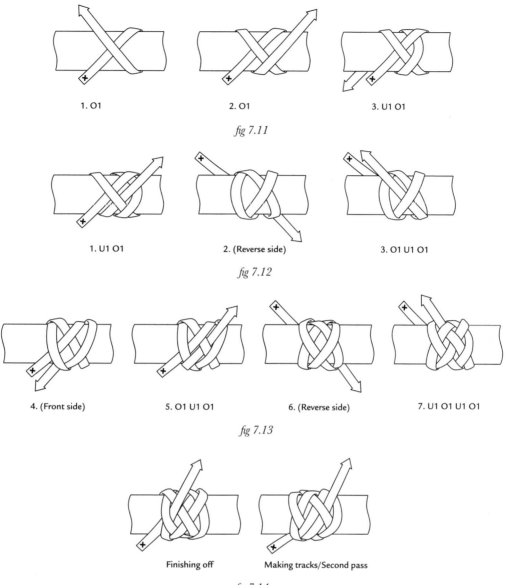

1. O1   2. O1   3. U1 O1

fig 7.11

1. U1 O1   2. (Reverse side)   3. O1 U1 O1

fig 7.12

4. (Front side)   5. O1 U1 O1   6. (Reverse side)   7. U1 O1 U1 O1

fig 7.13

Finishing off   Making tracks/Second pass

fig 7.14

It is generally much easier to tie turks-head knots around a long cylinder than any other shape. For this reason, it is usually best to first tie the knot around a mandrel, a cylindrical core of a diameter similar to that of the bolster. A wide wooden dowel, its diameter increased with tape if necessary, can often suffice. Once the knot is tied on the mandrel, it can be transferred to the bolster and tightened little by little. The mandrel can also make it easier to hold the lace in place when completing the initial steps. The 3-part 2-bight knot does not have enough weaves to be stable on its own, so must be held in place while it is expanded. To tie the 3-part 2-bight knot, follow the steps outlined in fig 7.11.

The first step in expanding the knot is often called "making tracks," and involves simply threading in the working end of the lace next to the original pass on the near side, following its under-over pattern.

When the top of the knot is reached, which will not take long on this particular knot, cross over two, then under the next, then follow that pass down the near side (fig 7.12).

When you reach the starting point again, it's time to begin the second part of the expansion, called "splitting tracks." First, take the working end and cross over two laces, then split the two parallel tracks from the previous step, going under the pass they cross over. Follow these strands, splitting them by going over the passes they go under, and vice versa. When you reach the top, which again will not take long with this knot, go over one, then under the next, splitting the remaining tracks as before until the starting point is reached (fig 7.13). It may be helpful to practice these techniques with a shoelace prior to working with leather.

After completing each expansion, rearrange the knot so that it is spread evenly about the surface of the mandrel. You may have to loosen the knot: if the knot is very tight on the mandrel, it will make the following expansion difficult. If you're planning on making a second pass on the knot, do so after the knot has been transferred to the actual bolster. The knot should not sit too tightly in this case, either. Once the knot, with all expansions and passes, is transferred and complete, tighten it with the help of an awl. Take care not to overtighten the knot, though, as doing so can overstretch the lace and create gaps.

In addition to the degrees of complexity, turks-head knots also come in a variety of styles, determined by the over-under pattern of the laces. The "over one under one" pattern can be rather limiting when weaving more complex knots. As the width of the lace approaches the thickness of the lace, there will inevitably be noticeable gaps around each weave. Also, the friction that all these over and under passes impose on the lace, while making the knot very tight, can stretch the lace as the knot is woven, making the gaps even bigger. Moving to an "under two over two" pattern is a simple solution to this problem, so I suggest you explore the gaucho knot (fig 7.15). (Several books are dedicated to these kinds of knots, if you wish to explore further variations.)

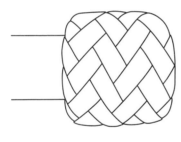

fig 7.15

The gaucho knot is based on the 5-part 4-bight knot, but can be applied to knots augmented from that base knot, such a 7-part 6-bight, etc. Basically, the knot is being expanded again, but on the far side rather than the near side (as described in the expansion technique figs 7.12 and 7.13 on page 193), and working toward an "over two under two" pattern.

- Start the first step by going over the standing end of the lace, then under one. Each successive step begins by going under one, except for the last step which starts by going under two.

- The first step will follow the original pass, except for going over two at the top of the knot.

- The following two steps will involve adding an under two before the final over two.

- Each successive two steps will involve adding an over two or under two alternately until the starting point is reached again.

In this example, a single-pass 5-part 4-bight knot is expanded to an 9-part 7-bight gaucho knot. After the base knot is tied (but not tightened), take the working end of the lace, wrap it around the standing end, and follow it up on the far side to the top of the knot. From there, when the top lace is reached, turn around and go under the next bight – but this time, instead of following the first pass exactly, use the pattern in Step 2.

With the exception of the first and last steps, notice how each pattern is repeated before proceeding to the next (e.g. steps 2 & 3, 4 & 5).

You can tie a herringbone knot using a similar algorithm. You can expand it using a separate lace, on the near side rather than the far side, and each step ending in under two.

	13-part 11-bight (from 7p6b)	9-part 7-bight (from 5p4b)
Step 1	O U O U O U O2	O U O U O2
Step 2	U O U O U2 O2	U O U2 O2
Step 3	U O U O U2 O2	U O U2 O2
Step 4	U O U O2 U2 O2	U O2 U2 O2
Step 5	U O U O2 U2 O2	U O2 U2 O2
Step 6	U O U2 O2 U2 O2	U2 O2 U2 O2
Step 7	U O U2 O2 U2 O2	
Step 8	U O2 U2 O2 U2 O2	
Step 9	U O2 U2 O2 U2 O2	
Step 10	U2 O2 U2 O2 U2 O2	

Laces for weaving knots should be cut from leather with as little stretch as possible. Also, it is very important that the knot lace not be skived, and that plaiting soap not be used. After the knot has been woven, smooth the surface by first rolling it lightly. Then round the edges

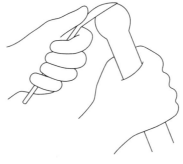

fig 7.16

by rubbing them with a metal spoon if the knot is cylindrical. If the knot is spherical, skip the rolling and simply rub it with a spoon (fig 7.16). Finally, thread the working end of the lace under the starting point (see fig 7.14 on page 193), pull both ends of the laces taut, then clip them to within 1mm ($^1/_{32}$") of the knot. If the lace has been dyed, dab the ends with dye, or simply color them with a matching permanent marker. Finally,

polish the knot with a small amount of leather conditioner to help it match the finish on the plaiting.

Forming a tight symmetrical knot takes some practice. If your first attempt is not satisfactory, simply untie it and try again. It may be necessary to experiment with different lace widths, knot types and numbers of passes to achieve a knot that fits the base perfectly.

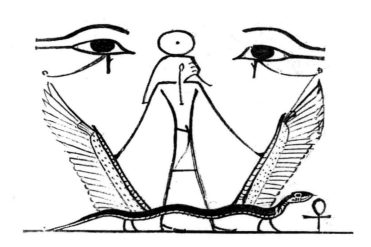

EASY FLOGGER

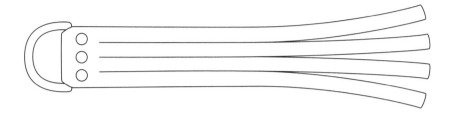

This incredibly simple little whip can deliver quite a sting. It is made from a single piece of chap leather cut into eight falls and fixed around a D-ring with rivets. It is held with the index and middle fingers, which can make it difficult to control. If you take the time to get to know it, though, it can be used accurately to deliver a variety of sensations. A smaller version can also be made with shorter falls, a 25mm (1") D-ring, and two rivets.

Tools

- Rotary cutter and ruler
- Drive punch
- Rivet setter and anvil
- Cutting board
- Hammer
- Measuring tape
- Water pencil

Materials

- Chap leather
- 3 x medium rivets
- 1 x 38mm (1½") D-ring

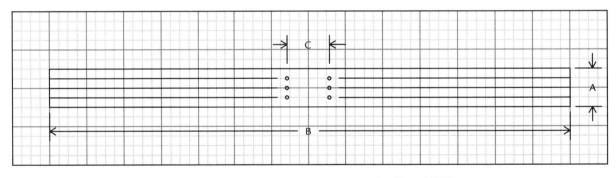

A = 40mm (1½")
B = 880mm (35")

C = 45mm (1¾")

Instructions

- Mark and cut the strap as shown.

- Make cuts along the marked lines with a rotary cutter.

- Punch all holes where marked.

- Assemble the flogger around the D-ring with medium rivets.

CROP

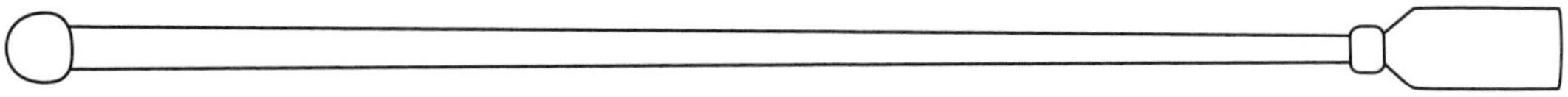

This unique crop can make a memorable impact. It is constructed with four vegetable-tanned leather laces plaited around a fiberglass core. Other materials can be used for the core, but fiberglass is light, flexible and easy enough to obtain. The most economical way to obtain it is usually to purchase a cheap two-piece fishing rod from a hardware or department store. Only the top half is thin enough for this job, and after the eyelets and sleeves are removed and the bottom and top ends are clipped off with a wire cutter, the core is ready to use. The prescribed length of the crop is 550mm (22"), but can easily be shortened or lengthened as much as the core will allow.

Tools

- Leather needle
- Lacing needle
- Shears
- Utility knife
- Australian strander
- Stitch chisel
- Awl
- Cutting board
- Rolling board
- Hammer
- Locking pliers
- Wire cutter
- Measuring tape
- Small foam brush
- Pen
- Small clean rag
- Spoon

Materials

- Light vegetable-tanned leather
- Top half of a separable fiberglass fishing rod
- Matching waxed cotton
- Artificial sinew
- Contact cement
- Solvent
- Dye
- Leather conditioner
- Plaiting soap
- Newspaper

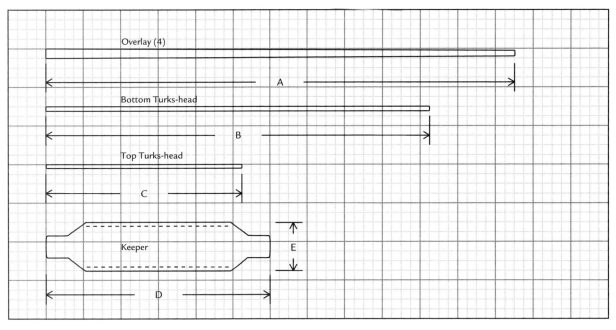

A = 1000mm (40") x 7mm (¼") tapering to 4mm (3⁄16")

B = 750mm (30") x 4mm (3⁄16")

C = 350mm (14") x 3mm (⅛")

D = 140mm (5½")

E = 30mm (1³⁄16")

Instructions

- Remove the eyelets and sleeves from the fishing rod with locking pliers.

- Use a wire cutter to clip off the bottom of the rod, then the top, shortening it to 550mm (22").

- Mark and cut the laces and the keeper.

- Skive the overlay laces.

- Dye all pieces and let them dry overnight.

- Puncture the wide end of each lace with an awl, and thread a length of artificial sinew through them with a leather needle. Pass the needle through the grain side on the first two, and the flesh side on the last two. Then wrap the artificial sinew tightly around the laces a few times and tie in place. This will orient the laces properly for the plait, and provide a secure location on which to mount the turks-head knot.

- Apply plaiting soap liberally to the laces.

- Place the bottom of the rod between the laces and plait around it (fig 7.5 on page 189).

- Bind the laces together at the top of the rod with waxed cotton.

- Roll the crop thoroughly.

- Mark lines 35mm (1³⁄8") to each side of the keeper's widthwise center on the flesh side.

- Apply contact cement to the flesh side of the keeper between the lines made in the previous step.

- Fold the keeper in half, flesh sides together, along the center line.

- Punch stitch slots on both sides of the keeper.

- Hand-sew the keeper together along both sets of slots.

- Trim the ends of the laces to 5mm (3⁄16") from the binding.

- Push the tip of the crop into the keeper as far as it will go.

- Fix the keeper in place by wrapping its bottom securely with waxed cotton (fig 7.17).

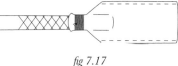

fig 7.17

- Thread a one-meter length of artificial sinew under the laces at the base of the crop a few times, then begin wrapping it around the bottom 12mm (½") very tightly, building up a small sphere for the turks-head knot to be woven over. Leave the start of the length of artificial sinew exposed, so that you can use it to tie the length in place.

- Trim the ends of the laces so that they are within a few millimeters of the awl punctures.

- Dip the sinew-covered portion of the base of the crop in contact cement and hang to dry. This process can be repeated multiple times until a base of sufficient size has been built up.

- Weave a 5-part 4-bight turks-head knot over the area where the keeper was bound to the crop.

- Weave a two-pass 5-part 4-bight turks-head knot over the bolster.

- Apply leather conditioner to the turks-head knots and the keeper. Polish well.

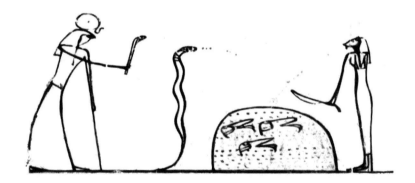

FLOGGER

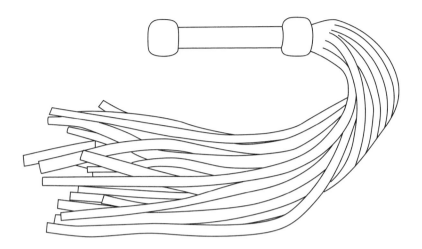

A flogger is a whip made of many individual falls. The sensations delivered by a flogger can range from soft and sensual to painful and severe. The flogger presented here has fifty falls 430mm (17") in length. The number, as well as the length and width, of the falls can be altered to make an endless variety of floggers. Also, the ends of the falls can be finished in a number of ways (rounded, pointed, knotted, etc.), each giving the flogger a different look and producing subtly different sensations.

Although not shown in this pattern, floggers often have a hanging loop protruding from the turks-head knot at the end of the handle. You can make one by tacking the loop onto the bottom of the handle core, then plaiting and tying the knot around it. A loop made of a simple garment or chap leather strap, fixed around the bottom of the handle after plaiting with a single small rivet (creating two loops in the style of the leash strap, see page 135), can make an effective, attractive, and replaceable strap to wear around the wrist and/or to hang the flogger from.

The falls are fixed to a wooden handle covered with a 12-lace handle plait and then finished with turks-head knots at the bottom and over where the falls are mounted. As was discussed on page 186, the handle is weighted with a lag screw and washers to help balance the flogger. Many experts prefer the balance point to be where the index finger lies when the flogger is held comfortably. Where the flogger is held is a matter of personal preference, therefore the location of the balance point must be determined by the user. When the flogger is placed on the balance point after assembly, it should tip in the direction of the falls. To balance the flogger, pick up one fall at a time until balance is achieved. Then, use the following formula to determine how much of each fall will need to be trimmed to achieve balance.

$$\text{Amount to be trimmed } = \text{ Length of each fall } \times \frac{\text{Number of falls picked up}}{\text{Total number of falls}}$$

For example, with fifty falls 430mm (17") in length, and two picked up to make the balance, 430mm x (2/50) = 17.2mm, so 17mm (⅝") will need to be trimmed from each fall to achieve balance. It's a good idea to start by making the falls slightly longer than what is intended, so you can adjust the balance by trimming the falls. The handle weight can be altered by changing the number of washers underneath the lag screw if necessary, but the amount of weight that can be added or subtracted is limited. With all this in mind, in the above example it may be prudent to first trim 10mm (⅜") from each fall and check for balance again before trimming the final 7mm (¼").

Alternatively, if balance is not desired, the lag screw can be omitted and the laces can be fixed to the handle with tacks, as described on page 186.

The overlay laces are cut around 100mm (4") longer than strictly necessary. This is to provide a decent handhold when plaiting the end of the handle. They can be shortened if desired.

Tools

- Lacing needle
- Shears
- Utility knife
- Carving knife
- Rotary cutter and ruler
- Australian strander
- Cutting board
- Rolling board
- Hammer
- Locking pliers
- Drill (9.5mm (³⁄₈") bit)
- Measuring tape
- Sandpaper
- Small foam brush
- Pen
- Water pencil
- Small clean rag

Materials

- Light vegetable-tanned leather
- Garment leather or suede
- Replacement furniture leg
- 13mm (½") tacks
- 19mm (¾") tacks
- 9.5mm x 64mm (³⁄₈" x 2½") lag screw
- 9.5mm (³⁄₈") washers
- Contact cement
- Solvent
- Dye
- Leather conditioner
- Plaiting soap
- Newspaper

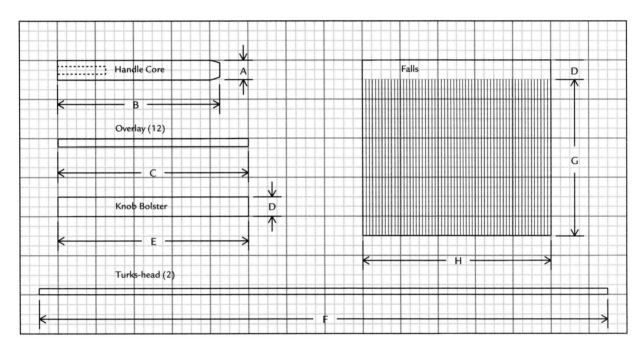

A = 20mm (¾")

B = 200mm (8")

C = 500mm (20") x 7mm (¼")

D = 30mm (1¼")

E = 600mm (24")

F = 2300mm (90") x 6mm (¼")

G = 430mm (17")

H = 500mm (20") (or number of falls x width of falls)

Instructions

- Drill a hole in the center on the handle stock, 9.5mm (³⁄₈") wide and as deep as the lag screw is long. If using a replacement furniture leg, remove the end cap and the threaded post with locking pliers, and increase the width and depth of the hole left behind if necessary.

- Shorten the stock to 200mm (8") and whittle it down to a diameter of 20mm (¾") with a carving knife. Sand

until smooth. Carve a slight taper on the top 10mm (³⁄₈") of the handle core, as shown in the pattern.

- Mark and cut the falls from garment leather or suede as shown, with a ruler and rotary cutter.

- Mark and cut the laces, bolster and cap from light vegetable-tanned leather and form the cap (see page 192).

- Skive the overlay laces.

- Dye the laces, bolster and cap and let dry overnight.

- Mount the overlay laces on the handle (see page 186).

- Hang the work at seated eye level, apply plaiting soap to the overlay laces, and plait (fig 7.7 on page 190). Once you reach the end of the handle, pull each lace tight and tack them in place with 13mm (½") tacks, 15mm (⅝") from the top of the handle. Because a 12-lace plait was employed, there will be six lace intersections running around the circumference of the handle. Tack each of these intersections.

- Trim the lace ends so they are flush with the handle core.

- Roll the handle, but do not put too much pressure on the rolling board, as it could loosen the plait.

- Check the lag screw for looseness and tighten if necessary. Do not overtighten.

- Clean the top and bottom 30mm (1¼") of the handle with solvent.

- Roll the falls onto the handle with a 30mm (1¼") overlap, and measure how much width they add to the handle. Remove the falls from the handle.

- Roll the knob bolster onto the bottom of the handle until the width it adds matches the width the falls added. Mark and trim the knob bolster if necessary.

- Apply contact cement to the flesh side of the knob bolster, and tack it on to the bottom of the handle with a 13mm (½") tack. The edge of the bolster should line up with the bottom of the lag screw bolt head, going over the top of the washers, if washers are used. Wrap the knob bolster tightly around the handle and tack it in place with a 19mm (¾") tack, remembering where the

wood begins if using washers. Secure the bolster with three more tacks around its circumference.

- Apply contact cement liberally to the flesh side of the cap and place it over the top of the lag screw. Let the handle dry overnight.

- Round the edges of the knob bolster with a utility knife.

- Color the exposed end of the handle core with a bit of dye or permanent marker.

- Apply contact cement to the top 25mm (1") of the handle and the flesh side of the bottom 30mm (1¼") of the falls, and place them on the top of the handle so that they overlap 30mm (1¼"). Tack them in place with a 13mm (½") tack.

- Wrap the falls tightly around the handle and tack in place with a 19mm (¾") tack. Tack the falls in place in approximately six places (keeping in mind that the bottom edge will be rounded, and also that the top 10mm (⅜") of the handle core is tapered, so avoiding these areas). Let the flogger dry overnight.

- Round the edge of the fall base with a utility knife.

- Weave a 13-part 11-bight gaucho knot (or as complex a knot as necessary) over the base of the falls (see page 194).

- Weave a 13-part 11-bight gaucho knot (or as complex a knot as necessary) over the bolster (see page 194).

- Clip and color the ends of both turks-head knots, then roll them and round them out with a spoon (see fig 7.16 on page 195).

- Apply leather conditioner to the turks-head knots and polish well.

- Balance the flogger as described on page 200.

SINGLETAIL

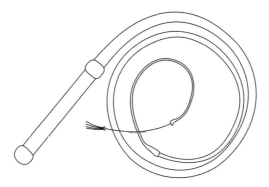

This final project is one of the most difficult and time-consuming in this book. It can take a number of days to complete because of the sheer number and length of the laces to be cut, skived and plaited. The first effort will be a learning experience, so be prepared for it to be less than perfect. An entire side of light vegetable-tanned leather will be necessary to cut the laces for this project, but the side can be used to make several whips.

This singletail is based on a classic bullwhip design with a covered wooden handle and a two-meter (six-foot) body. The belly of the whip is made of a four-lace plait around a twisted leather core. It is inserted into a hole in the handle, wrapped with a bolster, and covered with a 12-lace overlay tapering down to a 6-lace plait at the end. A fall and cracker can then be attached to the end of the 6-lace plait if desired. (These are essential if the whip will be used on more than one person, as it is impossible to properly clean body fluids from the body of the whip itself. The cracker should be replaced for each new person on whom the whip is used.)

Whips composed of more than one bolster and plaited intermediary layers are typically too heavy for the purposes of this book, though this is not always the case with kangaroo leather.

When a whip is cracked, the tip undergoes a lot of stress, as the cracking sound is actually the fall and cracker breaking the sound barrier. This is another reason for the fall and cracker: these components, which take the bulk of the stress, can be replaced when they wear out

Singletail whips are sometimes made without a fall and cracker to dull the intensity of the sensation and to reduce the chance of breaking the skin. Omitting these can, however, make the whip more difficult to crack. The fall described in this project is shorter than a traditional fall length to make the whip easier to handle, though extending it to 600mm or more is certainly possible.

To finish the whip without a fall and cracker, the top of the plaited section must be bound, leaving approximately 100mm of the laces unplaited. This can be done by wrapping it tightly with a 500mm length of artificial sinew forming a 7mm band, using a leather needle to interweave the last few turns in the laces beneath the band, tying it off, and dabbing the knot with a drop of cyanoacrylate glue. Trim the ends of the artificial sinew to 5mm from the knot, then slip a 15mm length of the appropriate diameter heat-shrink tubing (available at electrical supply and hardware stores) and heat it so that it is fixed in place. Further layers of heat-shrink tubing can be added if desired.

Pretty much any type of fine string can be used to make the cracker, but waxed cotton matching the whip is called for here. Making the cracker is very easy if you first make a small tool with a wire coat hanger. Clip the long side of the coat hanger with a wire cutter to make a 200mm length of wire, then twist it into the shape shown below with a pair of locking pliers (fig 7.18).

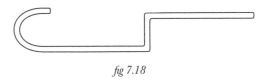

fig 7.18

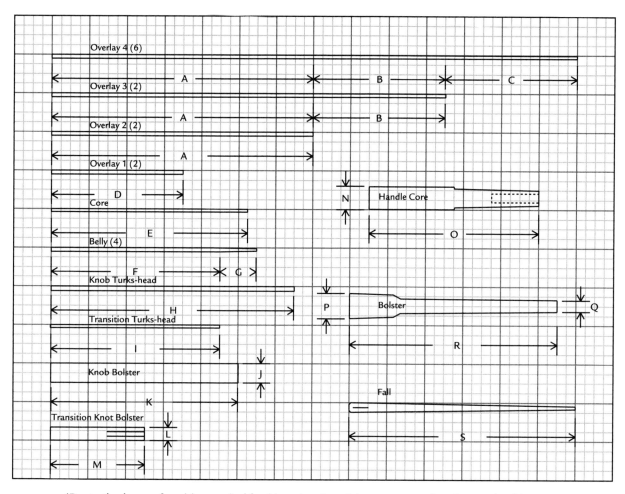

(Due to the degree of precision required for this project, imperial measurements have been omitted.)

X = Desired overall length of finished whip (2000mm)

A = 0.66X x 7mm

B = 0.33X x 6mm

C = 0.33X x 5mm

D = 0.33X x 7mm

E = 1200mm x 5mm

F = 1000mm x 7mm

G = 250mm x 7mm tapering to 4mm

H = 1500mm x 7mm

I = 1000mm x 4mm

J = 25mm

K = 350mm

L = 17mm

M = 160mm

N = 15mm-25mm

O = 180mm

P = 45mm

Q = 35mm

R = 500mm

S = 400mm x 11mm tapering to 3mm

Tools

- Lacing needle
- Shears
- Utility knife
- Carving knife
- Australian strander
- Beveler
- Awl
- Cutting board
- Rolling board
- Hammer
- Locking pliers
- Needle files
- Measuring tape
- Small foam brush
- Sandpaper
- Pen
- Small clean rag

Materials

- Light vegetable-tanned leather
- Heavy vegetable-tanned leather
- Replacement furniture leg
- 13mm (½") tacks
- Matching waxed cotton
- Artificial sinew
- Contact cement
- Solvent
- Dye
- Leather conditioner
- Plaiting soap
- Newspaper
- Round toothpicks

Instructions

- Drill a hole in the center on the handle stock, 9.5mm wide and 50mm deep. If using a replacement furniture leg, remove the end cap and threaded post with locking pliers, and increase the width and depth of the hole left behind if necessary.

- Shorten the handle stock to 180mm and whittle it down to the desired diameter with a carving knife. Keep in mind that the final diameter of the handle will be four times the thickness of the leather used plus the diameter of the handle core.

- Use a square needle file to create a 1mm-deep trench around the circumference of the handle, 90mm from the bottom. Use a carving knife to whittle a taper running from the trench to the top, leaving a 3mm or greater border around the hole.

- Sand each half of the handle until smooth.

- Mark and cut the core, laces and bolsters as shown, as well as a cap (see page 192) from light vegetable-tanned leather. The final 50mm of overlay laces 3, 2 and 1 should taper to a point to make for smoother transitions.

- Soak the core in a bowl of warm water for fifteen minutes.

- Clamp locking pliers onto one end of the core and fix the other end in place. A drawer or something heavy can help with this process.

- Twist the core, keeping it taut, until it cannot be twisted further without kinking.

- Stretch the core taut and let it dry overnight.

- Skive the belly and overlay laces. Do not skive the turks-head laces.

- If desired, dye the core, belly, overlay and turks-head laces, as well as the bolsters and cap, and let dry overnight.

- Tie the belly laces around the core, flesh sides together, in a square. Plait (fig 7.5 on page 189).

- Bind the ends of the laces with artificial sinew. Clipping off the core and ends of the laces is not usually necessary and only serves to make the transition more noticeable.

- Roll the belly thoroughly.

- Pour contact cement into the hole in the handle until it is full, turn it upside down and let it drain out, then let it sit for five minutes.

- Clean the bottom 50mm of the belly with solvent and push a toothpick into the center of the belly with the core.

- Push and twist the belly into the handle as far as it will go.

- Wedge two or three more toothpicks in the hole as needed to secure the belly, then break off their exposed ends.

- Build up the area where the belly meets the handle with artificial sinew to make a smoother taper.

- Tie the bolster in place (fig 7.19 on page 206) with artificial sinew, then roll thoroughly. The final width and shape of the bolster is determined only at this point. Although the narrow dimension which accommodates the diameter of the belly remains static, the wider dimension will vary with the handle diameter (45mm generally works with a 15mm handle core).

- Tack the ends of the overlay laces around the bottom of the handle, beginning with the six "overlay 4" laces. Once they are in place, continue by tacking on one of the

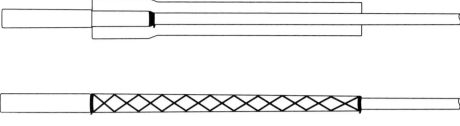

fig 7.19

"overlay 3" laces on each side of those six, then the "overlay 2" laces, then the "overlay 1" laces, which should meet up so that the laces cover the circumference of the handle evenly. Each lace must generally be tacked in place, slightly overlapping its neighbor in order to achieve even spacing.

- Hang the work at seated eye level and apply plaiting soap to the first quarter of the overlay.

- Start the 12-lace handle plait. Make sure that each time a short lace (overlay 1) is plaited, that the other short lace follows. If this does not occur, something has gone wrong with the plait and it will need to be backtracked.

- When the top of the handle is reached, switch the 12-lace handle plait ("under two, over two and under two") to a regular 12-lace plait ("under three and over three"). This transition will be covered by a turks-head knot.

- When there is only about 100mm of the short laces left unplaited, cross them over each other and pierce them with an awl. Run waxed cotton through the hole with a leather needle and around the belly and laces tightly several times, then tie off and clip the ends (fig 7.8 on page 191).

- Apply plaiting soap to the second quarter of the overlay and switch to a ten lace plait ("under three laces, and over two").

- When the plait becomes loose and bunchy or when only 100mm of the short laces are left unplaited, pierce and tie them off in the same manner as before.

- Apply plaiting soap to the third quarter of the overlay and switch to an 8-lace plait ("under two laces, and over two").

- When the plait becomes loose and bunchy or when only 100mm of the short laces are left unplaited, pierce and tie them off in the same manner as before.

- Apply plaiting soap to the final quarter of the overlay and switch to a 6-lace plait ("under two laces, and over one").

- When there is only 100mm of the laces left unplaited, bind them well with waxed cotton.

- Roll the whip well in at least three sessions, with the last one at least a day after plaiting the overlay.

- Clean the 20mm where the transition knot will be woven and the bottom 25mm of the handle with solvent.

- Mount the transition knot bolster by threading the lowermost strand, then the middle, then the uppermost, through the overlay laces around the transition area with the lacing needle. Since the strands are short, the lacing needle must be pushed underneath the overlay strand halfway first, then the bolster strand can be attached to the needle and pulled through. The bolster strands must each be woven under at least one overlay strand, and the interweaves should take place around the full circumference of the overlay. The bolster strands are then trimmed so that their length matches the circumference of the overlay.

- Apply contact cement to the inside of the transition knot bolster, wrap it very tightly around the overlay, and tie it in place with two lengths of artificial sinew.

- Apply contact cement to the flesh side of the knob bolster and tack it on to the bottom of the handle with 13mm tack. Wrap the knob bolster tightly around the handle and tack in place with a 13mm tack. Secure the bolster with three more tacks around its circumference.

- Apply contact cement to the flesh side of the knob cap, press it onto the end of the handle, and let it dry overnight.

- Round the knob bolster with a utility knife.

- Weave a two-pass 5-part 4-bight turks-head knot over the knob bolster (see page 193).

- Weave a 9-part 8-bight turks-head knot over the transition knot bolster (see page 193).

- Clip and color the ends of both turks-head knots, then round them out with a spoon (see fig 7.16 on page 195).

- Apply leather conditioner to the turks-head knots and polish well.

Fall and cracker

- Mark and cut the fall as shown from heavy vegetable-tanned leather. It should be about 400mm long, tapering from 11mm down to 3mm. Clip the corners off the wide end and cut a slot about 20mm long, 10mm from the end. Then, shave down the flesh side of the top 60mm until it can be tied in a knot. The fall can then be bevelled or skived on all four sides to round out the length, dyed and left to dry overnight.

- Cut a 1500mm length of waxed cotton and tie the ends together.

- Hang the loop on a hook and pull it taut, with the cracker tool hooked on the knotted end.

- Twist the loop counter-clockwise by turning the cracker tool like a crank while keeping the thread taut until it begins to kink.

- Grab the twisted loop from the center and roll it away from you until the cracker is twisted together.

- Tie an overhand knot 120mm from the base of the cracker. Trim the ends 30mm from the knot and unravel them.

fig 7.20

- Apply plenty of plaiting soap to the fall. Leave this overnight, then wipe away any excess.

- Tie the fall to the cracker (fig 7.20).

- Thread the unplaited laces through the slot in the fall and push it on to the plaited section, then tie the fall in place (fig 7.21). If the lace threaded back through the fall slot in step 9 is not snug, use a lacing needle to thread that lace under the laces on the reverse side of the fall knot. Finally, clip the ends of the laces to 5mm from the knot.

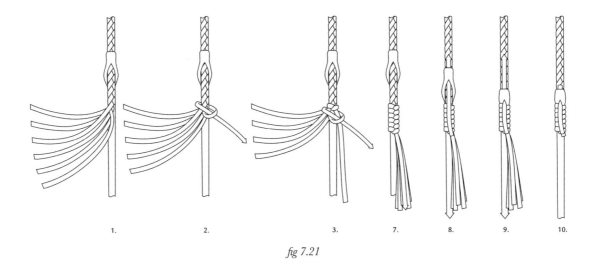

fig 7.21

AFTERWORD

Ritualcraft

Our purpose in this life can be reduced to three primary objectives: to love, to better ourselves, and to be happy. Most spiritual traditions honor each of these three, and a well-constructed play ritual can do the same.

Rituals

A ritual is simply a predetermined series of actions, often performed at a predetermined time and location. Rituals may be steeped in symbolism and are often based on myths. They can help tune in to the more primitive parts of the brain, a reservoir of archetypal symbols.

To participate in ritual is a fundamental human activity. We have an inbuilt desire to take part in them, and we construct them often without realizing that we are doing so. It could be hypothesized that the rapid growth of kink subculture is attributable to the lack of satisfactory rituals in the mainstream culture.

Play rituals

The notion of a "play ritual" may seem like a contradiction in terms, but play and ritual have much in common and are even rooted in the same area of the brain. Play is the foundation of the creative dimension of ritual, where form and pattern are respected, but options are creatively selected (Turner, 1983). The play ritual differs from most others in that its structure is determined consciously by the participants, allowing it to become a reflection of their individual paths.

Using a play ritual does not necessarily mean that the same activities are repeated over and over again. It simply means that there is a certain structure around which the activities are planned. Using a ritual can also help the participants feel more comfortable, which is important as this kind of exploration can often lead to feelings of vulnerability. Coming face to face with one's shadow is not unlike the shaman confronting his demons before his journey: a traumatic but informative experience.

Not surprisingly, rituals can have an ego-suppressing effect, which is often why they are used by organized religions to transform a congregation of individuals into a unified whole. This ego suppression is important for both participants in a ritual. The dominant's need to suppress ego may seem less obvious than that of the submissive, but all participants in a ritual or a scene are to some degree subsuming their personal impulses and desires to the greater goal of the scene.

When designing a play ritual, consider using elements from long-established rituals, which can give the play ritual a certain archaic power. It can be as simple as a few gestures or words prior to play, or as complex and precise as a Japanese tea ceremony. It is good form to include in your ritual some words, thoughts and/or gestures of respect for its originators.

Although every culture has its own set of rituals, a few common elements recur in many forms: ritual cleansing, ritual dress, and signs of respect are particularly applicable to play rituals.

As you design your ritual, do some research and consider carefully, because these recurring elements are often some of the most potent parts of the play ritual. Complex protocol can be important in some service-oriented relationships, but even simple rituals can shift the mind into the proper gear.

One goal of most religious traditions is to restore unity between us and our spiritual source. (Mystical experiences are important in this discussion, as a well-designed and well-executed play ritual can actually drive the participants to a mystical or ecstatic communion with one another and the divine.) The ways in which traditions pursue mystical experience generally divide them into two schools of thought, the ascending mode and the descending mode, though some traditions incorporate both.

Those that fall into the ascending category have an other-worldly orientation, focusing on finding salvation outside the physical world. For their adherents, time is generally best spent in prayer or meditation, often denying the physical world in an attempt to connect with the divine. Those in the descending category find salvation on earth, and tend to be focused on the physical world. For members of these groups, the focus is more on the experiential, with less emphasis on the other-worldly.

Both ascending and descending currents are important to our development, and engaging in both seems to be much more effective than either alone (Wilber, 1996). Incorporating elements of both ascending and descending currents creates a complete, or integral play ritual, which can lift the participants toward the mystical. Adding a period of meditation is an ideal way to give the play ritual an ascending component: we must first free ourselves from the physical world in order to come back and fully embrace and inhabit it.

The ascent

To meditate simply means to quiet the mind while remaining aware. In this state, one can achieve a heightened awareness of the body, or even disidentify with or dissociate from it. When the body is reinhabited, the meditator may experience increased vitality, awareness and sensitivity. Thus, in general, ascending before descending makes for a greater experience. Whether this means being bound and deprived of your senses, or sitting in zazen with your partner, the ascent is worth the trip.

Meditation can be more difficult than it sounds. Here is one technique that has worked well for me and for other novice meditators.

Set a timer for a short period of time, perhaps ten or fifteen minutes, with the intention of meditating until the timer sounds. Adopt the zazen posture on a small firm cushion by first crossing the legs in the half lotus position, or however they can be comfortable. Only the buttocks should be supported by the cushion, so that the knees are lower than the hips. (If assuming this position is difficult or impossible, adapt until you are comfortable. Sitting in a chair is a fine alternative.) Sit very erect, as though being pulled up by the top of the head, keeping the ears in line with the shoulders.

Lay your left hand over the right, palms up, matching the middle joints of the middle fingers, and touch the tips of the thumbs lightly together to form an oval. Hold the hands against the body with the thumbs at the height of the navel and the arms slightly away from the body, as though holding an egg under each arm without breaking it (Suzuki, 2006).

Keep your eyes relaxed, open and unfocused, pointing down at a 45° angle. Tuck your chin in slightly and let your tongue rest on the roof of your mouth just behind your teeth. Breathe naturally and deeply from your abdomen, through your nose if possible. Clear your mind of any thoughts and concentrate on, or even count, your breaths. Thoughts will no doubt begin to surface; this is completely normal. Recognize that a thought has surfaced, and let it pass away without frustration.

The more you practice meditation, the easier it becomes. When a quiet mind is achieved, the ego has been suppressed. With no ego, who is still aware of the passing moments? That is the true Self.

Zazen is only one of the many wonderful ways to meditate, and is presented here because of its simplicity and effectiveness. And meditation is by no means the only applicable ascent activity. Centering prayer, yoga and even a mindful walk all have ascending qualities. As was discussed in Chapter IV, being bound can help quiet the mind, so spending the ascent in bondage can be a valuable addition to the ritual. However, if you find bondage exciting, quieting your mind in this situation can be difficult. Being able to quiet the mind despite being thrust into such a subjectively stimulating situation requires mental discipline that few posses and even fewer exercise.

This period of ascent via meditation intensifies the descent via play. First we withdraw from the physical world, then reenter it as archetypal characters to enact our stories and scenes. Ascending can allow for a presence of mind which is necessary to extract the most from these experiences. Meditation can also help lift repression barriers and bring awareness to dissociated aspects of the psyche, facilitating this kind of play.

The descent

Whether the descent takes a ritual form as well or shifts into free expression, the specifics should be constructed according to the needs and desires of the participants. Although overly structuring the descent can end up leaving little room for spontaneity, doing so allows for a clear mind: thus, there is value to ritually based scenes planned to the last detail, dialogue and all.

While a satisfying scene can propel the submissive into an altered state of consciousness often referred to as "subspace," the dominant is rarely so lucky. Less experienced dominants may find that the intense focus needed to enact a scene prevents them from entering ritual consciousness, although some find that this difficulty eases as they become more comfortable with the physical mechanics of play. In the meantime, a meticulously planned ritual scene can allow the dominant to disengage some of the mental machinery necessary for running a scene and make room for "topspace" – though dominants should take care to leave a little consciousness available to monitor the safety protocols.

Ritual forms

Beyond the similarities of their individual elements, most rituals share a few common overall themes and structures which you can draw upon for inspiration. Most can be broadly categorized into one or more of four types: transformation, worship, sacrifice and punishment. These ritual forms carry a lot of weight with us, and can effectively be used as the basis for scenes. Transformative rituals include rites of passage, initiation and resurrection; in play, transformation could involve ordeals, tests and trials. Worship-based rituals could involve the submissive worshiping the dominant as an embodiment of the divine, or both joining in worship. A sacrificial play ritual could involve the dominant offering the submissive in a theurgical context. Rituals of punishment could be said to be the progenitor of our subculture, and could involve torture, imprisonment, humiliation, service, or any combination of these four.

When we get dressed and assume our roles, we are acting in a mythological theater, connecting to events and characters that recur throughout human history. The reasons we have the desire to act out these stories are likely as diverse as the fantasies themselves, but underlying them is a deep-seated human desire to play make-believe. Psychiatrists have been using role-playing to help treat a variety of disorders for decades with demonstrably positive results, and "mythological role playing" is said to rejuvenate the psyche (Horgan, 2003). Wanting to pretend that we're not who we are is innate in all of us.

From an interior perspective, when we costume ourselves in a second skin of fetishwear, we are reenacting on a fundamental level our own incarnation. The awe and excitement we experience when confined and transformed by these garments recreates that which the spirit undergoes when bound in a body. And when we surrender to another, we feel that we have as little control over the experiences thrust upon us as the spirit has in inhabiting the body. We feel locked into the ordeal for the duration, which is at once terrifying and wonderful.

Solo

Although this book has been written with the couple in mind, rituals can of course be designed for one person or a larger gathering. The ascent of a solo ritual would be very much the same as what a couple would engage in, but the descent would necessarily differ. Although some of the projects in Chapter VI can bring a new dimension to solo play, another unique way of enriching this experience is with a yogic technique called "Mula Bandha." This technique involves drawing up the pelvic floor (pubococcygeus), and is somewhat similar to "Kegel" exercises. These muscles can be found fairly easily by attempting to stop the flow of urine, though repeatedly stopping urine flow should be avoided. Strengthening the pelvic floor can help control and prevent ejaculation in males, and can lead to an increase in sexual pleasure and more intense orgasms in both sexes. With regard to solo play, rhythmically contracting and relaxing these muscles not only strengthens them, but can also heighten sexual energy and awareness, and can even bring some to the point of orgasm.

A final word

The role that sexual contact plays in these rituals can vary widely and be quite complex. For many, bondage, discipline, dominance and submission are completely distinct from genital sex, while for others they are a prelude to or a part of their sexual practice. One can see a certain symmetry between our primary objectives and our sexual motivators, described by the tantric traditions as procreation, pleasure and liberation. Freud theorized that all our desires have a sexual root, and while this may not be the case, it is easy to see how the awe and excitement we experience while engaging in these rituals is tied to our sexuality.

Awe is an emotion often associated with religion, and can be loosely defined as fascination mixed with fear. We are wonderstruck by our own beauty and that of our partner(s). We are fearful of the unknown realms we are about to explore and the limits we are about to test. Awe shakes us loose from our regular mode of thinking, and allows us to experience the groundless true nature of reality.

May these experiences be abundant on your journey.

Appendix I – Rivets per strap

¼"	6.4mm	One small rivet
⅜"	9.5mm	One medium or large rivet
½"	12.7mm	One medium or large rivet
⅝"	15.9mm	Two small rivets or one medium or large rivet
¾"	19.1mm	Two small rivets or one medium or large rivet
1"	25.4mm	Two medium or large rivets
1¼"	31.8mm	Two medium or large rivets
1½"	38.1mm	Two medium or large rivets
1¾"	44.5mm	Three medium or large rivets
2"	50.8mm	Three medium or large rivets

Appendix II – Conversion table

Inches to Millimeters	1" = 25.4mm	1mm = .0394"
Yards to Meters	1 yd = .914m	1m = 1.094 yd
Pounds to Kilograms	1 lb (16oz) = .454kg	1kg = 2.20 lbs

Appendix III – Leather weights

1oz	.4mm	$\frac{1}{64}$"
2oz	.8mm	$\frac{1}{32}$"
3oz	1.2mm	$\frac{3}{64}$"
4oz	1.6mm	$\frac{1}{16}$"
5oz	2mm	$\frac{5}{64}$"
6oz	2.4mm	$\frac{3}{32}$"
7oz	2.8mm	$\frac{7}{64}$"
8oz	3.2mm	$\frac{1}{8}$"
9oz	3.6mm	$\frac{9}{64}$"
10oz	4mm	$\frac{5}{32}$"
11oz	4.4mm	$\frac{11}{64}$"
12oz	4.8mm	$\frac{3}{16}$"

References

Horgan, J., 2003. *Rational Mysticism*. New York: Houghton Mifflin.

Hornung, E., Abt, T. & Warburton, D., 2007. *The Egyptian Amduat: The Book of the Hidden Chamber*. Zurich: Living Human Heritage.

Newberg, A., D'Aquili, E. & Rause, V., 2001. *Why God Won't Go Away*. New York: Ballantine Books.

Nunley, J.W. & McCarty, C., 1999. *Masks: Faces of Culture*. New York: Harry N. Abrams, Inc

Suzuki, S., 2006. *Zen Mind, Beginner's Mind*. Boston: Shambhala.

Turner, V., 1983. Body, Brain, and Culture. *Zygon*, 18(3), pp. 221-245.

Wilber, K., 1996. *A Brief History of Everything*. Boston: Shambhala.

Acknowledgments

I am philosophically indebted to many, but above all Ken Wilber. I have also been deeply influenced by the life and work of Carl Jung.

I would like to thank Ann and Alexander Shulgin for their books *Pihkal* and *Tihkal*. Their sense of exploration and their willingness to share their knowledge with the world is an example I can only try to follow.

I would also like to thank everyone who took the time to teach me. Though I am primarily self-taught in the realms of sewing and leatherworking, the information and advice I received along the way from shopkeepers, coworkers, and of course my mother (who introduced me to sewing at an early age), has been invaluable.

I would like to thank my editor, Janet Hardy, for her insight, expertise and patience.

I would also like to thank Eoin Hickey and Chris Skinner for their support and invaluable design advice.

Finally, I would like to thank my darling Julie, my muse, inspiration, and biggest fan. I love you, Julie.

"No man, when he hath lighted a candle, putteth it in a secret place,
neither under a bushel, but on a candlestick,
that they which come in may see the light." – Luke 11:33 KJV

FIGURES

INDEX

NOTES

NOTES

NOTES

NOTES

Other Books from Greenery Press

BDSM/KINK

At Her Feet: Powering Your Femdom Relationship
TammyJo Eckhart & Fox · $13.95

The Compleat Spanker
Lady Green · $12.95

Conquer Me: girl-to-girl wisdom about fulfilling your submissive desires
Kacie Cunningham · $13.95

Erotic Slavehood: A Miss Abernathy Omnibus
Christina Abernathy · $15.95

Family Jewels: A Guide to Male Genital Play and Torment
Hardy Haberman · $12.95

Flogging
Joseph W. Bean · $12.95

The Human Pony: A Guide for Owners, Trainers and Admirers
Rebecca Wilcox · $27.95

Intimate Invasions: The Ins and Outs of Erotic Enema Play
M.R. Strict · $13.95

The Kinky Girl's Guide to Dating
Luna Grey · $16.95

The (New and Improved) Loving Dominant
John & Libby Warren · $16.95

The Mistress Manual: A Good Girl's Guide to Female Dominance
Mistress Lorelei · $16.95

The New Bottoming Book
The New Topping Book
Dossie Easton & Janet W. Hardy · $14.95 ea.

Play Piercing
Deborah Addington · $13.95

Radical Ecstasy: SM Journeys to Transcendence
Dossie Easton & Janet W. Hardy · $16.95

The Seductive Art of Japanese Bondage
Midori, photographs by Craig Morey · $27.95

The Sexually Dominant Woman: A Workbook for Nervous Beginners
Lady Green · $11.95

SM 101: A Realistic Introduction
Jay Wiseman · $24.95

GENERAL SEXUALITY

A Hand in the Bush: The Fine Art of Vaginal Fisting
Deborah Addington · $13.95

The Jealousy Workbook: Exercises and Insights for Managing Open Relationships
Kathy Labriola · $19.95

Love in Abundance: A Counselor's Advice on Open Relationships
Kathy Labriola · $15.95

Phone Sex: Oral Skills and Aural Thrills
Miranda Austin · $15.95

Sex Disasters... And How to Survive Them
C. Moser, Ph.D., M.D. & Janet W. Hardy · $16.95

Tricks... To Please a Man
Tricks... To Please a Woman
Jay Wiseman · $13.95 ea.

When Someone You Love Is Kinky
Dossie Easton & Catherine A. Liszt · $15.95

TOYBAG GUIDES:
A Workshop In A Book · $9.95 each

Age Play, by Bridgett "Lee" Harrington

Basic Rope Bondage, by Jay Wiseman

Canes and Caning, by Janet W. Hardy

Clips and Clamps, by Jack Rinella

Chastity Play, by Mistress Simone *(spring 2014)*

Dungeon Emergencies & Supplies, by Jay Wiseman

Erotic Knifeplay, by Miranda Austin & Sam Atwood

Foot and Shoe Worship, by Midori

High-Tech Toys, by John Warren

Hot Wax and Temperature Play, by Spectrum

Medical Play, by Tempest

Playing With Taboo, by Mollena Williams

Greenery Press books are available from your favorite on-line or brick-and-mortar bookstore or erotic boutique, or direct from Revel Books, www.revelbooks.com. Most Greenery titles are also available in electronic form from your favorite ebook retailer. For more information, visit the Greenery Press website at www.greenerypress.com.